SAFE PASSAGE

SAFE PASSAGE

MAKING IT THROUGH
ADOLESCENCE IN
A RISKY SOCIETY

JOY G. DRYFOOS

OXFORD
UNIVERSITY PRESS

OXFORD
UNIVERSITY PRESS

Oxford   New York
Athens   Auckland   Bangkok   Bogotá   Buenos Aires
Calcutta   Cape Town   Chennai   Dar es Salaam   Delhi
Florence   Hong Kong   Istanbul   Karachi   Kuala Lumpur
Madrid   Melbourne   Mexico City   Mumbai
Nairobi   Paris   São Paulo   Singapore
Taipei   Tokyo   Toronto   Warsaw

and associated companies in
Berlin   Ibadan

First published by Oxford University Press, Inc., 1998
198 Madison Avenue, New York, New York 10016

First issued as an Oxford University Press paperback, 2000

Oxford is a registered trademark of Oxford University Press

Library of Congress Cataloging-in-Publication Data

Dryfoos, Joy G.
Safe passage : making it through adolescence in a risky society /
Joy G. Dryfoos.
p. cm.
Includes bibliographical references and index.
ISBN 0–19–511256–3 (Cloth)
ISBN 0–19–513785x (Pbk.)
1. Teenagers—United States.   2. Teenagers—
Counseling of—United States.   3. Juvenile delinquency—United
States—Prevention.   4. Drug abuse—United States—Prevention.
5. Teenage pregnancy—United States.   6. High school dropouts—
United States.   I. Dryfoos, Joy G. Adolescents at risk.
II. Title.
HV1431.D794   1997
362.7'083—dc21   97–36424

3 5 7 9 10 8 6 4 2

Printed in the United States of America
on acid-free paper

CONTENTS

FOREWORD

Joy Dryfoos has been a major contributor to our understanding of adolescent development, its serious problems, and ways to overcome them. This book builds on her cumulative experience, knowledge, and judgment to make a powerful case for all our youth.

Adolescence is a time of profound biological transformation and social transition characterized by exploratory behavior. Much of this behavior is adaptive, but when carried to extremes, and especially if it becomes habitual, it can have lifelong adverse consequences. Many dangerous patterns, in fact, commonly emerge during these years such as substance abuse, premature and unprotected sex, the use of weapons, alienation from school.

To have a promising future, adolescents must find a valued place in a constructive group; learn how to form close, durable human relationships; earn a sense of worth as a person; achieve a reliable basis for making informed choices; express constructive curiosity and exploratory behavior; find ways of being useful to others; believe in a promising future with real opportunities; cultivate the inquiring and problem-solving habits of mind necessary for lifelong learning and adaptability; learn to respect democratic values and the elements of responsible citizenship; and altogether build a healthy lifestyle.

These requirements can be met by a conjunction of institutions that powerfully shape adolescent development, for better or worse—families, schools, community-based organizations, and health care organizations. Working models of effective programs for young adolescents can be observed in some communities, a few of which have been scrutinized by evaluative research. Dryfoos highlights programs and strategies that show promise of setting young people on the path toward healthy adulthood.

A variety of organizations and institutions can provide supplements or surrogates for parents, older siblings, and an extended family. Across the country there are many examples of such interventions. Churches, schools, universities and community organizations can build constructive social support networks that attract youngsters, including seriously disadvantaged ones, in ways that foster their health, their education and their personal capacities. All this bears strongly on healthy alternatives to school failure, substance abuse, and violent gang membership.

Communities can provide attractive, safe, growth-promoting settings for young adolescents during the out-of-school hours—times of high risk when parents are often not available to supervise their children. More than 17,000 national and local youth organizations, including those sponsored by religious groups, now operate in the United States, but they do not adequately provide opportunities for this age group. These organizations can expand their reach, providing enjoyable opportunities for youth, offering activities that convey information about life chances, careers, and places beyond the neighborhood; and engaging them in community service and other constructive activities that foster education and health. All this requires support from both public and private sectors.

It is essential to train health and educational professionals with a thorough understanding of the developmental needs and behavior-related problems of adolescents. Historically, the relevant professions have been skimpy on preparation for the specific needs and opportunities of this crucially formative phase.

In this important book, Dryfoos illuminates the nature of adolescent problems and useful ways to prevent serious damage. She clearly describes multicomponent interventions that are effective (especially full-service community schools). Moreover, she includes many practical examples of effective programming, introduces interesting and committed youth workers, and offers her well-tested "what works" analysis. One chapter each is devoted to what parents, schools, and communities can do to support Safe Passage. Attention is paid to state and federal roles in supporting youth development efforts.

In the end, Dryfoos comes out strongly for comprehensive programs, with emphasis on full-service community schools. She advocates joining forces—combining the educational reform movement with the movement of the helping professions to create stronger school-based institutions. She wants to bring down the walls between what we can do well clinically and what we can do well in the classroom.

Overall, Dryfoos shows practical ways of meeting the essential requirements for healthy adolescent development through frontline institutions: family, schools, health sector, and community organizations. These in turn can be greatly facilitated by government at all levels, business, universities, media, scientific and professional organizations. Preventing much of the damage now occurring would have powerful, beneficial, social, and economic impacts.

We can fulfill the promise of these precious early years if we have the vision and the decency to invest responsibly in all our children. In a wary and contentious society, what could bring us together better than our children—all our children; girls as well as boys; poor as well as rich; minorities as well as majorities. This will surely be one of the greatest challenges to our nation in the next century.

David Hamburg
President, Emeritus
Carnegie Corporation of New York

PREFACE

A couple of years ago, Joan Bossert, Editorial Director at Oxford University Press, said to me, "Why don't you write an update of *Adolescents at Risk?*" She was referring to a book, published in 1990, that documented the patterns of risky behaviors among American adolescents and summarized the success of programs in changing those behaviors. A lot has happened in the world of teenagers, in the world of adults, and in my own life since that book came out. Much more information is available about the lives of young people and the programs and schools that serve them. The social and political climate that shaped those programs has shifted in complicated ways, creating a backlash against federally supported interventions and shifting the burden on to states. People seem to be somewhat at a loss as to how to deal with those pervasive youth problems related to sex, drugs, and violence.

During this interval, I personally have become much more interested in firming up the connection between the quality of education and the services young people need in order to make use of that education. I am more concerned than ever about the growing gap between advantaged and disadvantaged young people in their probabilities for success.

Safe Passage: Making It Through Adolescence in a Risky Society is an update—and much more. This book focuses primarily on successful efforts that help young people to emerge from their childhoods as responsible adults. The major premise here is that this society has access to programs that work to assure that adolescents achieve "Safe Passage"—programs in schools and community agencies; programs that involve all kinds of youth workers; programs supported by local, state, and federal public and private resources. The question then is: If we know what to do, why do we still have so many young people with such overwhelming problems that they have little hope of succeeding in life?

My answer is that we have not organized our schools and our communities to meet the needs of contemporary children, youth, and families. This book examines various approaches to creating new kinds of institutions that are built around schools but that are much more than schools—places that will serve as enrichment centers, hubs, and neighborhood safe havens.

ORGANIZATION OF BOOK

Part I describes the status of youth; our knowledge of their needs; what their families, schools, and communities are like; and how they view their world. I look at the current research on high-risk behaviors and school performance, and summarize the experiences of contemporary 10 to 17 year olds. A distinction is made between young people who are vulnerable because of their life situations, and those whom we call resilient because they have the capacity to overcome the odds.

Part II concentrates on youth programs of all kinds. I start with visits to five successful programs that I selected (out of many possibilities) to illustrate current approaches to assuring adolescents Safe Passage. You will meet some interesting youth workers who designed these programs and who work hard to implement them. Several of these programs are full-service community schools—new kinds of comprehensive institutions that in my view have the potential to become major components of the Safe Passage Movement. I describe a range of school-based efforts and review relevant organizational issues such as governance and turf. I also look at the "state of the art" in current school reform and school restructuring—issues basic in discussions of Safe Passage. Then I turn to a review of more traditional or "old-fashioned" approaches, programs that focus on one behavior at a time, such as preventing delinquency, substance abuse, teen pregnancy, or AIDS.

Part III focuses on what works to assure Safe Passage and what doesn't. Many common components of successful programs surface from this analysis. Studies of programs past and present reveal complex issues that must be resolved in the process of large-scale replications.

Finally, Part IV moves to the call for action, with visions and strategies that need to be pursued if young people are to be assured Safe Passage in the future. I start with the role of parents and discuss how they can build stronger relationships with their teenagers. Then I present my own vision of a full-service community school along with suggestions for how schools can become more effective. I also look at the potential of community-wide initiatives that plan and implement comprehensive programs for children and families. Resources and leadership for these school and community efforts rely on the commitments of the states and the federal government. I review the possibilities and problems in overcoming bureaucratic hurdles caused by the fragmentation in public agencies and the lack of policies that foster youth development. The final chapter in the book summarizes all of the above and then calls for a bold new initiative that will enable parents, schools, communities, and youth themselves to launch a Safe Passage Movement.

GOALS

The goal of this book is to stimulate readers to find ways to get involved in changing the prospects for a large segment of American youth. Many people lack the means to examine the lives of youth and do not understand how many barriers we have placed between them and success. Few people are acquainted with the youth workers who struggle so hard to help these young people overcome these barriers. Thus, one objective of this book is to raise the consciousness of the general public.

Another objective is to celebrate youth work, to encourage the hands-on youth workers—the teachers, social workers, street outreach people, health practitioners, case managers, and others. I hope that exposure to new ideas and examples of successful programs will stimulate people who want to replicate them in their own backyards.

In the language of this book, parents are treated as the most important category of youth worker. Parents need a lot of support these days because their children are exposed to threatening social conditions over which the parents feel they have no control. Parents are the most articulate advocates for youth—they desperately want their own children to succeed, and they are sympathetic to the plights of all children.

Although my previous work has been aimed at the research community, this book seeks a much wider audience. It is not my intention, however, to ignore my friends in academia. I have tried to annotate accordingly so that this book can be used as a text in courses on adolescence, education, social welfare, psychology, and other areas. College students should be stimulated to think more broadly about their involvement with the Safe Passage Movement and their own potential for effecting social change. Significant roles for universities in interdisciplinary professional education and community development are stressed.

Decision makers at all levels are also a prime audience for this work. Legislators and public administrators hold the future of our young people in their hands. I want to inspire them to use their powers and their resources in the most rational and humane ways, to help this generation thrive and become useful citizens. I want to convince them that youth workers know what to do if they are given the resources to do it. The American public should be demanding that their public officials respond to this call.

ACKNOWLEDGMENTS

In 1986, the Carnegie Corporation set me loose from the restraints of working in an organization or a university by giving me a grant to start what has become the long-term Youth-at-Risk project. Their financial support has made it possible for me to write three books and more than sixty articles, editorials, and commentaries over the past decade. They have enabled me to travel all over the country, visiting programs and attending conferences, getting to know the youth workers, youth researchers, decision makers, and the youth themselves about whom I write. I am particularly indebted to Vivien Stewart, my program officer, who has maintained her interest in my work through the long years. Her probing questions and responsiveness to new ideas have really kept me on my toes. David Hamburg, retiring president of the Carnegie Corporation, has strongly supported this project, and I have been influenced by his own important contributions to the field of adolescent development. Gloria Primm Brown has been a reliable advisor about interesting new developments in youth services; Avery Russell, a consultant on communication and style; Tony Jackson, an important source for material about middle schools; and Bernadette Michel, helpful administrator at the Carnegie Corporation. This book, of course, represents my own views and not necessarily those of the foundation.

I mentioned that Joan Bossert of Oxford University Press stimulated me to write this book. She and others at Oxford have been very helpful in assisting me through the arduous editing process, particularly William Jake Klisivitch and Kimberly Torre-Tasso.

Much of the "nitty-gritty" labor that had to be undertaken for this book was performed by Fonda Lifrak, my assistant and young friend. Among many other tasks, she contacted all the programs we could identify to find out what they did and whether they had ever been evaluated. During this process, she became an authority on youth programming and community schools. Fonda also worked with the photographers who contributed to this book and with Deborah Kates to set up "shoots" for some of the pictures.

We must have communicated with thousands of people in compiling the information presented here. Many are acknowledged in the text and the notes—too many to acknowledge. Several other people who have been particularly helpful include Martin Blank, Cynthia Brown, Lynn Curtis, Paul Dryfoos, Iris Dudman, Kevin Dwyer, Hal Lawson, Bill Shepardson, Ruby Takanishi, Bill Treanor, Gary Walker, Joann Weeks, and the staff of the Childrens' Aid Society and their community schools. On a personal level, I must mention my good friends who have encouraged me to keep going and are always willing to discuss relevant issues: Nancy Balaban, Shirley Barrett, Jeanette Bertles, Mary Sciocia, and Judy Seixas (and their significant others). And most of all, I am indebted to George Dryfoos, who not only read and commented on each chapter but also made sure our household ran smoothly and quietly while I sat upstairs at the computer doing this work.

This book is dedicated to Rose Rodgers-Dryfoos, our latest granddaughter, for whom Safe Passage must be assured. She, along with her wonderful sister Amy, will be a true child of the twenty-first century, an Asian American, Jewish Protestant, with a strong personality and a searching intellect. My greatest desire is that she be allowed to grow up in a fine democratic society that will be responsive to all young people.

J. D.

September 1997
Hastings-on-Hudson, New York

PART I

YOUTH TODAY

Susie Fitzhugh, Photographer

1

SAFE PASSAGE: WHAT DOES IT MEAN?

Ensure, insure, assure, secure mean to make an outcome sure. Ensure implies a making certain and inevitable; insure stresses the taking of special measures beforehand to make a result certain or provide for any probable contingency; assure implies a making sure in mind by removing all doubt and suspense; secure implies action taken to guard against attack or loss.

—Webster's Seventh New Collegiate Dictionary

Parents the world over want assurance that their children will be able to grow into responsible adults who can enter the labor force, become effective parents, and participate in the social and political life of the society. That is, after all, the parents' primary job, to ensure Safe Passage to their offspring from infancy through adolescence to adulthood.

In some societies, the roles of parents and other caretakers are rigidly prescribed, defined over centuries by religion and culture. Parents rule and control their children until they marry, and even then the younger family is heavily influenced in its behaviors by the supervision of the older one. In our country, the situation is very different—this is not a homogeneous society. Our diverse religious and cultural traditions lead to differing developmental paths, but these paths are also altered by social status, gender, race, neighborhood, region, and individual characteristics. Poverty is a major determinant of life course. Today, many children rapidly reject the values of their immigrant families after they are exposed to the compelling American youth culture. The traditional rites of passage, going from childhood to adolescence to adulthood, are changing dramatically as the society is shaken by enormous shifts in population, technological adjustments, family reconfigurations, and other economic and social events.

It is difficult to capture the mood of this country as we enter the twenty-first century. I often feel we are sitting atop the vast fault of a trembling earthquake. We don't know how to move away from the fault, nor have we made plans to deal with the consequences of the earthquake that will inevitably change the configuration of our society. These uncertainties make it even more difficult for families to protect their young and prepare them for the future.

THE RIGHT TO SAFE PASSAGE

The barriers to Safe Passage are profound. The twenty-first century will be launched in the United States under dangerous social conditions—growing poverty, crime, urban disarray, rural isolation, limits on employment opportunities, and racial enmity. Our country is not isolated from the impacts of turmoil in the rest of the world—bloody ethnic conflicts, starvation, mass migrations, the AIDS epidemic, and faltering economies. Even the worldwide environment appears to be entering a period of agitation, where harmful air, warming seas, and destructive hurricanes presage things to come.

Americans are already engaged in an ideological war over the meaning of government and the role of Congress in assuring equity, opportunity, and family support. Many young people have no sense of the future, operating under the assumption that little is expected of them. Even some of those youth who are lucky enough to live in my suburb, Hastings-on-Hudson, New York, appear perplexed when asked about what roles they envision for themselves after they reach adulthood.

Safe Passage is not a guaranteed right. It is a privilege. White suburban children growing up in Hastings have higher odds for future success than the disadvantaged, nonwhite children growing up in the contiguous city of Yonkers. Yet not every child in Hastings will make it, nor is every disadvantaged child in

Yonkers a potential failure. The objective of this book is to spell out in great detail all the work that has to be done to turn this privilege into a right.

I do not believe that families can overcome obstacles to Safe Passage for their children without help. In the raging welfare debates, many conflicting views of the strengths and motivations of families can be discerned. At one extreme is the view that families on welfare will overcome their dependency if they are thrown off of the welfare rolls and are forced to find jobs to feed their children. The other view is that these families, mostly headed by young single mothers, need long-term intensive support including basic educational training, child care, job preparation, and job placement services if they are to shed their dependence. The same argument is taking place over how to help vulnerable children, those who are not "making it." Should we let them "sink or swim," or should we be devising programs that will promote positive outcomes? Clearly, I am a "program person." The odds are too stacked against disadvantaged people to be sure that they will make it in this demanding society without considerable support and assistance.

The strongest argument for intervention is that the country as a whole will benefit if all children are assured Safe Passage. Your children will have a much better chance of living in a viable society if other people's children are able to participate as workers, parents, and citizens. This challenge calls for joining together all the human and institutional forces necessary to guarantee that children can grow into effective adults.

NEEDS OF YOUTH

Throughout the ages, researchers, writers, and philosophers have tried to capture the tumultuous transition from childhood to adulthood during that period known as adolescence. Almost everyone who has ever put pen to paper has had something to say about his or her own adolescent experiences. Indeed, one of the best ways to define what adolescents need is to think about your own history, what you expected, and what you received. In reviewing my own life, I am indebted to my parents for endowing me with the expectation of success. They never appeared to doubt that I would make it. The key word in my upbringing was "responsibility," a concept we learned early through examples. My parents were community leaders and central figures in a large extended family, and we were encouraged to do our part through household chores and jobs in the community. Anyone who grew up during the Great Depression will tell you that certain aspects of the experience built character. Everyone was struggling together, and the huge gaps between rich and poor that we see today were not evident to the children.

Recently, a group of renowned researchers brought together by the Center for Youth Development and Policy Research of the Academy for Educational Development came up with a surprisingly simple answer: "What young people really need on a daily basis is safe places, challenging experiences, and caring people."[1] We could stop right there and just figure out how to achieve those goals. But further expansion of these obviously simple ideas may lead to more clearly defined interventions that might ensure Safe Passage. So here is the preliminary agenda for our discussion:

- We all know that parents play a major role in shaping the futures of their children. No fact is more clearly documented than the importance of effective adults in the lives of young people. Every child must be connected to a responsible adult—if not a parent, then someone else.

- To be equipped for adult roles, young people must have access to cognitive learning, including the development of critical thinking and reasoning skills. Without basic intellectual proficiency, children will have great difficulty overcoming other barriers to successful maturity.

- Academic achievement alone is not sufficient. Social skills are necessary for relating to peers and the adult world. Young people have to develop social competence, including the ability to deal with pervasive peer and media influences.

- Young people need room to experiment. They have to be allowed to experience decision making about their own behaviors and values.

- Instilling high expectations and offering real and visible opportunities for success are crucial in motivating youth.

- To enter the labor force, young people have to be exposed to the world of work through career training, volunteer community service, and jobs.

- The welfare of young people can be assured only by safe streets, safe schools, and safe communities.

For most children, all of these needs must be dealt with simultaneously. No one single component—no "magic bullet"—is powerful enough to turn around the life of a young person. We have to make sure that we cover all the ground and that these pieces are woven together into a more holistic approach to adolescents. You will encounter the concept of *comprehensiveness* frequently on these pages—it means simply bringing together an array of interventions to increase the power of the component parts.

But more than parents must be involved in this effort. Although parents and siblings are the starting point, teachers, youth workers, police, health practitioners, people in business and government, the media, churches—indeed, the whole community influences young people as they go about shaping their lives. And, of course, other young people, those ubiquitous peers, very strongly influence youth behaviors.

This book focuses on practices and programs that foster the healthy development of youth, on interventions that can make a difference in the lives of young people. Most of these efforts concentrate on the critical period between childhood and adulthood—the preteen and teen years, roughly between the ages of ten and eighteen—often referred to as adolescence. Of course, we know every period in a child's life is critical and what happens during the earliest years shapes life's script, what is to come. Early childhood development has been a rich field for researchers and practitioners.[2] A strong case has been made for Head Start, parenting education, home visiting, and family preservation programs, based on the importance of intervention beginning at age zero. So for the purposes of this discussion, let's treat it as a given that effective parenting right from the start can make a huge difference. But this book is about teenagers, with a heavy emphasis on "middle-age" youth—those in middle and junior high school. These children are old enough to experiment with risky behaviors but young enough so that preventive interventions can make a significant difference. They are moving away from parents' controls and toward a reliance on outsiders to help them shape their lives.

PROGRAMS TO MEET THE NEEDS OF YOUTH

I have already used the term *intervention*, meaning an organized effort to change some aspect of human behavior and to improve the probabilities for success. In my vocabulary, interventions can best be described as *programs*, a catch-all term for organized efforts based on a set of objectives that have defined outcomes. Our society has a myriad of programs, ranging from programs that encourage mothers to obtain early prenatal care to programs that teach senior citizens to line dance. The vast Department of Defense is an aggregation of very costly programs. In recent years, the term *programs* has been endowed with negative connotations by the "nay sayers" who assert that programs cost too much, are a waste of taxpayers' money, don't work, and only make their users more dependent. Some people believe that parents—not social agencies or schools—should take full responsibility for taking care of their children. These people's criticisms have come largely during political discussions that favor passion rather than reason. Demagogues who cast social programs in a poor light never seem to find fault with "their" programs, such as subsidization of tobacco growers, esoteric weapons development, special highway construction, or corporate tax breaks. They don't seem to worry about programs in churches like Wednesday Night Bingo or Boy Scouts or those offered to the public by the National Rifle Association. One gets the impression that programs for "them" are bad, while programs for "us" are perfectly acceptable.

In fact, the concept of program is an organizing principle, not a political or moral theory. Computer hacks are well-acquainted with the programs that make their computers work (or at least claim to). I think of schools as a collection of programs, with specific goals for each classroom and even for each child within the classroom. All the other activities that go on in schools are also programs: physical education, music and art, special clubs, Honor Society, health education, driver education, and the biggest program of all—competitive sports.

A related term that gets bandied about is *categorical programs*, targeted interventions aimed at a specific behavior. It is true that, in this country, every new problem has been addressed by a new program. The latest initiative has to do with the prevention of violence. In response to the horrible threat of homicide and related dangers in our schools, streets, and communities, a whole new generation of programs is being promulgated. Many of these efforts involve classroom-based curricula that teach negotiation skills and conflict resolution.

Over the past twenty-five years of program watching, I have observed the initiation of new categorical programs to prevent delinquency, teen pregnancy, substance abuse, suicide, injury, HIV/AIDS infection, and, now, violence. At the same time, I have seen other categorical programs marketed for the promotion of self-esteem, abstention, health education, life skills, and social competency. Each category has its own funding stream, government agencies, and local advocates. This has led to the promulgation of literally thousands of different programs so that young people are bombarded sporadically with messages about what they should and shouldn't do. Such fragmented approaches have not been very successful at changing the life styles of contemporary adolescents. Yet categorization has a kind of energy of its own, stimulating specialized practitioners to create carefully designed curricula and targeted activities. And certain categorical programs have produced some useful components that can be applied across categories.

For many years, I have been studying programs because they can directly affect the way children grow up. Programs are malleable; they can be altered according to changing conditions and expanded knowledge about what makes them work. When I visit an effective school or a busy youth center, I can feel its vitality and excitement. It's stimulating to take in the sights and sounds of young people going about their activities and watching the skills of the caretakers who teach or counsel or just have fun. Not all programs are so wonderful. One can also learn from visits to dismal schools and poorly organized youth programs. My reactions are often heavily swayed by what I see on the walls reflecting the environment that has been created for the students, and often by the students. Schools and recreation centers that are full of children's artwork and cultural displays tell me the people here are really engaged by what they do, while blank gray walls and poorly lit rooms tell me a different story. The decor does not always reflect the quality of the program, but it certainly provides a clue as to what might or might not be going on there.

Most programs that I have looked at fall under the category of *prevention programs*—activities aimed at preventing certain behaviors that lead to teen pregnancy, or substance abuse, or delinquency, or that focus on promoting school achievement and "good" behavior.[3] Practitioners often distinguish among primary, secondary, and tertiary prevention.[4] Primary prevention efforts are universal; they are directed toward the entire population—for example, billboards that promote safe driving, or school-based drug-free zones. Secondary prevention efforts are more targeted, focusing on specific groups of people who appear to be at risk for a certain problem, such as group counseling of children of alcoholics, or mentoring for slow learners. Tertiary prevention is similar to treatment—for example, counseling for identified drug users, or medical treatment for young people with sexually transmitted diseases (STDs).

Literally millions of adults work in thousands of programs in institutions that touch the lives of young people. A unique characteristic of social organization in the United States is the huge number of public, voluntary, nonprofit, and private agencies that are involved with youth services. There are 85,000 public and 25,000 private elementary and secondary schools; 400 national organizations such as the Girl Scouts, YMCA, and 4H, with many local chapters; at least 17,000 community-based programs, including grassroots independent organizations, religious youth organizations, adult service clubs, sports organizations, senior citizen groups, and museums; and, among public-sector institutions, about 6,000 libraries and numerous recreation and police departments that offer youth service programs.[5]

How does one capture the quality and character of all this activity in one short volume? We have searched the nation for a few exemplary programs that demonstrate how safe passage can be assured. Later you will encounter five outstanding programs that represent various approaches to youth development and that have been shown to be successful at meeting the needs of young people. Keep in mind that good programs are being replicated throughout this country, programs that serve as prototypes of the efforts that will be essential as we prepare to deal with the complexities of the twenty-first century.

CREATING A SAFE PASSAGE MOVEMENT

Youth workers are among the most significant members of our society, yet they rank very low in visibility and recognition. Everyone has heard of Donald Trump, Joe Namath, and Madonna, but few of us can identify Michael Carrera, Luis Garden Acosta, and Deborah Scott, just some of the people you will meet on these pages. In every community, you will find teachers, counselors, nurses, recreation leaders, employment advisors, ministers, librarians, police officers, physicians, volunteers from business and the community, all kinds of folks whose lives center on helping young people. Part of the Safe Passage mission is to raise public consciousness about this cadre of significant people without whom children have little hope of making it. I want you to share my delight in observing youth work at its best, watching the way that committed individuals approach their work with young people, determined to help them succeed despite many barriers.

I will be frank about my own agenda here. I really believe that it is possible to assure every child a future, to create a Safe Passage Movement. We know how to fill each one of the pressing needs of young people. We have access to successful models of parenting, schools, communities; we know how to teach, counsel, promote social skills; we have experience with connecting young people to the labor force. We don't need any rocket scientists to show us how to put the pieces together to form comprehensive programs that work. We know what has to be done. The challenge is how to put the research into practice.

Surely the intention of the American public is to produce a new generation of effective adults. Why isn't that happening? I can think of several reasons. First of all, some people do not understand that they are sitting on a faultline; they do not acknowledge that millions of children are unlikely to make it. Second, many Americans are being misled by politicians and demagogues to believe that social interventions don't help these youth. They are wrong. The oft-repeated accusation that we are "throwing good money after bad" is incorrect. Taxation is seen as a burden, with little recognition that everyone's long-term quality of life will suffer if publicly supported programs are allowed to wither away.

I hope to offer you convincing evidence that social investment in programs that work is both a constructive public policy and a strong ethical personal position. I hope to recruit you to this optimistic movement that will celebrate the contributions of youth work; build stronger and more effective institutions; involve families, schools, communities, and youth themselves; and use scarce resources rationally and productively so that every child gets an even chance to succeed in life. Now, let's get into the heart of the matter and see what's going on with young people across the nation.

Beth Berkowitz, Photographer

2

YOUTH IN FAMILIES, SCHOOLS, AND COMMUNITIES

The situation of young people in America is deeply intertwined with the social and economic changes that are underway. During all periods of transformation . . . young people are in the forefront as both beneficiaries and casualties.

—Michael Sherraden, *Youth Participation in America*

lthough it is not my to intent overwhelm you with statistics, I do feel that it is necessary to review the important facts and figures about the life styles and the views of adolescents today. An understanding of the rapidly changing social environment in which young people are being reared is essential to developing the context for a Safe Passage Movement. My experience over many decades of trying to influence policy has taught me that numbers can be very persuasive, especially when they summarize significant social phenomena, such as "40 million Americans have no health insurance" or "almost 15 million children are being raised in very poor families."[1] In my past work, I have generated several national estimates: In 1970, 5 million low-income women were in need of organized and subsidized family services;[2] in 1975, 1 million teens became pregnant during the year; and in 1990,[3] 7 million youths between the ages of 10 and 17 would fail if they didn't have immediate attention.[4]

You may notice that the various data sources I will cite use different specifications—for example, each study looks at a slightly different age group (e.g., 10 to 15, 12 to 17, 15 to 19). I concentrate in this book on "middle-age" youth when possible, with a heavy focus on eighth or ninth graders. As for definitions of race and ethnicity, the vocabulary changes frequently. In my time, I have counted Coloreds, Negroes, Blacks, and African Americans; Latinos and Hispanics; Indians and Native Americans; Whites and Euro-American Caucasians (the latest jargon). For this book, I have settled on African Americans, Hispanics, Whites, Native Americans, and Asians. This chapter provides a quick look at the teenage population as a whole, their families, their schools, and their communities—in other words, their lives.

THE ADOLESCENT POPULATION

We start with an overview of the number and social characteristics of young people in the United States.[5] Currently, almost 30 million young people are between the ages of 10 and 17. At this tender age, there are still more males than females, a condition that changes by age thirty, when the differential mortality rate begins to reduce the male population more rapidly. In recent years, homicide among young males has hastened this phenomenon.

In 1995, almost 15 million teenagers were between the ages of 14 and 17. The U.S. Census Bureau estimates that this number will grow to more than 17 million by 2010. Thus, the first demographic lesson for the Safe Passage Movement is to get prepared to deal with millions more young people in the future! And while the numbers of youth will grow, the numbers of old people will increase even more dramatically. This will leave proportionately fewer wage earners in the middle who will have to support more children and old people. And the votes of senior citizens will control many local school budgets and legislative bodies.

Race and ethnicity are very significant factors for understanding social change and in planning for the future. In 1995, two-thirds of teens (ages 14–17) were White and non-Hispanic, 15 percent were African American, 12 percent were of Hispanic origin, 4 percent were Asian, and less than 1 percent were Native Americans. Thus, one-third of our young people are not counted as majority White. By the year 2010, not much more than a decade away, it is expected that almost 40 percent of all youth will be non-White or Hispanic, with the projected growth rate much greater among Hispanics (60 percent) than African Americans (22 percent). This means that in the future more than one out of every six young people will be Hispanic, and about one in six, African American. The fastest-growing group are Asians. Although their numbers are still small, the Asian population in this age group is expected to double in the next decade. In comparison, the number of White, non-Hispanic teens will increase by only 6 percent during the same period. Since these projections are based on current immigration policies, it is possible that restrictive legislation could slow the growth of certain groups, particularly Hispanics and Asians.

The term *minority* carries less and less meaning as various ethnic and racial groups become majorities in certain cities and the White, non-Hispanic population becomes the smallest group. In most large cities such as New York, Boston, and Chicago, more than three-fourths of public school students are "minority." In inner-city schools, many students come from families that do not speak English. Among eighth graders, only a few (2 percent) are described as "limited-English proficient"; however, one in six live in homes where a language other than English is frequently spoken.[6] In some school systems, more than fifty different languages are represented by the children who enroll. Because significant changes are taking place in the racial and ethnic makeup of the population, the Safe Passage Movement needs to pay attention to issues related to diversity, culture, language, and integration.

FAMILIES

Youth now live in many different family configurations. When I was growing up, no one in my school had divorced parents. A few young people lived with their widowed mothers, but they were rare. It was expected that everyone went home to a Mom and Dad. In contemporary society, children come from families with all kinds of marital and nonmarital arrangements, which frequently change during the course of a year. Today, half of all marriages end in divorce, and more than half of all children will spend some time in a single-parent family.[7] About 69 percent of youth currently live in a family with two parents. Of these families, one in five do not include both the biological parents; most include the mother and a stepfather, and the rest are father and stepmother; about 2 percent represent adoptive parents. Fully 31 percent of all youth (more than 8 million) live with only one parent, typically the mother [but, increasingly, the father]. Among mothers who head families, about one-third were never married. Roughly half a million teenagers live in foster care.[8]

A very important change in American life is this decrease in the percentage of households that include married couples with children. Not only does this reflect the aging of the population and smaller family size, but also the fact that people marry later than they used to—or not at all. In 1960, close to half of all households were made up of couples with children, but this decreased to one-fourth in 1990. This decrease in child-centered households has ramifications for the future of suburbia, where we can already see the proliferation of private, adult-only enclaves, gated neighborhoods that may not feel responsible for the children in the larger community and resist supporting schools and other public necessities that don't service them.

Unfortunately, many young people are growing up in families with very low incomes. Almost one in five teenagers in this country—close to 6 million—are in families whose incomes fall below the poverty line, and about 4 million teenagers are in families that receive welfare. Almost one-third of poor teenagers are not covered by any form of health insurance. More than one-third of African American and Hispanic teens live in very disadvantaged families, as do 13 percent of White teens. Living only with your mother is a strong predictor of poverty. In one analysis, more than half of eighth graders who lived with their mothers were very poor, compared to less than 12 percent who lived with both mother and father.

Very few teenagers go home after school and find Mom there, waiting with that glass of milk and peanut butter sandwich. Mom is in the labor force and a major source of financial support for the family. In fact, mothers' wages are a major factor in keeping families afloat. Women's salaries, on average, have increased much more than men's salaries, and women are more likely than in the past to obtain higher education, thus entering the work force at higher wage levels in increasing numbers. Men's incomes have not risen substantially in recent years, so that the income disparity between the sexes is gradually disappearing. These trends appear to be continuing.

More than three-fourths of all women who have school-age children are in the labor force. This represents a huge shift since 1960, when only 39 percent of married women with children worked outside of the home. And families are smaller now than they were in the past, and more than half of all families have no children. Only 1 in 10 families has three or more children, half the rate in 1970. The average family size has come down from almost four to close to three.

With baby boomers moving into their 40s and their children having fewer babies, our population is aging. So the young people currently going into the labor force will be supporting a higher percentage of retired people than in the past.

SCHOOLS

Of the 30 million 10 to 17 year olds, 95 percent are currently enrolled—80 percent in public school and 20 percent in private school. About half a million are not currently enrolled in school, have not graduated, and would therefore be labeled "dropouts." The proportion of students who drop out of school rises significantly with age. Only 1 percent of 14 and 15 year olds have dropped out, compared to 6 percent of 16 and 17 year olds.[9] The rates are much higher for 18 and 19 year olds, who tend to get discouraged if they are still in high school after their age mates have graduated.

But the definition of "dropping out" is very fuzzy. Another way of looking at school success is whether a teenager gets through high school in four years.[10] In 1991, only 69 percent of young people completed high school within the standard four-year time frame. Thus, some 31 percent lagged behind the graduates, an even worse record than in 1985, when 28 percent did not graduate on time. This indicator is much higher in inner cities than in suburban areas. Young people who drop out before age 18 are disproportionately Hispanic; African American youth are less likely to drop out than others.

We can also look at the proportion of older youth, 18 to 24, who have completed high school. In 1994, some 86 percent of people in that age group had acquired high school credentials—80 percent through graduation and 6 percent by obtaining alternative certification, typically a GED, a general education degree obtainable through night school or other courses.[11] We will take a closer look at teenagers who leave school before graduating in the next chapter and show how school failure is connected to other problems faced by young people.

School achievement is a much discussed subject in this country, and studies present conflicting evidence about how well or how poorly American children do compared to other countries.[12] In terms of reading literacy at age 14, U.S. students scored higher than those in other countries, while in science and math they had lower scores. However, the range of scores was much greater in the United States than in any other country, reflecting the great diversity in our locally organized public educational system compared to national systems such as those in France and Germany.

Test scores in our schools show significant differences between achieving children and nonachieving ones, related to such factors as the quality of the school itself, parental education, family income, and family size.[13] But the historical gap in math and verbal achievement scores between White and non-White students has shown a marked narrowing in the past two decades, attributed to improvements in the quality and productivity of schools, including measures such as school consolidation, increases in per-pupil expenditures, integration of students, changing curricula, smaller class sizes, and better teachers.

Yet the test scores for eight graders have changed very little over the past decade.[14] About one-third read above grade level, half are average, and 14 percent are below grade level; in math achievement, the distribution is similar. And each year about 10 percent of middle and high school students fail at least one subject. Most eighth graders are involved in extracurricular activities—about half report school sports, 40 percent participate in orchestras or bands, and more than 20 percent work on school newspapers and yearbooks. More than 60 percent of eight graders reported positive feelings about their schools: most said the teaching was good, the discipline was fair, and there was real school spirit.

While these eighth-grade students spend less than six hours per week on homework and less than two on outside reading, they report at least twenty-one hours watching television. About one in five goes home after school to an empty dwelling, and most of these teens spend more than three hours each day alone.

Most eighth graders expect to go to college, and almost one-fourth expect to attend some form of graduate school. And while few imagine that they will not complete high school, one in five thinks that high school graduation will be the end of his education or that he will go to a vocational or business school rather than a four-year college. By the time students are seniors, more than half are in college preparatory or academic programs, more than a third in general high school programs, and only a few in vocational programs. Two-thirds of those students whose parents graduated from college are in college preparatory programs, compared to just one-fourth of students whose parents did not complete high school. About 20 percent of high school students use computers at home—7 percent of those in the lowest income families and 53 percent of those in families with incomes over $75,000.

Almost one-third of students in public schools are classified as being a minority, but they are not uniformly distributed across school districts. More than half of the nation's 15,000 school districts have fewer than 5 percent minority students, and about 10 percent have 50 percent or more. Of the students in public schools, 75 percent in large cities are minority, as are 28 percent in the urban fringe and large towns and 18 percent in rural areas and small towns. In one out of every five school districts, one-fourth of the children live in poverty. The more affluent the district, the more likely that the students are White. In districts where less than 5 percent of the students are in poverty, 87 percent are White. In districts where more than 25 percent are in poverty, 37 percent are White.

COMMUNITIES

As would be expected, young people are found in all kinds of communities in the United States. About one-fourth of all adolescents live in central cities, half in suburban areas, and one-fourth in nonmetropolitan areas; only 5 percent of teenagers live on farms. The majority of White youngsters live in the suburbs, while Hispanic and African American youth are much more likely to live in cities.

A study conducted by Search Institute of a large sample of youth in small communities reveals certain relationships between the characteristics of the community and the status of the youth.[15] Students in sixth to twelfth grade filled out extensive questionnaires about their behaviors (substance abuse, unprotected sexual activity, suicidal ideation, delinquency, and school problems) and their experiences in their families, schools, communities, and peer relationships. Communities were rated as least healthy, average, and most healthy based on scores derived from the percentage of youth who reported high-risk behaviors. Not surprisingly, the healthiest communities were those where the students are most motivated and committed to their school work and have high aspirations. Where a majority of youth perceive that the school environment is positive, the community's atmosphere appears to be healthy. Other factors that are related to strong communities are frequent youth involvement with both religious and community activities—for example, in after-school programs. In the healthiest communities, the majority of the youth reported that their peers were not involved in negative or destructive behaviors.

Surprisingly, the communities did not differ on certain significant factors. Only about 40 percent of all respondents—regardless of the community's "health"—said that their parents monitored their activities or provided discipline. And almost half of the youth had "hedonistic" values (wanted to have a lot of fun, be popular, and spend money) in all three categories of community.

Young people do not live in a cocoon. The quality of life is different in a community like Hastings, where I live, from some neighborhoods of Yonkers, the contiguous city. Most young people in Hastings are engaged in school and vying to get into prestigious colleges. Yet some complain that there is "nothing to do." According to several teenage boys we talked to, the worst aspect of this village is its lack of a place to rollerblade. They claim that if they did their tricks in the middle of the village, the police would chase them away. Although a Youth Center was organized decades ago, few teenagers find it a congenial place to hang out, and in any case it is open only one evening each week. The plaza on the main street in front of the Veterans Headquarters and the woods of Hillside Park are where young people like to congregate, mostly to gossip and be seen, but also to drink and take drugs. The police track youth closely in this community. One officer is assigned full-time to work with high-risk youth. He claims that very few of the youngsters in town are actually delinquent. He is concerned, however, about a recent rise in drug use (marijuana), which he attributes to the influence of youth who have recently moved into the community from cities like Yonkers. He also feels that parents today are much too permissive, especially about marijuana use and alcohol, and not responsive when contacted by the police regarding the behavior of their children. Their parents get on the train in the morning to commute to New York City for their jobs and leave their children behind to fend for themselves.

I should note here that this community has been shaken by the occurrence of two suicides of teenagers within the past two years. One was known to be a troubled young man, but the death of an 18-year-old girl who was a good student and apparently had only recently gotten involved with "designer drugs" was almost inexplicable. As a result, some adults are beginning to raise questions about the social environment for youngsters here and trying to organize more contact with the younger people.

Yonkers is a city split down the middle by race and class. The east side is similar to Hastings. Those who live on the west side are more vulnerable. Guns are available there, and shootings occur. Young people can be observed hanging out on street corners, but there are also several after-school programs, privately operated youth centers, and Police Athletic League sports activities that draw many teenagers. Yonkers also assigns specially trained police to work with young people. According to the officers in the Youth Division, lack of parental supervision and involvement is one of the biggest problems they encounter. Children are found roaming the streets late at night with no guidance or supervision. In Yonkers, this situation has been attributed to "kids having kids," parents having children they were ill-prepared to rear.

The easy availability of guns, box cutters, and other weapons has greatly exacerbated the situation in Yonkers. The number of arrests for fights, robberies, and muggings is growing. And in recent years, youth officers have taken to visiting local middle and high schools to conduct weapons' searches in random classrooms.

Communities can act as protectors to young people. But when the problems mount, communities can be overwhelmed. When guns and drugs begin to proliferate, the situation goes downhill fast. Dr. Aaron Shirley, director of the Jackson, Mississippi, Comprehensive Health Center and a pioneer in school-based health care, described to me what was happening in his community:

> Up until a few years ago, you could walk down any street in Jackson and feel safe. Then crack arrived, pushed by outside dealers. Guns became readily available on the streets. Any kid could get one. Now people are scared and it's hard to even get anyone to come out to a community meeting.[16]

When parents are afraid to confront the troublemakers in the neighborhood or are otherwise unable to act responsibly in their children's interests, other institutions have to take over for them. In chapter 12, we will look at how communities are approaching the challenges of the twenty-first century and are trying to implement comprehensive school and community strategies that will assure Safe Passage.

VOICES OF YOUTH

What do young people think about their families, friends, schools, community, and country? Contrary to the media portrait of American teens, many young people like and respect their families, enjoy being with them for recreational purposes, and receive a lot of encouragement and stimulation at home. For most teenagers, of course, friends dominate their social scene. Peers have very strong influences on some young people, though not on all. Let's meet a few young people from different parts of the country.

Mary Anne

Mary Anne lives in a small town in the Midwest. Always a little ahead of her age group, at 15 she is in tenth grade. Her father owns a hardware store, and her mother teaches first grade. She has a younger sister and a younger brother and lives with her family in a small house on the outskirts of town.

> I have to be out on the road every morning at 7:05 to catch the bus to the Regional High School. The kids on the bus are very rowdy, in the morning there's a lot of talk about what everyone did the night before. Some kids have hangovers. I never go out on school nights.

Mary Anne wants to be a pediatrician. She is on the academic track, a member of the National Honor Society, the French Club, and the Community Service

Club. She plans to go to the state college and hopes to do well enough to get a scholarship for medical school. On weekends and in the summers, she babysits for a family down the road.

> I don't have much fun. I'm always either studying or working. Most of the kids who were my best friends in elementary school are kind of wild. I can hardly wait to get out of here and get on with my life.

Roger

Roger rides on the same school bus with Mary Anne and, at age 15 is also in tenth grade. He is one of the more boisterous riders, projecting his loud voice over the others. He wears a football jacket, baggy pants, and a jaunty cap on backwards.

> I like my good times. A few beers, joking around with my buddies, and after that a little entertainment with my girlfriend. Of course, I'm in training right now, and in this school they make you keep your grades up if you don't want to be kicked off of the team.

Roger lives on a small dairy farm with his father and his grandparents. His older brother and sister have left home, and his mother died of cancer two years ago. Roger's father has a job in town in a small factory in addition to tending to the farm.

> My dad is a good guy. He took care of my mom when she was so sick, and now he takes care of his old parents. But that doesn't leave much time for me. He's a little hard to talk to and expects me to be as good as he is, which I don't really want to be.

Roger has a girlfriend who lives in town. He has been pressing her to "make out," but she is afraid that she will get pregnant. Her sister had a baby at 15 and is stuck at home.

The future is not clear to Roger. He doesn't know what to do after he finishes high school in two years. One option is to stay on the farm and expand it, another is to get a job in the factory where his father works. He thinks he might qualify for a football scholarship if he keeps up his winning record, but that's a long shot.

> My guidance counselor in school is a neat guy. He encourages me to improve myself, to expect more in the future than I do. No one in my family has been to college yet. Maybe I'll be the first.

But in the meantime, Roger's greatest yearning is for "wheels."

> I want a car so bad it hurts. Stuck way out there in the country, I can hardly ever even get to see my girlfriend except around the school.

LeRoy

Transportation is the least of LeRoy's problems. He lives close to the bus stop in the middle of Chicago's public housing projects and can actually walk to his school, Junior High School 118. Although he is 15, he has been left back twice, and so he is just entering eighth grade.

> I'm the biggest kid in my class, but definitely not the toughest. A lot of them carry guns and knives. They are really scary. I have to cut through the back lots so I don't bump into them going to school. At least when I get in the building, I feel a little safer.

LeRoy's mother works downtown in a department store, and his father is employed by the city as a clerk. He has one little sister. LeRoy is in a special education class in a school with 2,500 students.

> My folks spend a lot of time helping me with my homework, but sometimes I just don't get it. I was real sick as a little child and missed a whole year of school and never did catch up with the other kids. The teacher is real nice, she gives me attention, but most of the other kids are crazy. They make so much noise and jump around all the time, I can't stick with my work.

Music provides LeRoy's happiest moments. As soon as he gets home from school, he turns on his CD player and plays his favorite tunes. He loves MTV, watches it every afternoon while he babysits for his little sister (who also watches it).

> I love those MTVs that have action, people dancing around in the street, having such a good time. I wish I could be there instead of stuck in this apartment with nothing to do. I want to be a famous musician when I grow up . . . probably a drummer.

Daniel

Daniel is 11 years old and lives with his mother and older brother in a suburb of Portland, Oregon. His parents are separated, and he spends every weekend with his father and his father's girlfriend.

> I never know where to leave my things, at Mom's or at Dad's. All of them are always so busy no one has any time for me.

Daniel is small for his age, and feels a lot of stress both about his appearance and his only average performance in school. He is troubled by frequent bouts of asthma and is allergic to many foods. When his parents have the time, they encourage him to "do better," but their interest in him is inconsistent and sporadic. Daniel would like to work with computers eventually, but he doesn't have access to one at home or at school. Because he does not act out in school, his teachers do not pay much attention to him.

School is so boring. Next year I can go to another school, but I hear that it's dangerous there. Maybe I should get a knife.

Some of his friends smoke and drink, and he is just beginning to join them at their homes after school for "parties."

I had a beer the other day at George's house, and it made me feel really good.

CONTEXT FOR THE SAFE PASSAGE MOVEMENT

These vignettes illustrate both the variability in the lives of youngsters and the universality of their needs and aspirations. They give relevance to the statistics—every number is simply an aggregate of many different lives, each having unique qualities and special challenges. As we review what is known about the lives and aspirations of young people, and the array of interventions to assist them to achieve Safe Passage, we must keep in mind the context of family, school, and community.

All young people rely heavily on their families for support. Not all of them get it. Most families are struggling just to maintain their economic security, and some lack the time to attend to their children. And from day to day and year to year, many children are unsure of who will take care of them.

School experiences, too, can have a major effect on the lives of teenagers and their hopes and future expectations, and the people children meet at school can influence them in both good and bad ways. And while test scores do not tell the whole story, they are useful indicators that warn us that American children need more rigorous educational opportunities if they are going to be competitive in the twenty-first century. As Lynn Olsen reminds us in *Education Week's* annual summary of the status of our schools:

> Many children in our poorest urban and rural areas attend schools that lack even the barest necessities, from up-to-date textbooks to functioning toilets. Some of these school systems spend thousands of dollars less per child than those in more affluent suburbs.[17]

Of course, where young people live makes a huge difference in their life scripts. Healthy communities are those with excellent schools, safe streets, adequate transportation, nice houses, and plenty of resources to stimulate, entertain, and nurture youngsters. But many young people are forced to live in unhealthy communities because they are poor, African American, Hispanic, Native American, or immigrants. Deprived White children, particularly in rural areas, confront equally difficult situations. A Safe Passage strategy must help young people overcome the barriers they face because of where they live and who they are. In the next chapter, we focus on specific behaviors that profoundly affect the lives of contemporary youth. We need to understand who does what and what difference it makes, always keeping in mind the positive picture that most teenagers are doing reasonably well and do not require intensive interventions in order to make it.

Film still from movie "Girls Town,"
Phyllis Belkin, Photographer, Courtesy of October Films

3

VULNERABLE YOUTH: SEX, DRUGS, AND VIOLENCE

I want to die from natural causes. Because of all the violence there is today I don't know if I will live long enough to die of natural causes. I think we were brought into this world to love each other not to kill one another.

—Lestina Hill, Rayser High School, Memphis, TN, in The Rising Tide

Which adolescents are in jeopardy of not making a successful transition into adulthood? Many people maintain that all adolescents are at equal risk because they are all exposed to the same hazardous influences, and are all going through phases of adolescent development that make them vulnerable. Others would assert that young people growing up today are located in very different environments depending on their gender, race, ethnicity, social and economic status, family strengths, access to good schools, and community climate. I am firmly in the camp of those who believe that young people fall into very different risk groups, a distribution heavily influenced by poverty and race. Children right here in the United States are growing up with vastly different odds of making it.

One of the riches of our country is the plethora of different approaches to programs and research, yet no one research study has produced a comprehensive picture of youths at risk. Because we have separate categorical programs, we find specialized researchers for almost every kind of problem. Universities perpetuate this situation through departmentalizing—psychology, social work, public health, education, educational psychology—and academic journals follow suit. As a result, we have carved up our adolescents into many disconnected pieces, often losing sight of the real people we are claiming to care about and treat.

RISKY BEHAVIORS

In discussions of the health of American teenagers, one often hears the phrase "new morbidities," which means the negative outcomes that result from early sexual involvement, substance use, and violent behaviors. These problems are called "new" to distinguish them from the "old" morbidities that formerly affected young people, such as acne, obesity, and head lice. Yet, the old morbidities are still with us, and the past was not as innocent as we are led to believe. In my own youth in Plainfield, New Jersey, more than half a century ago, young people also indulged in sex, drugs, and certain forms of delinquency. The consequences, however, were not as dangerous, or at least we were unaware of the consequences. We did not know that smoking might lead to cancer, and the connection between drinking and driving was rarely made explicit. Drug use was mostly confined to "reefers" (marijuana), a substance openly used in the park across the street from my high school in the early 1940s. Boys claimed that they "made out" with a few girls who "put out," but this was more likely gossip than reality. The unlucky girls who got pregnant were bundled off to maternity homes, where they delivered babies that were immediately put up for adoption; few of those girls ever returned to high school. In any case, no one we knew ever died from sexually related diseases, and of course guns were not readily available to young people.

Today almost every teenager at one time or another tries some form of these behaviors. And no teenager is immune from the consequences of random violence or stressful family conditions. In this chapter, we start with a series of snapshots of the most prevalent high-risk behaviors. An important source of information drawn on here is the Youth Risk Behavior Survey (YRBS) conducted by the Centers for Disease Control, which looked at a national sample of high school students. I rely heavily on reports from the 1995 survey that included compilations by sex, race, and grades (ninth to twelfth).[1] We can see the big picture in Table 3.1, which summarizes the rates specifically for 14-year-old males and females. First I will discuss the high-risk behaviors of current students; later, I will compare the differences in vulnerability between students and dropouts.

Substance Use

Most high school students report that at some time in their lives they have used alcohol, drugs, or tobacco. More than 71 percent of high school students

TABLE 3.1 Percent of Male and Female 14 Year Olds Involved in High-Risk Behaviors, 1995

Behavior	Male (percent)	Female (percent)
Substance use		
Current smoking	32%	30%
Current drinking	47	44
Heavy drinking	28	20
Current marijuana	24	17
Hard drugs	5	1
Sexual Activity		
Sexually active	41	32
Use condoms (if sexually active)	66	59
Delinquency		
Adjudicated	7	1
Carry weapon	34	9
Carry gun	14	3
Fight	55	37
Depression		
Suicide thoughts	18	34
Suicide attempt	7	15
School problems		
One year behind	26	21
Two years behind	5	3

Source: Centers for Disease Control and Prevention, "Youth Risk Behavioral Surveillance—United States, 1995." *Morbidity and Mortality Weekly Report*, September 27, 1996, 45:ss-5; and U.S. Census Bureau, "School Enrollment," *Current Population Reports*, Series P-20-479, Table A-3, pp. A-16–A-20, 1993.

Current means at least once during past month. Heavy drinking means five or more drinks on one occasion during past month.

report that they have tried cigarettes, 42 percent have smoked marijuana, 27 percent have had a cigar, 7 percent report trying cocaine, and 80 percent have had at least one drink of alcohol at some time during their lives. But a much smaller proportion report heavy and frequent substance use during the previous month.

CIGARETTES

About 35 percent of students had smoked at least once during the thirty-day period prior to the survey, and 16 percent had smoked almost every day. Frequent smokers were more likely to be in eleventh and twelfth grades and more likely to be White than Hispanic or African American. Females smoked at levels similar to males.

MARIJUANA

One-fourth of all students reported that they had used marijuana at least once during the previous thirty days. Males were significantly more likely to be users than females (28 percent versus 22 percent), with higher use among African American males (37 percent) and Hispanic males (32 percent) than White males (27 percent). While use goes up with age, 17 percent of females and 24 percent of males in the ninth grade said that they had smoked marijuana in the previous month.

CIGARS

A special survey reported on by the Centers for Disease Control in 1997 asked teenagers whether they had ever smoked cigars.[2] Much to the dismay of health advocates, fully 27 percent of 14 to 19 year olds had smoked a cigar at least once in the previous year, and almost 3 percent had smoked more than fifty. Respondents reported that part of the reason for the rising popularity of cigars was to obtain the wrappers and refill them with marijuana. This news fits in with the general pattern of increased smoking among teenagers despite intensified anti-smoking campaigns.

COCAINE

Reported current cocaine use by high school students in the YRBS is low. About 3 percent of the students claimed to have used cocaine during the previous month, with slightly higher levels of use acknowledged by males, particularly Hispanic males (9 percent).

ALCOHOL

During the preceding month, more than half of all students drank alcohol at some time, and one-third admitted to having five or more drinks on one or more occasions. These heavy episodic drinkers were more frequently males (36 percent) than females (29 percent). Hispanic students reported the highest rates of heavy drinking, with little difference between males (39 percent) and females (36 percent). White males also have a high rate (39 percent); the rate for White females is 32 percent. African American youngsters have lower rates, 13 percent for females and 25 percent for males. All of these rates indicate a serious drinking problem among today's youth. No one—adult or teen—can have five drinks in a row without negative effects.

USE ON SCHOOL PROPERTY

The students were asked whether they were ever involved in any of these behaviors while on school property. Some 16 percent had smoked cigarettes, 9 percent had used marijuana, and 6 percent had actually drunk alcohol while at school during the past month. Almost one-third had been offered, sold, or given an illegal drug on school property during the past year. These experiences were particularly prevalent among Hispanic males (47 percent), indicating just how available these substances are to adolescents even in places that seem to be protected environments.

EARLY INITIATION OF SUBSTANCE USE

About one-fourth of all high school students had already smoked a cigarette when they were 12 or younger, one-third had finished a drink, and 8 percent had already tried marijuana. Ninth graders were the most likely to report early initiation, proving the extent to which high-risk behaviors are starting in younger and younger children. For example, 28 percent of ninth graders smoked before age 13, compared to 22 percent of twelfth graders.

TRENDS

Substance use among adolescents has been tracked for several decades by the University of Michigan, the National Household Survey on Drug Use, and the YRBS. Although there was a significant decline in the 1980s, in recent years increases in cigarette and cigar smoking, and marijuana and cocaine use have been reported, as well as an upturn in the amount of binge drinking. Students report less concern about the consequences of substance use than in the past, and greater access to the sources of supply in school and out in the community. Peer disapproval of marijuana has also declined, from a high of 70 percent among high school seniors in 1992 to 58 percent in 1994.

The leading cause of death among all young people, however, is unintentional injuries due to alcohol-related motor vehicle accidents. The rate has dropped significantly in recent years, apparently due to the use of seat belts, safer autos, reduced speed limits, and enforcement of drunken driving laws, particularly among those under age 21. Yet drivers between the ages of 16 and 20 who were involved in fatal crashes were more likely than any other age group to have been under the influence of alcohol.

Sexual Behavior

More than 50 percent of all high school students report that they have had sexual intercourse, and 38 percent say that they have had intercourse within the past three months and are currently sexually active. Over 50 percent of the currently sexually active students claim that they use condoms, and 17 percent say they relied on birth control pills the last time they had intercourse.

Male students (54 percent) are only slightly more likely to say that they have had intercourse than female students (52 percent), with much larger differences in the earlier grades than the later ones. Among ninth graders, typically 14 years old, 37 percent had already had intercourse once—32 percent of females and 41 percent of males, a spread of 9 percentage points. By twelfth grade, 66 percent of females and 67 percent of males reported having had intercourse, only a 1-point difference between the sexes.

The gender divergence is reversed among those who report that they have been sexually active within the past three months. Some 40 percent of females compared to 36 percent of males were currently sexually active, possibly reflecting the fact that many teenage females have sex with older males. African American students report much higher levels of current sexual activity—51 percent for females and 58 percent for males—compared to Hispanics (39 percent of both) and Whites (38 percent females and 32 percent males).

Condom use during last intercourse is more likely to be reported by male students (61 percent) than female students (49 percent). Conversely, 20 percent of females and 14 percent of males' partners used birth control pills as their method of contraception. We don't know from this survey how many students used both methods simultaneously, but clearly a significant group did not use any.

One measure of risk for sexually transmitted diseases is the number of sex partners students have had during their lifetimes. Four or more is the cutoff point used in this survey. Almost 18 percent reported four or more partners, with the highest rates among African American females (22 percent) and males (52 percent). This reflects the early age of initiation of sexual intercourse among African American boys. Some 41 percent of them reported that they had experienced sexual intercourse for the first time prior to the age of 13, a much higher proportion than for the high school population as a whole, of whom 9 percent reported early initiation.

A clear outcome of sexual activity is parenthood. Females under the age of 20 accounted for half a million births in 1993. Girls under age 15 had 12,554 births, and those between 15 and 17 had 190,535. The birth rate for 15 to 17 year olds was 38 per 1,000, indicating that about 4 percent of girls in that age group had a baby. About 8 percent of African American 15 to 17 year olds became mothers in 1993 compared to about 7 percent of Hispanic and 2 percent of white, non-Hispanic teenagers that age. Most of these births were to unmarried young women. Many of the fathers were several years older, and many of the pregnancies resulted from rape, incest, and other forms of forced sex.

TRENDS

The reported rates of sexual activity among adolescents increased dramatically during the past several decades, particularly among White youth, who have almost "caught up" with African American youth. Girls are now reporting rates almost as high as boys. In recent years, the incidence among all teens has begun to decrease, while condom use has increased significantly, perhaps in response to concerns about contracting HIV.

The adolescent birth rate dropped in the early 1980s, rose in the early 1990s, and now appears to be declining. By 1995, the birth rate had fallen to 57 births per 1,000, from the peak of 62 per 1,000 in 1991, an 8 percent drop. Although we do not have access to the most recent data, it appears that the abortion rate among teenagers has also declined, suggesting a dip in the total pregnancy rate. The estimated pregnancy rate among sexually active teens has decreased in recent years, presumably due to the improvement in contraceptive use.[3]

Violence

The Youth Risk Behavior Survey included questions about the use of weapons by students, and the incidence of reported weapon-carrying is remarkably high. More than one in five students reported that they had carried some kind of weapon—a gun, knife, or club—during the thirty days preceding the survey, and about half of them claimed to have carried the weapon on school property. Males (31 percent) were much more likely to report weapon-carrying than females (8 percent), with few differences accounted for by age or race among males. However, 16 percent of African American females reported carrying a weapon, compared to 13 percent of Hispanic and 5 percent of White females.

One out of three of the weapons was a gun. Almost 8 percent of all students reported carrying a gun within the previous month—12 percent of males and 3 percent of females. Close to one out of five, some 19 percent of African American males, reported carrying a gun, as did 17 percent of Hispanic males and 10 percent of White males.

Physical fights are very common among students. Almost half of all males and a third of females had been in a fight during the previous year, and 4 percent reported being injured. About 16 percent had been in fights on school property.

More than one-third of the students had property stolen or deliberately damaged on school property, and 5 percent felt too unsafe to go to school. Younger students and Hispanic students were most likely to say that they hesitated to go to school because of unsafe conditions.

Many of these gun-toting young people turn up in juvenile justice statistics. More than 2 million juvenile arrests were made in 1993 throughout the country, and, according to the Department of Justice, almost 1.5 million of these cases were handled in Juvenile Court. This represents a dramatic increase over 1988, when there were fewer than 1.2 million cases.[4] More than 5 percent of all 10 to 17 year olds were taken to court, with the rate reaching 11 percent at age 16. Males were almost five times more likely to be arrested than females (9 percent versus 2 percent), but the number of young women in the juvenile justice system is growing rapidly. Although twice as many White teenagers were arrested as African Americans, the juvenile arrest rate for African American youngsters (12 percent) was three times the White rate (4 percent). One in five of those arrested was detained in secure facilities.

TRENDS

The most alarming fact about teens and violence is the rise in the homicide rate for 14 to 17 year olds, which has gone from 7.0 to 19.1 per 100,000 in just a decade.[5] Among African American males the rate has risen from 44.3 to 139.6, and among White males it has risen from 7.0 to 15.6. This dramatic rise is attributable to the availability of handguns beginning in 1985. James Fox, an expert on juvenile crime, asserts:

> The problem of kids with guns cannot be overstated. A 14-year-old armed with a gun is far more menacing than a 44-year-old with a gun. While the negative socializing forces of drugs, guns, gangs and the media have become more threatening, the positive socializing forces of family, school, religion, and neighborhood have grown relatively weak and ineffective.[6]

Depression

This chapter started with a quote from a high school student who claimed, "I don't know if I will live long enough to die of natural causes." Given the threatening environment surrounding these students, it should not be surprising that many teenagers feel beleaguered. Almost one in four high school students reported that they had thought seriously about attempting suicide during the previous year, and almost 9 percent had actually attempted suicide. Females were more likely to think about suicide than males (30 percent versus 18 percent) and more likely to try to kill themselves (12 percent versus 6 percent). The rates for attempted suicide were strikingly high among Hispanic females— 20 percent—compared to 11 percent of other groups. No differences were reported in age in regard to thinking about suicide, but actual attempts were more prevalent in ninth grade (10 percent) than in twelfth (7 percent). Although girls are more likely to report suicidal feelings than boys, the actual suicide rate is more than four times higher among boys. In 1993, the rate (per 100,000) for 15 to 19 year old males was 18 compared to about 4 for 15 to 19 year old females. White teenagers have somewhat higher rates than African Americans.

According to a recent review of the health of adolescents, the presence of developmental, behavioral, or emotional problems among youth under age 18 ranges from 17 percent to 22 percent.[7] It is estimated that approximately 5 million adolescents have emotional or behavioral problems. In fact, about 1.8 million teens have been designated as eligible for special education classes in schools. Among all children in special education, about half are learning disabled, one-fourth speech impaired, 12 percent retarded, and 9 percent emotionally disturbed.

TRENDS

Measures of "suicidal ideation" were not available prior to the initiation of the Youth Risk Behavior Survey. Practitioners report that the demand for personal counseling continues to mount and that young people are "more depressed than ever." Suicide is the third leading cause of death among teenagers. Although the rates are still very low compared to deaths from auto injuries and violence, they have been rising slightly in recent years.

School Failure

In the previous chapter, it was pointed out that young people rarely drop out of school before the age of 17, at least officially. Experiences that lead to dropping out, however, start much earlier. One of the strongest determinants of dropping out is being behind in school—sitting in classrooms surrounded by younger and higher-achieving students. Many children can overcome one year of being left back, but two or more such experiences of failure leave the child feeling only marginally connected to school and virtually predict the collapse of any sense of a positive relationship with the school.

The U.S. Census collects data on the age of youths and their years in school. For each grade, there is a "model" year. For example, 14 year olds are typically in the ninth grade. Using these census figures, one can compute the number of young people for each grade who are older or younger than their peers. In any recent year among 10 to 17 year olds, about 25 percent were one year older and 5 percent two or more years older than their classmates. We can only assume that older students were left back, although in some cases they started school at a later age than their age group. For those who are two years behind, it is a safe assumption that it's due to academic failure.

Males are much more likely to be kept back than females, particularly African American males. By the ages of 15 to 17, more than half of all African American males are behind their age peers. Among Hispanic males, 46 percent in that age group are below modal grade, as are 36 percent of White males. About one-third of African American females across age groups are behind, as are one-fourth of Whites and Hispanics. In terms of numbers, 7 million students between 10 and 17 are one year behind, and nearly 1.5 million are two years behind. Of those who are two years behind, 61 percent are males, 57 percent are White, 27 percent African American, and 16 percent Hispanic.

A detailed study of eighth graders found that about 30 percent of that group were one year older than their peers (who were 14), and 6 percent two or more years older.[8] In this group, 18 percent reported that they had been held back at least once, and, of these, 13 percent reported repeating two or more grades (2 percent of the total). Repeaters were much more likely to be found in families where the parents had limited education and were poor. The study found:

American Indians [sic], Hispanics, and blacks are more likely than Asians and whites to repeat a grade. Among those who ever repeated, Asians and whites are more likely than blacks to report repeating kindergarten. Limited-English Proficient (LEP) students are more likely than others to repeat grades, 30 percent of LEP students repeated at least one grade compared with only 17 percent of non-LEP students.[9]

One problem confronting disadvantaged students that is rarely noted is summer loss. A program that tested participants before the summer break and when they returned to school in the fall found that the average student had dropped six months behind over the summer months.[10] Without daily stimulation, much of the school-year learning was lost.

WHO DOES WHAT?

Almost every young person has tried one or more of the risky behaviors described here, with potentially negative consequences. But that piece of information doesn't really create a framework for thinking about solutions. Many researchers who have studied adolescent problems have concluded that problem behaviors significantly overlap. And any sensitive observer can probably figure

---

SNAPSHOT: HIGH-RISK BEHAVIORS AMONG TEENS TODAY

Substance Abuse: More than one-third smoke frequently—16 percent smoke every day. One-fourth use marijuana frequently. More than half use alcohol frequently. Almost one-third are very heavy drinkers. Substances are readily available and often used on school property. Heavy drug use among high school students is minimal.

Sexual Behavior: Half have had sexual intercourse. Rates go up with age—by twelfth grade, few differences exist between males and females. Almost three-fourths use condoms or pills, but many are still not protected. Teen birth rates have peaked and are declining.

Violence: Twenty percent of high school students carry a weapon, and 12 percent of males carry a gun. Fighting is a common experience. Many students feel unsafe in school.

Depression: About one in four young people think about suicide. Close to one in ten report suicide attempts.

School failure: Few 10 to 17 year olds drop out, but 25 percent are one year behind their modal grade, and 5 percent are two or more years behind. Almost 20 percent of eighth graders have been left back.

Trends: Over the past decade, the most significant changes in high-risk behaviors have been the increase in weapon carrying and homicides. Minor fluctuations have been displayed in the use of substances, the prevalence of unprotected early sexual activity, minor delinquency such as truancy, and school failure. All high-risk behaviors start earlier than ever.

out that some young people are in trouble while others are doing well. We know that those young people involved in one kind of behavior, like drugs, are very vulnerable to getting involved in other kinds of behavior, like truancy or early unprotected intercourse.

Many articles have been written on this subject, so I will only summarize the major conclusions here:[11]

- Early initiation of any negative behavior generally predicts that other problems will follow.

- Substance abuse is closely related to delinquency.

- Almost all incarcerated youngsters report some involvement with drugs.

- Heavy alcohol, smoking, and marijuana use appear to co-occur with early unprotected intercourse.

- Young people who initiate sex at early ages, have multiple partners, and do not use protection, are often under the influence of alcohol or drugs when they participate in sexual activity.

Dropouts appear to be involved with sex, drugs, and violence to a much greater degree than enrolled high school students. Falling behind in school is a strong predictor of dropping out and is associated with all of the high-risk behaviors reviewed here. Depression and stress, as measured by suicidal ideation, are strongly related to early intercourse. Sexual abuse is implicated in this pathway, as it is related to both unprotected sex and depression. Failure in school reflects low expectations and a kind of hopelessness that are associated with suicidal thoughts and attempts.

An Old Estimate

I have long been interested in figuring out the patterns of occurrences of high-risk behaviors and the overlap between one behavior and another. For the book *Adolescents at Risk*, I developed a set of "synthetic estimates" of the proportions of 10 to 17 year olds who "did it all" and of those who seemed to be relatively risk-free. The estimates were synthetic because no one survey could produce the numbers I needed, so I constructed approximate figures based on the results from several different surveys.

As of a decade ago, I estimated that about 10 percent of 10 to 17 year olds were at extremely high risk because they simultaneously were delinquent, failing in school, abusing drugs, and having early unprotected sex; 15 percent were at high risk because they did all of these things, but had not yet been arrested and placed in the juvenile justice system; 25 percent were at moderate risk because they were occasionally truant, weren't doing very well in school, experimented with drugs and alcohol, and had sexual intercourse; and 50 percent were at low or no risk because they appeared to be doing reasonably well in school and were not involved in any behaviors with potentially negative consequences.

Today's 14 Year Olds

A decade has passed, and as we have seen, not much has changed in the status of young people. What has changed is the availability of survey data to check out that synthetic estimate and add some new factors to it. I thought it would be useful to narrow down the age range and attempt to profile one group right in the middle of our target population—namely 14 year olds—most of whom are in ninth grade. This is the transition year into high school, the time that many observers believe is the "make-or-break" point for young people. These 14 year olds may move into high school with little difficulty and adjust well to the different structure, or they may be quite intimidated and drift inwardly, or they may take up with a group of peers who are acting out and experimenting with risky behaviors. Some adolescents appear to fall into each of these patterns on different days, depending on their moods and their opportunities.

We know that many young people are at very low risk. They rarely take chances or experiment with behaviors that they know can have dangerous consequences. Using data from several large-scale studies conducted by the Search Institute, the configurations of risk indicators can be determined.[12] In a national sample of ninth graders, 22 percent reported no involvement with any of the at-risk behaviors (including substance use, sex, depression/suicide, antisocial behavior, school problems, vehicle safety, and bulimia). Another 29 percent had one such indicator, 18 percent had two, and 31 percent had three or more. A more recent survey of Michigan youth, using the Search Institute methodology, produced evidence of more youths being at high risk. Among ninth graders, 20 percent were not at risk in any behavioral areas, 22 percent were at risk in only one, 17 percent in two, and 41 percent in three or more.[13]

These two studies provide great insights into the patterns of risky behaviors. For example, in Michigan, 18 percent of the ninth graders were at risk because of school problems (frequent absence and a desire to drop out). Some 48 percent of those with school problems reported excessive alcohol use, compared to 17 percent of those without school problems. Some 66 percent of those with school problems were involved in unprotected sexual activity, compared to 33 percent of those without school problems.

I have allocated the problem behaviors among the 14 year olds to sort out who does what according to the studies mentioned above and other sources of information. Table 3.2 presents the numbers and percentages of 14 year olds who are at very high, high, moderate, low, and no risk.

VERY HIGH-RISK YOUTH

According to my estimates, very high-risk youngsters are those who have entered into the juvenile justice system within the past year, who carry guns, and/or who use illegal drugs such as cocaine. About 10 percent of all 14 year olds fall into this category. It is estimated that among these young people more

TABLE 3.2 Estimates of the Number and Percent of 14 Year Olds in 1995 According to Risk Groups

Risk Group	Number	Percent of Total
Total	3,571,000	100
Very high risk (do it all)	357,000	10
High risk (do most of it)	892,000	25
Moderate risk (experiment)	892,000	25
Low risk (occasional)	715,000	20
No risk (no involvement)	715,000	20

Source: Population: U.S. Bureau of the Census, *Statistical Abstract of the United States 1996*, Washington, D.C.: U.S. Department of Commerce, Table 16, p.16, 1996. Risk group percents: estimates derived by author based on Table 3.1 and other sources.

than 50 percent have been arrested at least once during the year. Almost all have access to guns. At least 80 percent drink, 40 percent use illegal drugs, and 90 percent are sexually active without using protection. About 40 percent are depressed, and many have attempted suicide. Only a few have officially dropped out of school, but 40 percent are two or more years behind and the remainder one year behind. Thus, one out of ten 14 year olds are in serious trouble, already labeled delinquent and a school failure. To change their life courses will require case management and treatment of the most intensive kinds.

HIGH-RISK YOUTH

Another 25 percent of all 14 year olds are at high risk. Although they have not yet been involved with the juvenile justice system, some of them are particularly vulnerable because of delinquent and antisocial behaviors. They are heavily involved with drinking, smoking, and marijuana; behind modal grade in school and often truant; and frequently have unprotected intercourse. Others might be identified as at elevated risk for mental health problems. These adolescents are involved in similar risky behaviors, but they also are extremely depressed as indicated by suicide attempts. These high-risk youngsters—one-quarter of all 14 year olds—are in great jeopardy unless they receive immediate, intensive interventions that will act as deterrents to further involvement in behaviors with negative consequences.

MODERATE-RISK YOUTH

Moderate-risk young people make up another quarter of the 14 year olds and are involved in one or two high-risk behaviors. They may be behind in school and occasionally truant, or drink once in a while, or experiment with marijuana, or have sex (rarely without contraception), or feel depressed from time to time.

These young people are clearly vulnerable because of their behaviors and need considerable support in order not to deepen their involvement with risky behaviors in a way that would put their futures in jeopardy.

LOW- AND NO-RISK YOUTH

About 20 percent of 14 year olds are at low risk. They might take a drink once in a while or cut a class, but they are not in any serious jeopardy because of their behaviors. A few are sexually active, but they always use contraception. Another 20 percent of all 14 year olds are at no risk. They report no high-risk behaviors, no depression, and no school problems.

These young people, more than two-fifths of their age cohort, are currently protected from the most deleterious consequences of the new morbidities. But they are surrounded by many of the negative factors that may promote antisocial behavior. They are also in jeopardy of being victimized by other youth. And their resilience is strongly dependent on the stability of their families, the quality of their schools, and the safety of their neighborhoods—all factors that can change.

By applying the estimates of risk status in Table 3.2 to the total number of 14 year olds (about 3.6 million) we can get an idea of the relative size of various target populations. Over one-third of all 14 year olds (more than 1.2 million) appear to be at high risk. They have little chance of making it to adulthood without a great deal of attention. Another large group, about 25 percent (almost 2 million), are in jeopardy of not making it if they intensify their involvement in risky behaviors as they go through high school. Finally, the largest group, 40 percent of all 14 year olds (more than 1.4 million), are at little or not risk, and if they continue to live in supportive families and attend good schools, they should make it through adolescence without major difficulties.

These estimates differ from previous ones in several ways. First of all, they only encompass 14 year olds. In several areas, the prevalence has risen since the estimates of a decade ago—for example, both substance use and sexual activity rates have increased in this age group. As a result, more young people are vulnerable than in the past. The bottom line is that more than one-third of 14 year olds, the turning point of adolescence, are at very high risk of failing to make it unless they receive immediate, intensive attention. This at-risk group is not difficult to identify and should be the primary target for social interventions that work toward the assurance of Safe Passage.[14]

COMMON CHARACTERISTICS OF HIGH-RISK YOUTH

Extensive quantitative and ethnographic research sheds light on the lives of high-risk youth, low-risk youth, and another group of great interest, disadvantaged young people who make it against all odds—resilient youth. If we examine the predictors or determinants of the different behaviors—for example, frequency of illegal drug use, unprotected sex leading to parenthood or sexually transmitted diseases, or extended absences from school—we find a similar list of factors, no matter what the subject. I do not mean to imply that every sexually active 14 year old is involved with alcohol, nor is every boy who cuts school in ninth grade likely to become a criminal, but rather that young people heavily involved in behaviors that have potentially damaging consequences share many common characteristics.

Early "Acting Out"

High-risk behaviors start at very young ages. Recent surveys have shown earlier and earlier initiation by youths of substance use, sexual intercourse, and antisocial activities. In one urban area, 10 percent of 7 year olds had already committed a street offense, such as bike theft or purse snatching. The earlier the start, the more serious the later problems and the more likely that one type of behavior will lead to another (alcohol use at 10, sex at 12). Aggressive behavior in preschool is an indicator of future maladjustment. A first-grade teacher once told me that she could pick out the children who would later become troublemakers from the way they acted in her classroom.

Absence of Nurturing Parents

It's not the number of parents, it's the quality of the parenting. High-risk youth lack nurturance, attention, supervision, understanding, and caring. They do not have adequate communication with responsible adults. The lack of books and computers in the home and of access to libraries limit the potential of these youth. Children of parents with drug or mental health problems are at particularly high risk.

Evidence of Child Abuse

Child abuse creates vulnerability to a whole array of negative outcomes. Young people who are in the juvenile justice system, in runaway or homeless shelters, or in foster care all report having experienced extremely high rates of sexual or physical abuse during their childhood years. A very high proportion of girls who become mothers while still in their teen years have been victims of rape and incest at early ages.

Disengagement from School

Young people who are failing in school, have been left back, or have already dropped out are extremely vulnerable. School problems can be detected as early as first grade, when poor reading ability has been shown to relate to other difficulties. Problem behavior rates—especially teen pregnancy and delinquency—are much higher in schools that are disproportionately attended by minority populations and segregated. These schools often have low expectations for students, oppressive environments, high suspension and expulsion rates, and discouraged teachers who produce students who "act out" more frequently. And, of course, dropouts are at significantly higher levels of risk than all other young people.

No new research is needed to identify high-risk students. The knowledge of age and grade in any classroom will produce a list of those behind modal grade. Being two years behind in school is a sure indicator of trouble ahead.

Easily Influenced by Peers

When other supports such as families and schools are lacking, young people are more easily influenced by peers. Susceptible youth seek peer approval by being "badder," committing more violent acts, and being disruptive in school. They look to gangs as a substitute for family. Some studies have shown that problem behaviors are associated with "unconventional" versus "conventional" behavior. Vulnerable youth conform to what they perceive to be peer norms and peer culture in opposition to what they perceive to be societal norms. However, opposition to social norms may be a rational response to certain issues—for example, in my lifetime, opposition to the Vietnam War was initially perceived as "unconventional" behavior.

Depression

A strong link has been shown between various forms of "acting out" and depression. The depression appears to be stress related, reflecting sexual and physical abuse and neglect, family problems, neighborhood violence (drive-by shootings), and detachment from school. High-risk youth see little future for themselves or their generation. Homeless and street youth are particularly vulnerable.

Residence in Disadvantaged Neighborhoods

Rates of severe problem behaviors are elevated in poverty areas. Gun violence, drug sales, teen parenthood, sexually transmitted diseases, and school failure are all prevalent in low-income neighborhoods, where young people lack access to social resources such as churches, viable businesses, community police, and community centers. Nothing is left of the old stable community except decaying school buildings. Schools are underfinanced and, with few exceptions, of much lower quality than in upper-income areas. Mobility is very high; families move frequently, another factor that predicts falling behind scholastically.

Certain high-risk behaviors such as excessive alcohol use and driving while intoxicated are not associated with low socioeconomic status. Not all high-risk youth are in disadvantaged families, but young people growing up in poverty in inner cities and in rural areas are much more likely to be at high risk than those living in middle-class and suburban areas. Poverty, rather than race or ethnicity, is a significant marker for risk.

Nonexposure to the World of Work

Many high-risk youth do not know anyone in the labor force. They lack role models—family members or friends who have prepared for a career and found gainful employment. The young people themselves have no idea of how to enter the labor force, have unrealistic dreams about the future (many believe that they will be famous basketball pros or rap artists), and have no access to career options.

RESILIENT YOUTH

I have stated that young people can be assigned to very different risk levels according to the incidence of their behaviors. The 35 percent of 14 year olds at high risk of not "making it" share significant common characteristics having to do with family, school, community, and individual factors. Not every young person in a dysfunctional family, not every student in an inferior school, not all children growing up in disadvantaged neighborhoods fail to thrive. A relatively new area of adolescent research focuses on this special population: resilient, invulnerable, successful-despite-the-odds young people.

The small unknown number of "survivors" who have made it have been studied by several prominent researchers, most notably Emmy Werner[15] and Norman Garmazy[16] in the early 1980s, and, currently, Robert Blum,[17] Michael Resnick,[18] and J. David Hawkins.[19] These successful youth also share common characteristics that are the flip side of those identified among the young people at highest risk.

Attachment to a Caring Adult

The best-documented fact in the extensive U.S. literature on youth is the importance of social bonding between a young person and an adult. The responsible adult may be either or both parents (single mothers can perform this function very well), a grandparent, a teacher, or any other mentor. Consistency, caring, encouragement, and maintenance of contact through childhood and adolescence are all important factors.

Independence and Competence

Many children who make it despite all odds appear to have a strong streak of independence. They can make decisions and solve problems on their own, seeming to have a built-in competence that helps them overcome barriers that arise in poor social environments. Others describe them as having "sunny personalities." During periods of stress, resilient youth appear to be able to distance themselves from their troubled families.

High Aspirations

Autobiographical accounts contribute to our understanding of how the dreamer becomes the doer, how the disadvantaged youngster who wants to be a scientist finds out how to get on the achievement track at the earliest age and realizes her dream. Usually, an adult is involved in helping turn the aspirations into reality.

Effective Schools

A supportive and challenging school can act as a significant influence in the life of a disadvantaged youngster. As researchers express it, "The effect of all the other variables is through education"—in other words, when other factors such as family structure, socioeconomic status, and race are taken into consideration, access to a strong educational system is a crucial factor. Caring teachers with high expectations for students can act as buffers against the outside world and help young people to achieve their goals.

LOW-RISK YOUTH

At least 40 percent of U.S. youth appear to be on the achievement track—they have strong supportive families, go to effective schools, and live in safe neighborhoods. These fortunate youngsters are more likely to be White non-Hispanics and to reside in suburban areas with many social resources. They are surrounded by protective factors. But these factors are not immutable. All families are at risk of change, and family members can be devastated by life events: sudden death, divorce, illness, unemployment, and, increasingly, random violent acts.

When I was a child long ago, my life script was fairly well-assured from birth; I was solidly in the middle class with clear expectations regarding educational achievement and, ultimately, marrying the right guy. Life is much more hazardous as we approach the twenty-first century, and my little granddaughters face a much more uncertain future because of sweeping economic, social, demographic, and even climatic changes. So all children growing up today are vulnerable, and even those at low risk for problem behaviors require protection against stress and violence and may need social supports in the event of negative change.

ARE THESE DISTRIBUTIONS UNIQUE TO THE UNITED STATES?

Sir Michael Rutter, a professor at the University of London, has been the "guru's guru" in the study of adolescent behaviors for many decades. Early on, he identified the importance of early school experience and attachment as primary factors in psychosocial development. His views on how the trends in the United States compare to those in Western Europe and the rest of the world have great credibility. Recently, he observed that, on the whole, crime, drug taking, attempted suicide, and depressive disorders among young people have become pervasive throughout the world.[20] But significant differences can be observed in the United States in regard to murder rates, teenage pregnancies, and abortion. "The conclusion of virtually all scientific commentators [regarding the murder rate] . . . lies in the greater availability of murder weapons, namely guns." The level of sexual activity in the United States does not explain the higher pregnancy rate, since it does not differ from the level in Western Europe. Instead, he believes the differences are attributable to the much lower use of contraception in the United States, reflecting both lack of accessibility and conflicting attitudes. So far as changing moral values are involved, the trend in Europe has been toward an *increase* in tolerance toward sexuality and personal behavior, but a *decrease* in tolerance for illegal acts such as carrying a gun.

Comparing the relative status of adolescents with a Dutch colleague, I was interested in his statement that in his country it was "unthinkable" for a girl to become a mother during her teen years. All the social institutions in Holland— families, schools, health providers, churches, media—are lined up to assist young people to practice safe sex by providing them with both the information and birth control they need when they decide to become sexually active. Can you imagine a time in the United States when it will be "unthinkable" for a young person to get into so much trouble? Can we ever line up all our social institutions to be responsive to the needs of our children?

MOVING TOWARD SAFE PASSAGE

This brief review of which adolescents are at risk can be useful for laying out a framework for designing more effective and targeted programs. In fact, we must use our research base for shaping strategies for Safe Passage. Rather than continuing to address the problems of adolescents in fragmented pieces, we must turn to more comprehensive solutions that deal with the underlying issues found in families, schools, and communities. We have seen how the highest-risk youths have been forced to fend for themselves without parental nurturing or community supports. Yet some children get "rescued" by forming attachments to responsible adults at home or in school. These facts alone should point the way toward systematizing "caring" so that every young person is assured consistent nurturing and support.

The status of young people growing up in the United States today is uncertain. Ours is a high-risk society moving further and further away from dealing with the problems implicit in all that I have described: children on the margins, beset by growing poverty, homelessness, dangerous streets, racial tensions, and lack of access to the powerful school and community institutional supports they need.

It is ironic that while so many children are failing, so many educational, health, and mental health practitioners of every description are working hard in so many programs to prevent that failure. You might characterize this situation as the best and the worst of America, a country with such great contrasts between the haves and the have-nots, the doers and the takers, the believers and the skeptics. So let's now visit some exciting places, look at full-service community schools and schools in general, and review specialized prevention programs in community agencies and schools that address the problems of sex, drugs, and violence.

PART II

PROGRAMS TODAY: THE CONTEMPORARY SCENE

4

VISITS TO FIVE OUTSTANDING SAFE PASSAGE PROGRAMS

She is just like a second mother to me. I will never forget this lady. She's been such a big part of my life. I don't think she really understands how much she means to me. This lady is God's angel. She works and works and stays on my case about sex, school, and life—period. She's been such a blessing to me . . . and she believes in me, although she may get upset with me, because she loves me and wants the best for me.

—Participant in Quantum Opportunities Program

To single out any one program and designate it as exemplary is not a simple assignment. So many excellent efforts are going on all around the country. Yet I wanted to be able to take you inside a couple of places and share the experiences of being there, picking up the "vibes" from the program providers and the participants. I looked for exemplary programs that concentrated on teenagers; that could provide evidence that the program assured Safe Passage by promoting educational outcomes, preventing new morbidities, and demonstrating high expectations for youth; and that represented a variety of types and locales that I could visit. These five were selected:

Centro Sister Isolino Ferre, a youth and family center with a police sub-station (Koban) in Caimito, Puerto Rico

Quantum Opportunities Program, an after-school enrichment program run by Opportunities Industrialization Centers in Philadelphia

El Puente, a high school in a community center in Williamsburg, New York

Caring Connection, a comprehensive, multicomponent, multi-agency program run by the Marshalltown School District in Marshalltown, Iowa

Turner Middle School, a university-assisted community school run in collaboration with the University of Pennsylvania in Philadelphia.

CENTRO SISTER ISOLINO FERRE, CAIMITO, PUERTO RICO

On the way out of San Juan, Puerto Rico, as the hills begin to steepen, one comes to a little town of 20,000 called Caimito.[1] This community, like so many others, is experiencing marked deterioration in the quality of life for families due to the increasing rates of drug use, guns, domestic violence, unemployment, and poverty. In the middle of the village, along a winding and rutty road, however, you will find the Centro Sister Isolina Ferre, a Puerto Rican settlement house. Entry to the Centro is directly from the street marked by a suburban-looking pink cement house with a curious sign on the wall—KOBAN. This indicates that the building contains a police presence, organized to be responsive to the needs of the community.

Centros have been in existence since 1968 in Ponce (a major city on the south coast of the island), and in 1987 this one was organized in Caimito. Sister Isolina Ferre, the "patron saint" of the Centros, started this movement with a belief that strengthening families and communities and improving access to education and employment were the keys to helping neighborhoods overcome the problems of crime and delinquency. An important component in this approach to promoting youth competency has been the use of youth advocates, or "intercessors"—young, street-wise community residents who advocate for youth.

The Koban—which means ministation in Japanese—was added to the Centro after the current director, Sister Teresa Geigel, went to Japan to explore the model as part of a visit organized in 1988 by the Milton Eisenhower Foundation.

The idea is to place police officers in nonthreatening situations that will promote responsible behavior and prevent delinquency. In Caimito, a police officer resides with his family in the Koban, which also houses offices for two other police officers, several youth advocates, and a program director. The police officers are fully uniformed and carry guns.

All police in Puerto Rico are employees of the Commonwealth, and the decision to support the Koban was made at the San Juan Police Command, which assigns the three officers to the project and supplies a police car and office equipment. Additional cost for the Koban activity is $75,000 a year, more than half of which comes from state-side funding through the Eisenhower Foundation. These funds support the advocates, project director, and building maintenance. The Koban was built with a grant from the U.S. Department of Housing and Urban Development, and the Centro buildings were purchased and remodeled by the governor's office and private donations. The annual budget for the Centro of approximately half a million dollars is funded by a mix of federal, state, and local funds. A community board that includes parents and leaders oversees this program to ensure that the police and the Centro work smoothly together and are responsive to the neighborhood.

The Koban activity is only a small piece of the Centro. A palm-tree-lined driveway from the street goes down to a central building that accommodates the offices and classrooms. Behind that building is a large campus encircled by six curious-looking outstations. Each little house is built on the base of two truck trailers, which support a peaked wooden roof, added on to create an A-frame structure. Several of the units are specialized classrooms—for computer work, cooking, pottery, and intensive educational enhancement. One of the classrooms incorporates the *only* library in Caimito, open to all who want to use it. One unit is spacious enough to be used as a small gym, and another is completely set up for infant care. One building is devoted to apiculture, the art of extracting honey from bees. To the side of the campus is a basketball court, apparently much used by the clientele of the Centro.

When I asked Sister Teresa who designed the odd-looking buildings, she admitted that she did. "You see, I found out I could get the truck trailers for nothing and I just had to figure out a way to put a roof over them." This "can-do" approach typifies Sister Teresa's approach to problem solving.

At the end of the large property is a huge nursery, the Horticultural Project, set up by the Centro with support from the Conservation Trust of Puerto Rico. As a condition of the grant, the Centro had to promise to produce 100,000 baby trees to replace those destroyed in a hurricane. On our return visit, Sister Teresa couldn't wait to show us how the nursery had grown into a major community development project, employing fifteen local women to produce a vast array of houseplants and exotic trees to sell at the Centro. Another addition was just being built, a house for teenage mothers where they would be taught parenting and homemaking skills.

The Centro offers ten programs run by a staff of sixty-six. During the day,

an alternative school program successfully works with dropouts on school remediation, the acquisition of GEDs, office clerk training, and computer skills.
The young mothers can join classes and other events because their children are
being cared for in the nursery. Immunizations and screenings are provided by
the health department, the only place in Caimito where public health services
are offered. After school, a special program for 6 to 12 year olds gives many
youngsters their first exposure to the arts, along with educational remediation,
sports, and Hispanic culture. During our visits, we observed many teenagers in
classrooms, working in the nursery with the plants, and "hanging out." Many
women were crowded into a cooking class featuring desserts. The whole place
was humming with activity.

The work of the Koban and the work of the Centro are closely coordinated.
The police officers make home visits along with the Centro advocates, and all
work together to involve young people and their families in activities offered by
the Centro. According to Sister Teresa:

> Each arm of the program supports and enhances the other. When the team visits
> a family, the police bring a sense of authority and the advocates a sense of
> sustenance. But the family is introduced to the police as a friend to trust, not
> to fear. The young people overcome their antagonism and get to know the police
> as counselors, sports instructors, and in many different ways, since the police
> are thoroughly integrated into all parts of the Centro program.

The Koban police officers are also a presence in the local schools, turning
up at recess to play ball with the students or to work with the school administrators to get truant students back to school. In some cases, Koban officers
accompany school social workers on home visits to truants.

The staff have many stories about people they have helped. Hundreds of
young people have been supported to stay in school. Others have used the
Centro as a safe haven, as a place to gain new skills, and as a point of referral
to community agencies. One advocate told us:

> We are well-connected in the community, and when we work with the police
> we can produce results. We visited one family that had a long history of domestic
> violence. The husband was known to be abusing his wife. We—the policeman
> and I—had to move fast to find alternative housing until the problem could be
> dealt with.

In another situation, the Koban police convinced the local public works department to fill a dangerous pothole. The primary purpose of all the interactions
is to promote strong families, to prevent youth problems, and to improve the
social environment. The staff's mantra—"prevention is our philosophy"—reflects the orientation of Sister Teresa and the Centro movement.

The Eisenhower Foundation made an effort to track the crime rate in the
Caimito area from 1990 to 1993, starting with the initiation of the Koban.

During this period, the number of serious crimes decreased by 26 percent in the immediate neighborhood served by the Centro while in the rest of the precinct the rate increased almost 3 percent. At the same time, the crime rate decreased by 9 percent in the rest of San Juan, clearly demonstrating a significant difference in the locality of the Koban. Sister Teresa ascribes the changes in the crime rate to

> a decrease not derived from an increase in arrests and incarcerations; it has happened because of prevention activities, . . . officers interacting with youth . . . patrolling the narrow, winding streets and conducting community-oriented police activities. The officers act as mentors and surrogate parents to youth.

Sister Teresa believes that the success of the Koban is due to its being situated in the center of town life and the availability of the advocates to act as a bridge between the police and the community. She warns that

> police officers come with a mentality geared toward intervention, and it takes a lot of training in prevention techniques and infinite patience to achieve the understanding needed for the job.

The Centro has already trained hundreds of Puerto Rican police officers to work in Kobans and housing projects throughout the island. It has also played host to hundreds of police officials from around the world who are eager to initiate community-police programs.

A visit to Centro Sister Isolina Ferre is an inspiring experience. Sister Teresa is a dynamic woman, clearly a problem solver of the first order. When presented with a new challenge, she moves quickly to meet it. Currently, she is organizing to buy a large piece of property that abuts the Centro so she can expand successful programs such as the Horticultural Project. She would like to introduce young people to agriculture, a goal very much in keeping with the stated needs of the Commonwealth of Puerto Rico to interest people in the development of small farms. But this is not a one-woman operation. Sister has surrounded herself with many committed and well-qualified staff members who carry out their functions with great enthusiasm.

QUANTUM OPPORTUNITIES PROGRAM

When other Philadelphia teenagers are hanging out on street corners or sitting in front of television sets or hassling each other over a pair of sneakers, a group of young people gather in the afternoons after school to attend the Quantum Opportunities Program (QOP).[2] This effort is located in the national headquarters of the Opportunities Industrialization Centers of America (OIC) on a busy street in the heart of the city. On the day we visited, about thirty teenagers were huddled over computers, busily applying themselves to programmed educational enhancement, or getting help from their counselors. What was going on here?

QOP is described by its designers, Benjamin Lattimore, director of Literacy Programs, OIC, and Robert Taggart, president of Remediation and Training Institute, as an innovative, four-year, year-round program that provides learning opportunities, development opportunities, service opportunities, and summer jobs to small groups of youth from disadvantaged families. The theory is that intensive and varied interventions are necessary to make a difference in young people's lives, and that the adults who deliver these services must be both nurturing and tough. Financial incentives further the chances for success. As Ben Lattimore puts it:

> How do you treat your own kids? You reward them when they behave well, and punish them when they don't. It's a simple idea, and certainly not novel. But it works.[3]

QOP is designed to provide education, community-service experience, and social skills over a four-year period no matter how much or how little each student participates. In other words, QOP is there for them for as many or as few hours as they choose to attend.

Beginning in 1989, QOP was launched as a five-site demonstration project in Philadelphia, Saginaw, Oklahoma City, San Antonio, and Milwaukee, with each location's activities organized and administered through the local OIC chapter. OIC, founded thirty-four years ago by Reverend Leon Sullivan to help African Americans gain entry to the labor force, now serves seventy affiliates and is the country's largest job-training, technical-assistance, literacy, and social development organization.

With support from the Ford Foundation, the program initially enrolled twenty-five youths in each of the pilot five communities. These youths were selected randomly from a list of students who were from welfare families and who were the most at risk for school failure and dropping out. From the beginning, a rigorous evaluation process was built into the program plan to assess what was working and what was not. Andrew Hahn of Brandeis University tracked the pilot program from beginning to end, and produced a series of reports that carefully document every stage of this process. First- and second-year postprogram studies were also conducted by Hahn and colleagues at Brandeis, and by Robert Taggart, who developed the educational self-learning, self-paced curriculum. Some sites did better than others. Milwaukee (the only site that was not an OIC affiliate) failed after several years due to staff changes as well as a lack of institutional support and leadership. But overall, the QOP program seemed to hold great promise after the first four-year pilot was completed.

The results from 1989 to 1993 at the four pilot sites (Milwaukee was eliminated) showed that, when compared to similar students who did not participate, QOP members were

- more likely to graduate (63 percent versus 42 percent).

- more likely to go on to postsecondary education (42 percent versus 16 percent).

- less likely to drop out (23 percent versus 50 percent).

- more likely to receive some sort of academic honors (34 percent versus 12 percent).

- less likely to become parents while in school (24 percent versus 38 percent).

- more likely to be involved in community service, to be hopeful about the future, and to consider their lives a success.

Some sites were definitely more successful than others, with Philadelphia the most successful. But even at sites where services were sporadic, just a little program involvement seemed to produce positive impacts on the students. As one student put it, "Without QOP, I wouldn't be a college-bound student. I'd be a hustler on the corner."

The cost for the original experiment worked out to about $15,000 per individual over the four years.[4] Average participant QOP hours on programs reached 2,300 over the four years, yielding an average per-hour cost of about $6.50. A cost-benefit analysis revealed that for each dollar spent on the QOP, $3.68 is gained in public benefit if the students go on to finish college, and $3.04 if they do not complete college.

According to Hahn:

> QOP debunks the myth that nothing works for economically disadvantaged, minority adolescents. QOP's key finding is that these young people will stick with the program, especially if the adults stick with them. In one site . . . 24 of the original 25 youth were still actively involved [at the end of the four-year cycle].[5]

Many factors contributed to the success of the pilot project, including the small size of the experimental groups, a case-management approach starting at age 13 in ninth grade, financial incentives, use of multiple approaches, dedicated staff, multiyear funding, and treatment integrity (sticking to the design).

Based on the pilot results, the U.S. Department of Labor (DOL) is funding a new multisite program which began in the summer of 1995 in five additional sites: Houston, Memphis, Washington, DC, Fort Worth, and Cleveland. In addition, the Ford Foundation is funding QOP sites operated by OIC in Philadelphia and in Yakima, Washington. The OIC National Office provides technical assistance to all seven sites.

The Philadelphia Story

The program I visited in 1997 was the Philadelphia replication, located at OIC national headquarters. (The original Philadelphia site was up the street at the OIC affiliate.) Our guide for the day was Deborah Scott, manager of Literacy Programs for OIC and coordinator of QOP. Several months prior to our visit, some fifty ninth-grade students had been selected as participants from Benjamin Franklin High School and another fifty as a control group. The expectations are that, in every year over the four-year period, each participant will receive 250 hours of education by participating in computer-assisted instruction, peer tutoring, and homework assistance; 250 hours of service activities by participating in community-service projects, helping on public events, or holding regular jobs; and 250 hours of development activities such as life- and family-skills training, planning for college and jobs, and joining in family and community recreation.

The QOP process starts with an educational assessment to determine the entry level for the students. The Comprehensive Competencies Program developed over the years by Robert Taggart encompasses several hundred units of computerized courses, covering K–12 basic subjects as well as career and personal skills. Print materials and CD-ROMS are also available to enrich learning. The site is organized according to plan, with at least one computer for every three students and individual records for each participant. Andre, one of the students, showed us his personal files.

> Every day when I come here, I can check in here and see how far I've come. I had to start with fourth grade arithmetic, but I've already moved up to eighth grade.

The expectation is that each student will receive a lot of tender loving care from the staff. Three counselors were carefully selected—African American men of diverse backgrounds. One was a teacher, another a social worker, and the third a salesman. All staff members wear beepers and have 800 numbers so the participants can contact them at any time. Before the program officially started, Scott and the counselors visited the homes of many of the students to secure parental consent and to inform the families about the benefits of the effort.

Deborah Scott describes the Quantum Opportunities Program as a "tough love" program, where no matter how little or how much you attend, once you are randomly selected, "once in QOP, always in QOP," even for students who are incarcerated or do not show up. The staff follows up on everyone. At the beginning, each student goes through a three-day orientation, and parents are invited for a Parents Night at the center, when they can walk through exactly what their children experience at QOP every day. Students and parents must sign a four-year "contract" with QOP committing themselves to the program. Staff also must agree to stick it out for the whole four years. Scott told us:

None of the staff are married or have their own children. All our time is required for paying attention to the needs of the QOP kids. Believe me, this is 24-hour duty.

One of the hallmarks of the QOP program is that the participants earn stipend money. This money is put into an accrual bank account, and each student receives a bank card. A student can conceivably earn up to $5,000 by the end of the four-year program—serving not only as as an incentive for participation but also as a means of teaching money-management skills. Students can use a certain amount of their money freely, but they must also save a portion.

As the students arrive from school, they sign in. Each hour of participation yields a "salary," starting at $1 and increasing to $1.33 over time. After completing 100 hours, they receive a $100 bonus and an equal amount invested for them in an interest-bearing Quantum Opportunity Account, which can only be used for certain approved items such as college or training. The facility is open from 2 to 7 P.M. weekdays, and generally from 10 A.M. to mid-afternoon on Saturdays for special events.

At the QOP after-school center, we spoke to several of the students (Tiffany, Paul, Lakeisha, Andre . . .). What we heard over and over again was that the students loved coming to the center. As Paul, an oversized 14 year old, told us:

I usually cut my last class at school so I can get here early. I wish I could come to QOP all day long since I don't really learn nothing in school. We hardly get any homework. I learn a lot in this place. I love working with the computers.

Lakeisha, a very enthusiastic young women, reported:

We have so many substitutes in school. They don't have any idea what to do. Here I got my great counselor who keeps me going all afternoon long. I see him every day. When things get bad at home, he comes over to my house to talk to my mom. I really trust him.

Although the students receive a stipend for each hour they attend QOP, it did not appear to be the primary incentive that brought these students to the QOP center. Instead, it seemed that the intensive attention received from the staff and the pleasant atmosphere were the real draws.

Earlier in the day we visited their school, Benjamin Franklin High School. This is a grungy urban school where graduation rates are as low as the morale. It was reported that 400 of the 800 female students were already mothers in a building that has only twenty-nine slots in the nursery for students' child care. Our visit with the principal, Tilghman Moore, was marked by an interruption from a school staff member who reported that a teacher had literally disappeared.

We later learned that several months after our visit, Dr. Moore allowed QOP to open a small office in the school so that QOP staff could be on hand during the school day to help students with immediate problems.

Quantum Significance

QOP has been a breath of fresh air in a world populated by skeptics. This exciting and commonsense program (albeit expensive) integrates technology, education, counseling, caring, and evaluation to achieve the best results for targeted at-risk students. Its careful design and controlled evaluation have produced invaluable tools for practitioners who want to influence the lives of very disadvantaged young people. It proves these young people will take up the offer to enter into a structured contract that requires work, concentration, consistency, and long hours.

The contract with staff to commit to four years is another key component of the program's success. One staff member commented on "the extent to which staff turnover can rupture a program's sense of integrity and security, and lead to emotional disinvestment on the part of youth."[6] It is vital to have a shared vision among the designers, implementers, and evaluators. And bonding and creating group solidarity with adolescents, major elements of this program, are a lot easier when they are in ninth grade than when they are older.

The QOP practice summed up by Debbie Scott is to "never give up on a kid." A QOP "graduate," Jackie Jones, now a poised and articulate 19 year old majoring in psychology, recalled to a reporter from *Youth Today:*

> QOP helped me to understand the person that's inside; to trust people and understand the world and be a better person by helping others—not just to gain information for myself . . . but to pass it on.[7]

Reverend Leon Sullivan, OIC's founder and chairman, is convinced that

> to give up trying to help our next generation is to forsake the American dream. QOP shows that even the most economically and educationally disadvantaged youth can succeed with faith in the future, hard work and a helping hand.[8]

This will be an interesting program to watch over the next several years, to see what can be learned from replication, and whether these lofty principles can be applied across a larger universe.

EL PUENTE

El Puente is both a school and a community-based organization. El Puente means the bridge, an appropriate name for a facility located at the entrance to the Williamsburg Bridge, which links the borough of Brooklyn to Manhattan.[9] Yet many of the young people who crowd into El Puente every day have little experience crossing that bridge, either literally or figuratively. The major goal of

El Puente, as articulated by its founder and president, Luis Garden Acosta, is to empower young Hispanic immigrants to cross that bridge.[10]

The Academy for Peace and Justice

The building we visited is the original El Puente site, set up in the early 1980s in what used to be St. Mary of the Angels church. It has recently evolved from a community center to a school and now serves as the location for the El Puente Academy for Peace and Justice, one of New York City's thirty-five small, theme-based New Vision Schools. As Acosta explained to a *New York Times* reporter,

> Unless we were able to create a safe bridge (*el puente*) for growth and empowerment, our children would never be safe. But from the very beginning we knew we would have to take on the educational system. If we didn't deal directly with the educational system, nothing would change.[11]

Built on years of community organization and neighborhood involvement, this new venture brings innovative schooling to 130 ninth through twelfth graders (the first class will graduate this year). El Puente Academy was founded by Frances Lucerna, principal of the school and cofounder of El Puente. The academy, an integral part of the total El Puente organization, is open twelve months a year from 8 A.M. to 9 P.M. The Academy is seen by its founder to be an academically and developmentally focused school as opposed to a second chance or alternative school. As one observer noted, schools like El Puente "aren't aiming simply to be mainstreamed into the city's factory style of education. They want to displace it."[12] Engaging the classroom as community and the community as classroom, teams of students create community-development projects promoting peace and social justice.

El Puente Academy works to:

- create a place for young people where they feel safe, respected, and cared for so they can learn.

- build a young person's positive sense of self through the curriculum.

- integrate book learning with community projects, with family, and with community.

- give back to the community—nurturing a sense of responsibility to others.

In this school without walls, where space is scarce, classroom areas change according to need, from a traditional desk and chair setup for a language arts class to desks being cleared away for a movement class—all in the same area. Every inch of the old church building has a function. Classrooms are carved out of the sides of the old church, with an open central space that converts from assembly hall to stage to exhibition area to social space depending on the need.

Offices are squeezed into corners. On the second floor is a small cafeteria with a kitchen that is supplied through donations that the students themselves obtained; and a studio area that is used for dance, aerobics, and martial arts. Throughout the building, on every available wall, are imaginative works of art. In the history classroom, students have drawn family trees and made masks from many cultures. Many African American and Hispanic leaders (Malcolm X and Che Guevara) are celebrated through portraits and murals. The high ceiling of the church leaves room for a floating dinosaur and colorful flags and banners.

More than half of the students at El Puente come from the neighborhood, as do many of the staff. Others come from nearby Brooklyn neighborhoods, opting for El Puente rather than Eastern District, a local high school with high failure rates. Half of El Puente's students are selected to attend the academy by New York City's Board of Education computer and half by El Puente itself. At entrance, 16 percent of the students at El Puente perform below grade level, 68 percent at grade level, and 16 percent above grade level.

The staff of El Puente is multicultural, and there is no hierarchy among directors, volunteers, facilitators (teachers), and part-time staff. Everybody teaches, including Lucerna and Garden Acosta. All facilitators must become certified, but all do not originally come from a traditional educational background. Unlike traditional New York City schools, El Puente has been allowed to select its own teachers during its start-up period.

The school is part of the New York City school system, and students take core courses in mathematics, English, social sciences, language, and science, and are strongly encouraged to take the Regents exams, for which they receive special tutoring on Saturdays and after school. The curriculum emphasizes team teaching and interdisciplinary cooperation.

We sat in on one English class where the students were reading aloud Lorraine Hansberry's *Raisin in the Sun*. Big, sprawling boys performed with great seriousness, and self-conscious girls responded with equal dignity. One boy remarked, "This sounds just like what goes on at my grandmother's house."

In a laudatory article in the *Village Voice*, Matthew Fleischer described how enterprising teachers bring the street into the school.[13] For example, El Puente students pursue environmental community service projects, in which they develop math and science skills by actually measuring the toxic perils that surround them. An environmental study of the impact of removing lead paint from the Williamsburg Bridge was a project of an epidemiology class. The environmental curriculum, created by a group called International Community Information and Epidemiological Technology, is implemented by Robert Ledogar, a retired volunteer and former UNICEF planner. He told us, "This is the most challenging job I've ever had and maybe the most useful. Every day I can see these students come alive."

One humanities class has made a documentary video on the dangers of a proposed incinerator for the nearby Navy Yard; an English class focuses on the hip-hop movement; and biology students work on immunization drives. Fleischer warns that "these renascent one-room schoolhouses do demand sacrifices . . . teachers must adapt to being generalists rather than specialists." He cites as an example an English teacher who also serves as an academic advisor and monitors after-school studies, all of which require "every shred of energy."

To attend El Puente, one has to become a "member" of the El Puente center, become involved in an El Puente community project, and go through an orientation process that focuses not only on what El Puente can offer but also on how every member is a vital resource who can help build El Puente and the community itself. The academy provides breakfast and lunch to its students. Half of the students stay for extended-day programs such as tutoring, leadership, and the arts. Other students from the community also come to El Puente after school. El Puente is in the process of expanding its wellness center to establish a family health clinic in partnership with the New York City Health and Hospitals Corporation and the New York University/Bellevue Center for Occupational and Environmental Medicine. It also has a partnership with 651 BAM Majestic, an affiliate of the Brooklyn Academy of Music (BAM), and is defined and funded as an arts center.

Parents are encouraged to be involved with the academy through a Parent Action Center, which runs leadership workshops, computer technology and other adult-education classes, and support groups. The center actively encourages relationships among the parents, who are themselves members of El Puente and the school. A Sunday Soup Kitchen has been organized, with students and staff volunteering to feed those in the area in need of a meal. Garden Acosta plans to make this a weekly event, with each staff member working one Sunday morning every six weeks along with the students.

Since the first class will not graduate until next year, high school completion rates are not yet available; but the prospects for the current crop of students are very encouraging. Fleischer reported a 100 percent passing rate for El Puente students at the end of the first year compared to Eastern High School, where only 25 percent of the students graduated.[14] David Gonzalez reported in the *New York Times* that after the school's first eighteen months, the students outscored their counterparts in other schools on basic measures of reading and mathematics.[15] A case study of El Puente conducted by Sharon Ramirez and Tom Dewar for the Kettering Foundation summarized the program elements that parents felt contributed to the success of their children as students. They mentioned the small size of the school, the safe and caring environment, the amount of individual attention and tutoring, and the open communication between the staff and the parents through frequent phone calls and home visits.[16] "They care. They really do. It's like a family. They keep track of what's going on, and they really try to teach." Ramirez and Dewar believe that El Puente has the potential for building and strengthening "social capital" in the Williamsburg area through networking, involvement with community development, and opportunities for young people to engage in civic participation. As Lucerna has stated, "Youth development cannot be separated from community development, and the goal must be self-determination."

How El Puente Got Started

The philosophy of El Puente is a crucial part of its success and vitality. Founded in 1982, the center was initially a response to the high rate of violence among teens in the area. Garden Acosta was a former member of the Young Lords, a militant Puerto Rican group formed in the 1960s, much like the Black Panthers. He grew up in the public housing projects, eventually went on to Harvard University Medical School, and became a hospital administrator. It was during his tenure as administrator at Woodhull Hospital that he became an eyewitness to the violence that was overwhelming the area. In one year alone, forty-eight neighborhood teens were killed in the gang wars that engulfed the Williamsburg streets. On top of the crime and poverty, Williamsburg is plagued by toxicity: Its pollution levels are almost sixty times the national average for residential neighborhoods. Thus El Puente was formulated not only as a center for self-enhancement but also as a meeting place for those concerned with environmental and other life-threatening issues.

As viewed by a Hispanic paper, the center "is a place where young people and their families see the worlds of the arts, medicine, education, sports, communication, and the environment intimately tied to the political and social empowerment of their community."[17] Every year, more than 1,000 Hispanic youth, parents, and grandparents are reached through a broad array of programs. The El Puente Dance Ensemble, organized by Frances Lucerna, performs throughout the city and is widely recognized for its innovation and high professional standards. The organization also sponsors an "I Have A Dream" Project in a local junior high school. It presently runs dropout prevention programs in three Brooklyn high schools; through its new Bronx Center (Youth Ministries for Peace and Justice), two other schools have become part of the growing El Puente family.

One example of El Puente's role in Williamsburg is the establishment of CAFE (Community Alliance for the Environment). Although the constituency of El Puente is predominantly Hispanic, the Williamsburg population also includes Hasidim (Orthodox-fundamentalist Jews) and people of Polish ancestry. After years of interethnic turmoil, environmental issues brought these groups together in a coalition to monitor and change the toxic environment of the neighborhood. Spearheaded by Garden Acosta and Rabbi David Niederman, executive director of the United Jewish Organizations of Williamsburg, young people and adults from these diverse ethnic groups joined together to oppose the placement of a garbage incinerator in their neighborhood.[18]

But El Puente is also a national organization with affiliates. In addition to El Puente of Williamsburg, El Puente Centers are located in other parts of New York City (Bushwick, Bronx, and Washington Heights); Revere and Chelsea,

Massachusetts; and San Diego. Not all sites are built around the Hispanic model; one of the Massachusetts models is Cambodian, and San Diego's is multicultural. In the spring of 1996, Acosta began publication of a national newspaper called *El Palante*, using the Young Lords icon as its logo.

El Puente has a $2 million annual budget, most of which goes for the academy. Funding for the school comes from the Board of Education on the basis of student enrollment. Additional money comes from public funding, including the New York State Department of Health and the Council of Arts, although there are private funds as well. El Puente also gets help from the AmeriCorp program, which supports twenty-two of its sixty-nine Brooklyn staff members (continued funding from this source is questionable at this time).

The Future

In 1998, the school will move to a large new facility in the Williamsburg area; the building is currently being renovated, with a multimillion-dollar budget derived largely from the New York City Board of Education. The new school building will house seventh and eighth graders in addition to the current upper grades, a day care center, a community library and technology center, as well as a family health center. Eventually, the hope is to establish El Puente as a human and community development center that houses a school for pre-K through 12.

Although the school is administered through a partnership with the Board of Education and New Visions for Public Schools, El Puente clearly "owns" and stays true to its philosophy. One feels that if turf problems were to arise with the Board of Education, the El Puente staff would look for other ways to support El Puente rather than compromise their ideas and ideals.

Although El Puente has not yet been formally evaluated, negotiations are underway with Public/Private Ventures, a major youth development research organization. Many questions remain. Although parental involvement is frequently mentioned, it is not clear to what degree parents are involved other than through their attendance at school functions or by attending their own classes and workshops. Given the time constraints on the staff, it seems unlikely that much attention is being paid to the processing of this experience to figure out where the program is going, what needs to be changed along the way, what is working, and what is not. Moving to a much larger structure will certainly change the atmosphere and improve the physical setting. But will the closeness and coziness of the academy be lost? El Puente as it stands now is a very exciting and inspirational place to visit, not only because of the dedication and charisma of its leaders and staff, but also because of the creativity and calm that seem to reflect what the academy instills in its students.

But not everyone sees El Puente as a miracle. The late Albert Shanker, then head of the American Federation of Teachers, expressed his concern that schools based on the vision of a small group of people would not be integrated into the school system and always remain outside.[19] He feared that these experiments might self-destruct, especially if the leadership moved on to other endeavors or the teachers burned out. He also worried about the proliferation of "do your own thing" curricula, which could undermine the idea of universal standards or what he called "common schooling." Deborah Meier, the founder of Central Part East and the country's leading advocate for "do it yourself" schools, believed that Shanker was poorly informed. As she says, "A good school is a good school, and the point is to engage the student in learning. No visitor to El Puente Academy for Peace and Justice could fail to observe the involvement of the students and the commitment of the staff."[20]

"The miracle of El Puente," says Garden Acosta, "is the bridge we've built for people to come back home and in a sense raise the village that raised them. We believe it takes children to raise the village."[21]

CARING CONNECTION

Go sixty miles out of Des Moines, Iowa, past rolling acres of cornfields and fertile farmland, and you come to Marshalltown. Drive down the broad, immaculate, tree-lined streets, with their sturdy clapboard houses on large plots, and you think you have arrived in what must be "middle America." The small downtown area still has some viable businesses, along with a handsome city hall and a large hospital. A glimpse of the Marshalltown Community High School set in a huge campus with new buildings furthers the impression of well-being. But a visit with folks at the Caring Connection quickly changes these first impressions as the staff describe the range of interventions they feel they must provide for Marshalltown youths.

Marshalltown *is* actually located in the middle of America, a small market town of 27,000 people. In its heyday, it was a bustling manufacturing city, but in recent years many of the plants have closed or relocated, taking their jobs with them. What remains is a smelly pork-processing plant and a few small tool-and-die industries. Older white families have moved out toward warmer climes, and Hispanic families have moved in, drawn by promises of jobs in the processing plant. An influx of Southeast Asians has followed. Behind the facade of Main Street affluence, you find the "barrio," with its extremely dilapidated housing, abandoned cars, and what are reputed to be dangerous streets. No one knows exactly the percentage of minorities in the city population nor the current poverty rate, but at least one school in Marshalltown has an enrollment in which 82 percent of the students are eligible for free or reduced-price lunches. The community is changing, and so are the children.

To respond to these problems, Marshalltown School District initiated the Caring Connection, a K–12 initiative that brings together the efforts of thirteen local and state agencies to "nurture students to become intellectually and personally empowered for citizenship in a changing world."[22] At the time of my visit, Todd Redalen, the director who is employed by the school district, expounded on the belief that "all students have the potential to find themselves in at-risk situations, not just those who are failing or come from deprived circumstances."

The Caring Connection provides services in the high school as well as in six elementary and two middle schools, and one alternative high school. According to Redalen, the effort started informally, building on dropout prevention and mentoring activities that were already in place in the high school. In 1990, when the Iowa state legislature approved the education department's School-Based Youth Services Program, a group in Marshalltown applied and received one of only four grants that were given in the state at that time (currently there are eighteen). The Caring Connection's grant was for $200,000 a year over four years. Additional funds for the program have come from Iowa's unique "allowable growth" provisions in the state education law, through which school districts are permitted to use their funds to develop special projects for high-risk youth; Marshalltown has dedicated $600,000 yearly to these purposes. Other grants cover special programs, most recently job training and employment.

In the Marshalltown High School, Caring Connection acts as a "one-stop shop." I was impressed with the size and scope of the program. One whole corner of the first floor of the school is occupied by the program's facilities. The entry is designated by a large sign, and a bulletin board carries notices of all kinds of activities and support services available in Marshalltown. A pleasant receptionist greets students and sends them to the appropriate place. A number of private offices ring the area, and there is also a large conference room. A well-equipped, specially designed classroom for tutoring is located on another floor.

The Caring Connection actually offers twenty different services through contractual arrangements with local agencies, including mental health and substance abuse counseling, family development, juvenile court liaison, runaway and independent living support, legal services, primary health care, service learning, and job training and placement.[23] The staff comprises twenty-seven individuals, almost all of whom are employed by a participating agency rather than the school system. In addition, many specialists are available through the agency contracts. For instance, a family development worker from Mid-Iowa Community Action does crisis intervention, works with families as a case manager, and facilitates support groups in the school; the Mental Health Center supplies a part-time therapist; and the Substance Abuse Treatment Unit does assessments, counseling, treatment, and follow-up.

The tutoring program is intensive, with a special room—called the Individual Assistance Center—equipped with computers and on-site tutors who can devote considerable attention to students who are having problems in their classrooms. The day I visited the special classroom, two students were learning how to use computers, and four others were getting help with math homework. Joshua, a reticent 16 year old, told me, "I can concentrate much better in here, and the teacher goes to the trouble to explain things that I just can't get in my regular class."

I met with the Caring Connection staff, who talked about working with other professionals both in the school and in the community. One of the social workers said, "You'd be surprised how much everyone wants to know more about things like mental health problems, substance abuse treatment, parent involvement, literacy programs, and the use of case managers. The teachers in this school are always eager to talk to us." Another told me, "Many of the parents in this community can't cope with their children. We have to spend a lot of time visiting with them and acting as liaison between the school and the home."

Every student who participates in Caring Connection is informed of options that may enhance his or her ability to successfully complete high school. Some students are able to arrange to attend school for shorter hours to accommodate employment, teen parenting, or other circumstances. Individual academic assistance is promoted, especially for those students returning from residential placements. A self-paced curriculum is available through the Individual Assistance Center to help students make up credit deficiencies, and special courses titled Community Living Skills and Vocational Skills are offered with flexible schedules. Modified school-within-school courses in English, World Cultures Speech, and composition are available for students with histories of low achievement.

Services are well integrated into the school. The principal is very supportive, and turf issues do not seem to be a problem. For instance, the job specialist teaches the vocational skills course for the entire school. Caring Connection staff are provided ample office space in the school and are encouraged to participate in meetings with school staff.

More than 1,000 students are served in this program every year. As a state grantee, this program uses the Iowa School-Based Youth Services record system. Evaluation data show a reduction in the dropout rate and evidence that the programs services attract former dropouts back into the school system. Among students who were at high risk of dropping out, those who made more than twenty-five contacts during the year with Caring Connection had a dropout rate of 3 percent, compared to 8 percent among those with few contacts.[24] A survey of students and parents showed very positive assessments of the program and the school, with 75 percent or more reporting better attendance and performance in school, reduction in use of substances, going on to college, not engaging in unprotected sex, and improved relationships with peers and family.

Caring Connection is an excellent example of a comprehensive program heavily supported both by the local school system and by the state department of education. The school superintendent is strongly committed to community schools and actively seeks the involvement of every resource in town; the school board is primed for action. Todd Redalen is a real "go-getter," responsive to the needs of the students (and the dropouts) in this community. He is continuously seeking new programs to expand the already large assortment he has put together. Marshalltown recently received a $643,000 school-to-work grant to expand the strong vocational education component that has been created by the staff of the Caring Connection. These funds will bring local employers into more formal partnerships with the school and enhance transition into the work force.

During my visit, Redalen invited me to meet with the school board and "some other folks," so I had the opportunity to talk with all the local movers and shakers who were interested in full-service schools. It was clear that, under the superintendent's guidance and Redalen's influence, a consensus had been formed that community schools are the way to go. The expectations in this community are that by the year 2000, all schools will house community-sponsored family resource centers in partnership with all community agencies.

The Marshalltown Community School System has a plan that spells out the mission, vision, and goals for students, the district, parents, community agencies, and "citizens." The Marshalltown effort is truly a community-based effort, but it is also a reflection of the unique leadership of the Iowa State Education Department in addressing the problems of high-risk students.[25] In fact, every local school board in Iowa is called upon to develop a plan to provide assistance to all students who have difficulty "mastering the language." The plan must ensure access to academic, cultural, and social skills necessary to reach the educational levels of which the students are capable. Finally, the plan "shall accommodate students whose aspirations and achievements may be negatively affected by sterotypes linked to race, national origin, language background, gender, income, family status, parental status, and disability."

In my view, Marshalltown exemplifies the "art of the possible"—all sectors of the community coming together to strengthen the capacity of the school system to produce strong and well-educated people. Other communities in Iowa have their own versions of community schools. It will be interesting to track what happens in the future to see whether the movement can successfully impact the state as a whole.

TURNER MIDDLE SCHOOL IN WEST PHILADELPHIA

Love them tender love them sweet,
why did they throw a baby in the street.
Baby so innocent, baby so small
why would you shove a baby under a car.
If you didn't want it you should have given it away so
the baby could have his/her stay.

Lateefah Williams, sixth grade

From the outside, the Turner Middle School looks like a typical city school building, surrounded by concrete and not very inviting. But the minute you step in the doors, you are captivated by visual delights. Every corner of the school is decorated with student work, celebrating both the talents of the children who produce the various mixed media and the teachers and volunteers who stimulate them to do it.

This public school is in the process of becoming a model of a "university-assisted" community school, the results of an eight-year partnership between the school, the West Philadelphia Improvement Corps (WEPIC), and the Center for Community Partnerships of the University of Pennsylvania (Penn). Once a declining institution like many Philadelphia schools, Turner has been revitalized by staff members whose imagination and commitment brought university and community people on to the premises to turn the school around.

Today Turner is organized into three small "learning communities"—Conflict Resolution, Community/Environmental Studies and Community Health. Each center operates like an academy, as a separate entity with about 250 students and nine teachers. Each of the learning communities involves community-service components.

According to the proposed small learning community plan, the students in the Conflict Resolution center learn conflict resolution skills and work in their communities with a program called Safe Corridors, which involves students and neighbors in ensuring safe passage on the main streets to and from school. By eighth grade, the students are expected to be able to conduct peer mediations. The Community Environmental Studies group focuses on both environmental issues and publishing. By eighth grade, these students are able to put out a community newspaper and work in environmental improvement projects. A Humanities center is operated during the summer only, as an institute that focuses on academic enrichment which includes exposure to computers.

The Community Health academy is the most fully developed. At the sixth-grade level, students run the school store (Fruits R Us and Vegetables Too). In seventh grade, students are involved in peer education and, in eighth grade, they are exposed to health careers through placements in local hospitals. Three students described their hospital activities to me: "Each week we are assigned to different people in the hospital who teach us what to do. The other day, we helped deliver trays to the sick people, and got them to eat it all up." The young man in the group liked working in the kitchen best so he could stand beside the dietician, figuring out what people should eat. All claimed to be able to take pulse readings, and one had a stethoscope draped around her neck like a real doctor. All three plan careers in the medical profession.

One academic project focused on the ecology of the neighborhood. Starting with an historic approach, the whole area was laid out on maps, block by block, to portray the city as it was in the past in the 1880s and its evolution over time. The students constructed models of early buildings to recreate the neighborhood at that time. Then, the students made models of current housing structures and placed them in their present state. Finally, they worked on envisioning the neighborhood of the future, with constructs of how housing could be improved and how local businesses could be organized to create an ideal living arrangement. All of this activity extended over years, and involved mathematics, history, English, and social studies, in an integrated curriculum.

As one teacher at Turner reported, "This school year was very challenging

. . . my goal was to connect mathematics to our Community History Project. Some of the activities were: walking and picture tours of community blocks, creating scale drawings of homes, writing classified ads, preparing a realtors' multi-listing of homes including details of construction, room sizes, tax infor- mation."[26] The class also learned to draw floor plans and classify commercial building functions, and visited the architectural foundation in the city where their work was on display.

Surrounding the academic centers are an array of activities that make this a community school and keep it open from early morning till late in the evening, six days a week. An after-school program lists Health Awareness, Landscaping and Beautification, Health Careers Exposure, Homework Center, Peer Mediation Program, and others courses. Saturday Community School provides students and their families with free educational, recreational, and cultural programs. On Tuesday evenings, special classes are held for adults according to their interests. A Summer Institute keeps the school going for about one-fourth of the students. A full-time social work office has been established, and medical and dental screenings are offered to all students.

Organized relationships are maintained with feeder elementary schools from which future Turner students will come. Turner students go into those schools to teach younger children. Seventh graders at Turner showed me the pictures that first graders had drawn during their book-reading session at another school.

The fruit and vegetable stand is open every day after school. The students purchase the supplies, organize the sale, and staff the stand. They learn how to take inventory, set prices, and build the stand each year. The students also operate a Takeout Store where after-school snacks are prepared and sold. The Turner school opens early with breakfasts for 160 students a day. A homework center accommodates fifty to eighty students a week. Access is provided to the gym before and after school.

Obviously, the operation of a community school such as Turner calls for considerable administration. Charles D'Alfonso, the principal, has been at his post for four years, following a principal who established the precedent for mak- ing Turner a community school. Marie Bogle, the director of the community school, has been there since its inception. (Philadelphia included funds for com- munity school administration in the education budget up until this year.) About fifty Penn students come to this school every week to perform community service as part of their coursework, as work-study students, as AmeriCorps members, and as volunteers. They act as assistant teachers, recreation aides, tutors, and social worker interns.

In visiting with D'Alfonso and Bogle, I was moved by their collaborative spirit and their belief that this institution will be able to overcome whatever obstacles may be put in their path—even severe financial constraints. Recently, this school lost its Title 1 funding because *only* 80 percent of students are eligible for free lunches (apparently, in Philadelphia, all students have to be in poverty). Turner School also lost community schools funding and some of its operating budget, cuts that were endemic in Philadelphia schools. It has just obtained, however, extra money for special education that could be used for some of the community school services. D'Alfonso says that when he gets desperate, he calls his friends at the University of Pennsylvania for help in getting grants.

Like many programs we visited, the hardest item to obtain was detailed evaluation data. After pressing, we were informed that the attendance rate at Turner had increased from 86 percent in 1993 to 89 percent in 1996, and this rate was much higher than in comparable schools in west Philadelphia. Suspensions decreased from 302 to 124 during the same period. Parental involvement in the school increased from 53 percent to 69 percent, reflecting changes in attitudes on the part of both parents and teachers. According to the Turner staff, "The whole building feels different." Effects on the Penn students who participate as volunteers can be measured by the comments of Amy Cohen, associate director of the Penn Program for Public Service: "Penn students get a whole new understanding of the world."

How the Turner School Got Off the Ground

We have to step back to take a look at Penn's role in getting this program underway. Lee Benson and Ira Harkavy are two academics who firmly believe (as followers of Francis Bacon and John Dewey) that knowledge should be sought for the benefit and use of building one's life and understanding one's community. They applied this philosophy to where they were, in a walled university located in a deprived urban neighborhood. As an article in *Education Week* put it, "They directed faculty research and student coursework toward solving pressing social problems in the university's backyard."[27] This led to the formation of the West Philadelphia Improvement Corps (WEPIC), a university-assisted neighborhood and school revitalization program.[28] As one observer noted, "The University of Pennsylvania realized it could no longer escape from its troubled inner city neighborhood. Instead, it's trying to be part of the solution."[29] The program is coordinated by the West Philadelphia Partnership, in conjunction with the school district and many other organizations. WEPIC began in one school in 1985 with an after-school neighborhood clean-up effort, and now includes three large comprehensive high schools, five middle schools, and five elementary schools. Turner's is the most fully realized project; however, Shaw Middle School and University City High School already have extensive WEPIC programs in place.

Class Act is a special newspaper supplement prepared by a group of students from Shaw Middle School and the University City High School for *The Daily Pennsylvanian*, a paper of the University of Pennsylvania. A recent article by student April Brown gives us a flavor of the program. "On Wednesday, October 19, I attended Shaw Middle School after-school Community Activities where they had African-American studies, basketball, drill team tryouts, math tutoring, and the 'Keeping Teens Healthy' program. Parents from the surrounding neighborhood came and students attended too. In the girls' gym, volunteers from the

University of Pennsylvania organized a basketball activity . . . with seven coaches from Penn. . . . The main reason why most people were there was because the volunteers wanted to try to get the kids off the streets of Philadelphia."[30]

Penn starts its work in the university classroom. Almost fifty academic offerings are defined as Community Service Courses. For example, Anthropology 205, Health in Urban Communities, introduces students to the history of community schools and the West Philadelphia community. University students develop curricula and teach health topics at Turner to middle school students, who are in turn taught to give these health lessons to their peers. The course also focuses on nutrition and improvement of eating habits. In Anthropology 210, Biomedical Science and Human Adaptability, Penn students teach Turner students to conduct demographic and family health surveys and to evaluate anthropometric data, such as body mass and fatness. Robert Giegengack, a renowned geologist, has developed a course, Urban Environment: West Philadelphia, that focuses on issues such as lead toxicity in order to improve the environment around the schools. Education in American Culture, designed by John Puckett, one of the leaders in the community-school movement, gets Penn students working directly with eighth graders in developing reading and video productions that illuminate the impact of social factors on schooling. Together they study the development of street car lines and the impact that the local trolley has had on the growth and development of their own community surrounding the Turner school.

I got the impression that once the university faculty become involved in these inner-city schools, it's difficult to stay away. I observed Dr. Giegengack at Shaw Middle School, where he stopped two strapping boys in the hall to ask them how everything was going in their lives. He likes hanging out at the schools because it brings such relevancy into his own teaching and his life.

Turner is an excellent example of a university-assisted school, and the other WEPIC schools show promise of equal distinction. Syracuse University recently published a directory listing more than 2,200 school-college partnerships. According to *Education Week*, "What sets Penn's work apart is both its academic focus and the comprehensiveness of its involvement."[31] In 1994, Dewitt Wallace–Readers' Digest awarded WEPIC $1 million to help three other schools adopt a similar model: University of Alabama at Birmingham, University of Ohio at Cinncinati, and University of Kentucky at Lexington. And WEPIC leaders have been instrumental in carving out a new field of community schools through technical assistance, publications, conferences, and cosponsorship of the Community School Summit in May of 1997.

LESSONS LEARNED

What can we learn from the programs we visited? Several things stand out. These efforts offer vital services to young people in facilities that they can easily get to. Two are located in community centers, two in schools, and one in a combination of both. What do these good programs have in common?

First of all, quality programs show that they work; they can document that the outcomes for the participants are improved. Quantum is truly unique because it is built on a solid research base that shows progress on many behavioral levels, particularly in graduation rates. El Puente and the Turner School are places where students are clearly engaged, and as a result attendance is markedly improved. In Caimito, crime rates have actually fallen. Marshalltown, although open to all students and dropouts, effectively targets high-risk youth. All of these places are safe havens. Anecdotal data from all sites suggest great advances in self-expression and self-competency among the participants, although one does tend to hear from the most enthusiastic people.

The important charge to any program is to produce promised effects and to accomplish announced goals. In the case of El Puente—the "bridge"—achievement was enhanced in an atmosphere where students were continuously motivated to become effective community leaders. At Quantum in Philadelphia, consistency and carefully constructed components, offered by caring individuals, had the potential to produce excellent long-term results (the program we visited was a new replication of a proven model). Turner School turned itself around to become a learning community and village hub. Caimito convinced the community that police could be a supportive force in the company of youth advocates. Marshalltown demonstrated that a firm partnership between school personnel and program personnel had great benefits and increased the capacity to draw in additional program components.

Of course, the theory has to be correct, or the program may not work. Each of these programs was painstakingly thought out by its creators and was designed to address specific youth, family, and community issues. El Puente is the invention of local community practitioners committed to the process of youth empowerment. Thus, every step of their approach is guided by their desire to give young Hispanics the opportunity to participate in their community life as educated and dedicated citizens. Caimito has a similar moral tone, perhaps reflecting the influence of its founders' religious connections. Disadvantaged youth are expected to grow in terms of cognitive and social skills as a result of being surrounded by caring people (including the police) and being offered a wide array of classes and activities in an attractive setting.

Given the attention to design, it is not surprising that a common attribute of these successful programs is that they were carefully planned; none just grew serendipitously. Some individual, or group of individuals, spent a lot of time trying to figure out what pieces were needed to accomplish what results. Having a planning year is very important for practitioners. All of these programs were flexible and reactive. They appeared to be able to adjust schedules, personnel, and policies to meet the needs of their clientele. They could absorb and implement new program ideas rapidly. When problems arose, they reacted as quickly as they could to alter the situation or to negotiate for change.

You cannot help being impressed by the people running these programs. Of course, leadership styles differ. Luis Garden Acosta is a charismatic man who has used his own life history to guide him in trying to change the life histories of young Hispanics who started out as he did. Debbie Scott, in her own distinct way, personifies this quality of "sticking with it." She made it pretty clear that her life at this time centers on "her kids," and she expects that other staff members will maintain the same dedication over the four-year term of their contracts. Todd Redalen personifies the new wave of Safe Passage facilitators who can work well within both the educational establishment and community-based efforts.

I would be remiss if I failed to say that although these programs are interesting, they are not perfect. I have reported what I observed in a short visit to each site and summarized the reports made available to me by the programs. My own bias pushes me toward painting portraits of youth development programs in glowing colors. All of them welcome visitors, and I would encourage you to go and see them or any of the other places I mention in the next three chapters.

In the next chapter, I take a closer look at one of the types of programs featured here—the full-service community school—similar to the Turner School, and then turn to school reform programs and, finally, to efforts to deal specifically with sex, drugs, and violence.

Bill Foley, Photographer

5

FULL-SERVICE COMMUNITY SCHOOLS

The goal is to be able to bring in employment services, health services, child welfare, detention services—all in one site and not call it anything. Yes, you will serve people who are in crisis, but most of it is prevention. It should get to the point that no matter what the issue, the response is the same, "Go to the Beacon."

—Geoffrey Canada, Director of the Rheedlen Foundation

A full-service community school integrates the delivery of quality education with whatever health and social services are required in that community. These institutions draw on both school resources and outside community agencies that come into the schools and join forces to provide seamless programs. Community involvement is an important aspect of community schools. School buildings are open extended hours every day—over weekends, over the summer—to respond to the needs of the children and their parents in a neighborhood.

The community school concept is not new. It has roots in early progressive thinking about reforming social institutions. One might perceive of these emerging "settlement houses in schools" as a marriage between John Dewey and Jane Addams. Over the past decade, a whole new wave of school-based programs began to emerge. It seemed that in different ways, program developers were trying to put together the best practices from all the diverse areas of youth development programming. These efforts appeared to focus simultaneously on both school-related and behavioral outcomes, preventing dropout and high-risk behaviors—or, to put it more positively, promoting school achievement, assuring good physical and mental health, and fostering positive youth development and family involvement.

In 1994, I wrote a book called *Full-Service Schools*.[1] I used that label to try to convey the idea of combining two separate social movements: the struggle to restructure education and the drive to integrate fragmented categorical programs. In my view, bringing those worlds together would result in schools that were neighborhood hubs where children could learn, and where they and their families could receive the necessary support so that the learning could "take." It is amazing to me how much has happened in the few years since I completed that book.

In this chapter, I review the various types of school-community partnership programs that are on the horizon, present several examples, take a look at the research, and discuss some of the issues that have come to the fore as these programs have evolved.

Here we look at an array of emerging models: school-based health centers, youth service centers, family resource centers, Beacons (schools that are open extended hours), full-service schools, and community schools. What these programs have in common is the provision of services by community agencies in school buildings with a view toward the creation of new institutional arrangements, of comprehensive "one-stop" educational and service centers. The prevailing terminology for the arrangements between the schools and the outside agencies includes collaboratives, cooperatives, partnerships, and contractual relationships.

The term *full-service* was first used in 1991 when, under the leadership of Governor Lawton Chiles, the Florida legislature passed a law supporting the development of Full-Service Schools.[2] A primary objective was to enhance the capacity of school health service programs to prevent teen pregnancy, AIDS and other sexually transmitted diseases, and alcohol and drug abuse. The legislation required the state Board of Education and the Department of Health and Rehabilitative Services (DHRS) jointly to establish programs in local schools to serve high-risk students in need of medical and social services.

DIFFERENT APPROACHES TO FULL-SERVICE COMMUNITY SCHOOLS

School-based health clinics are facilities operated in school buildings by outside health agencies and are staffed by medical personnel who provide primary health care, emergency care, mental health counseling, health promotion, and education. Several years ago, Congress's Office of Technology Assessment (since disbanded) issued a report on the health status of adolescents, documenting the consequences of the "new morbidities"—sex, drugs, violence, depression—and calling for greatly expanded access to comprehensive health care.[4] The report concluded that school-based health clinics were "a most promising recent innovation," excellent access points for young people to receive confidential primary health and social services, although the report noted insufficient evaluation. Currently, more than 1,000 school-based clinics are in operation, largely in disadvantaged communities.[5]

I admit to a partiality toward school-based clinics, having visited many and written extensively about them.[6] Beginning in 1983, when only ten such clinics were operating around the country, I became convinced that this system for delivering health services and intensive counseling right in the school building made a lot of sense. Since then, as support has been made available, school personnel have welcomed the partnerships that help them deal with the problems of increasingly high-risk populations. And the students feel cared for by trained practitioners who treat them with respect and confidentiality. It was my interest in school-based health care that led me eventually to embrace the broader concept of community schools.

School-linked services are referral locations outside of the school building to which school personnel send students or families for health and social services. The most common example is an Adolescent Health Center or a Planned Parenthood facility, located near a school, where students can go for reproductive health care along with primary health care and counseling. Almost any community agency such as the local health department or drug treatment center could be designated as "school-linked" if school personnel ever referred students or families to that source.

I do not believe that linkage is as effective as the colocation of services within the school building unless the ties are formal and intensive. Experience has shown that referrals frequently fail to turn up at the outside agency, and the agency frequently fails to follow up on the patient or client who does not show up. When a program is school based, follow-up is easily achieved and communication between the school personnel and service providers strengthened.

School-based youth centers are facilities within school buildings that are usually operated by outside agencies. These centers provide services such as after-school recreation and mentoring, employment services, substance abuse counseling, and group counseling. In some communities, schools are used as the location for Boys and Girls Clubs, the Police Athletic League, Girls Inc., and 4H after-school programs. In many others, the local recreation commission runs activities in the gym.

Family resource centers are facilities located in schools or community sites where parents can come for parenting education, literacy, employment assistance, immigration information, housing help, food, clothing, case management, health services, and early child care. Programs specifically for teenage parents are frequently located in these kinds of centers.

The *School of the 21st Century* was created in 1987 by Edward Zigler, director of the Bush Center at Yale University and a founder of the Head Start program.[7] This effort brings comprehensive family support services into elementary schools. The model calls for school-based, year-round, all-day child care for children 3 to 5 years old; after-school and vacation care for school-based children; family support and guidance through a home visitation program for new parents; and other support services to increase access to child care. The program is currently operating in over 400 schools in thirteen states and in England. This model has now been linked with James Comer's School Development Program (described in chapter 6) to create *COZI* schools that build on parental involvement, mental health teaming, and school climate changes through the middle school years. The end product of this collaboration should produce community schools like those discussed here.

Community schools exist in several forms:

- The *lighted school house* was pioneered by the Mott Foundation in Flint, Michigan, and throughout the country. It brings extended-hour learning, recreation, and social activities into the school building.[8] These community schools are strongly oriented toward addressing community needs, facilitating lifelong learning for people of all ages.

- *Beacons*, introduced in New York City through the Youth Bureau, import community-based organizations into forty schools to utilize the nonschool hours for community enrichment.[9] Each program is different, depending on the capabilities of the provider agencies and the particular cultural and socioeconomic needs of the community. Many have health clinics and employment programs; others encourage family participation, arts, and recreation.

- A *settlement house-in-the-school* approach has been created by the Children's Aid Society, also in New York City.[10] This version involves both school restructuring and the provision of one-stop services. It creates safe havens by bringing all the quality of old-fashioned settlement houses into school settings. I describe one of these comprehensive schools below.

■ Hal Lawson and Katherine Briar-Lawson, while at Miami University in Ohio, worked to create what they call *family-supportive community schools*, which place high priority on "two-generational" approaches that enhance the lives of the parents as well as the children.[11]

Other community schools are school-system-generated lighted schoolhouses that work to develop partnerships with community agencies so that the agencies contribute or contract services. All community schools are open for extended hours, over weekends, and over the summer. Some alternative, magnet, and charter schools share these characteristics.

University-assisted schools are those with which universities establish formal relationships and sponsor a range of activities. University faculty work with teachers on curriculum and with administrators on school restructuring; university students practice-teach in schools and offer after-school activities.[12] The Turner School in chapter 4 exemplifies this approach.

Cities-in-Schools (now Communities-in-Schools) is a large national organization that works with local communities (businesses, social service agencies) as a broker to relocate social workers and other staff into schools so they can act as case managers and mentors (see chapter 6).

School-based coordinating centers are family or youth centers where the school receives a grant to hire a coordinator who facilitates referrals to outside agencies.

Outside agencies are nonschool entities such as health departments, hospital/medical schools, universities, youth-serving agencies, community/neighborhood health centers, social service agencies, settlement houses, employment agencies, or Head Start programs. These agencies bring their own staffs and financial support into schools. Business, industry, churches, and media also are involved in partnerships with schools.

A *Full-Service School* is defined in Florida's innovative legislation as an

> integration of education, medical, social and/or human services that are beneficial to meeting the needs of children and youth and their families on school grounds or in locations which are easily accessible. Full service schools provide the types of prevention, treatment, and support services children and families need to succeed . . . services that are high quality and comprehensive and are built on interagency partnerships which have evolved from cooperative ventures to intensive collaborative arrangements among state and local and public and private entities.[13]

Many different approaches are presented here, which might suggest there are clear delineations between different kinds of school-based programs. In reality, however, the situation is not quite so clear. The latest versions of school-community partnerships have been labeled *extended schools* by one foundation and *successful schools* by another. For purposes of improved communication, I call these efforts *full-service community schools*, or just plain *community schools*.

SUPPORT FOR FULL-SERVICE
COMMUNITY SCHOOL INITIATIVES

Most of the innovative prevention programs and model school restructuring efforts taking place around the United States were created by individuals in universities or community-based organizations or national youth-serving agencies. States and foundations, however, have been the leaders in creating programs that bring human services into educational settings. In some states, including Florida, California, Iowa, and Kentucky, competitive grants have been awarded to school districts, which must then seek partners with whom to collaborate. In other states such as New Jersey, a community-based agency may be awarded the grant (be the lead grantee) and then seek a partnership with a school. Massachusetts's initiative focuses on promoting linkages among parents, schools, community agencies, businesses, and other community leaders.

More than $30 million is being spent each year in Florida on collaborative school-based projects and school health services. In 1995, it was reported that 220 schools in forty-nine districts were servicing more than 225,000 students as part of the Full-Service Schools program. About one-third of the full-service grantees offer primary health services, and many are family resource centers, case management, or recreational programs. The state expects all schools will be full service in a few years, as each one gradually brings in child care, vocational education, and mental health, along with health services. A recent state initiative in the juvenile justice system favored school settings that already offered other on-site services.

California's Healthy Start Support Services for Children Act was launched in 1991 with high ideals: "To be a catalyst in a revolution that will fundamentally change for the better the way organizations work together, the way resources are allocated for children and families, the nature and location of services provided, and ultimately, the outcomes experienced by children and families."[14] For each of four years, beginning in 1991, $20 million was awarded to projects in 171 school districts and 890 schools. The school districts created four types of collaborative programs: school-site family resource centers; satellite school-linked family service centers; family service coordination teams involving school personnel with project staff; and youth service programs that include school-based clinics. In 1995, the budget was doubled to $40 million, a signal of the strong support these school-community programs enjoy in the state legislature.

The state of New Jersey Department of Human Resources pioneered the "one-stop" concept with their School-Based Youth Services Program beginning in 1987. About $7 million in grants has been awarded to twenty-nine communities to develop joint school-community agency partnerships that incorporate core services into school centers. Five of the grantees are community mental health centers, and several are partnerships between schools and employment programs.

Kentucky's major school reform initiative in 1988 called for the development of family and youth service centers in schools where more than 20 percent of the students are eligible for free school meals. In 1996, $36 million was awarded to school systems by an Interagency Task Force of the Kentucky Cabinet for Human Resources. Small grants are given to 142 school systems for Youth Service Centers to set up in each school a designated room with a full-time coordinator to oversee referrals to community agencies for health and social services and to provide on-site counseling related to employment, substance abuse, and mental health. Kentucky also supports 303 Family Resource Centers in elementary schools, which offer parent education and refer parents to infant and child care, health services, and other community agencies. Seventy-five schools operate on-site combined family and youth service centers. Funding for all types of centers will increase to $50 million by 1998.[15]

In other states such as Connecticut and Colorado, family resource centers are being supported through various state initiatives and federal grants that deliver comprehensive services on school sites, including parent education, child care, counseling, health services, home visiting, and career training.

At least thirty-four states have opted to use their Federal Maternal and Child Health (MCH) block grants, or have created special funding initiatives, to support health agencies that operate primary health care centers in schools. The first federal grants for a small number of school-based health centers were made available through the Healthy Schools, Healthy Communities initiative of the Bureau of Primary Health Care in conjunction with the MCH Bureau.

In a separate initiative, the Bureau of Family and Youth Services in the Department of Health and Human Services administers a Community Schools Youth Services program.[16] Less than $14 million was divided up in grants to forty-eight community-based agencies in 1995 and 1997 to provide after-school activities. (No funds were included in the 1996 federal budget.)

A few cities have launched their own community-school initiatives. In New York City, Beacons are supported by the city youth agency with a budget of more than $22 million in 1997. Beacons provided the prototype for the Family and Community Endeavors part of the 1994 Crime Bill, based on the belief that offering after-school activities in high-risk communities would help prevent delinquency. The Community Schools program cited above resulted from that bill.

Foundations have played major roles in creating demonstration projects and in replicating the results. The Mott Foundation has funded its version of community schools since 1935 and currently supports a national center for training in community education. The Robert Wood Johnson Foundation first supported twenty-three school-based clinics and recently organized Making the Grade, an initiative in ten states to develop districtwide, comprehensive school health programs through joint efforts of the state departments of health and education. The Dewitt Wallace–Readers Digest Fund is heavily committed to the development of "extended-service" schools. It supports a cohort of university-assisted community schools, using the University of Pennsylvania program as the lead agency; an expansion of the Beacon model through the Fund for the City of

New York; replication of the Children's Aid Society's community schools in conjunction with Fordham University National Center for School and Community; and United Way of America to replicate its Bridges to Success model (see chapter 12). The Carnegie Corporation's Turning Point initiative in ten states is directed toward the reorganization of middle schools, and includes arranging for access to health and social services in the school or in the community. The Danforth Foundation's Successful Schools initiative puts together school reform with school-linked services and parental involvement efforts in five states. The Wilder Foundation is launching a major effort in St. Paul, Minnesota, to create a partnership among the local school system, city, county, state, and other foundations to establish five community schools during the next five years. Kauffman, Kellogg, and Stuart foundations also support school-based services in various forms.

EXAMPLES OF FULL-SERVICE COMMUNITY SCHOOLS

The new generation of community schools attempts to integrate quality education with support services. Following are a few examples from around the country.

Children's Aid Society: Salome Urena Middle Academy

In 1991, the Children's Aid Society (CAS) moved into Washington Heights in New York City to work with the local community school board to develop schools that were truly responsive to the needs of this very deprived area. Currently, two middle schools and two elementary schools are being operated with strong support from CAS and many other community agencies. In *Full-Service Schools* and subsequent articles, I have highlighted one of these schools, the Salome Urena Middle Academy (Intermediate School 218, referred to here as IS218), as an example of what I think schools should begin to look like in the future.[17] IS218 has received a lot of attention from the media, and it also has been visited by hundreds of interested practitioners, as well as foundation and policy people who are squired around by a technical assistance crew. In this chapter, I just want to update what others have written and report on how this effort has evolved and weathered its early years.

IS218 is located in a new building in Washington Heights that was designed to be a community school with air conditioning for summer programs, outside lights on the playground, and an unusually attractive setting. It offers students a choice of four self-contained "academies"—Business, Community Service, Expressive Arts, and Mathematics, Science, and Technology. The school opens at 7 A.M. and stays open after school for educational enrichment, mentoring, sports, computer lab, music, arts, trips, and entrepreneurial workshops. In the evening, teenagers are welcome to use the sports and arts facilities and take classes along with adults who come for English, computer work, parenting skills, and other workshops. A Family Resource Center provides parents with social services, including immigration, employment, and housing consultations. Twenty-five mothers have been recruited to work in the center as family advocates, for which they receive a small stipend. In addition, a primary health, vision, and dental clinic is on-site, as well as a student-run store that sells student products. These facilities, arrayed around the attractive lobby of the school, are open to the whole community. School-supported and CAS-supported social workers and mental health counselors work together to serve students and families. The school stays open weekends and summers, offering the Dominican community many opportunities for cultural enrichment and family participation.

During a recent visit to the school, I observed a scene that strengthened my conviction that community schools offer great hope for the future of our children and their families. In the library were "triads," hard at work over Spanish lessons. Each teaching team consisted of a child and a parent—the student was a police officer. IS218 had taken on the task of instructing the local precinct in the language of the neighborhood. The police officers, mostly white and non-Hispanic, reciprocated by inviting these families to visit the police station and stay in touch. This innovation combined important educational lessons with parental involvement and social supports and came about through the collaborative efforts of a school system, a community agency, and the local police precinct. The CAS coordinator facilitated the invitation to the precinct and arranged for the participation of the school in designing the instructional components.

The Recycle-a-Bicycle: Tools for Life program is another example of putting youth development and educational pieces together. Originally designed by a group called Transportation Alternatives to be part of the CAS After-School Program at IS218, it was then incorporated into the summer session and finally became part of the school curriculum. Old bikes are collected from the neighborhood, and IS218 students restore them and sell them to the community. The technical work involved in fixing the bikes is done under the auspices of an accredited industrial arts course, led by two well-trained instructors who offer workshops on repair, maintenance, safety, and environmental studies related to recycling and cycling. Students are graded for the course work, and can also earn stipends for time spent in the workshop repairing the bikes. An offshoot of this is the Earn-a-Bike program, available to all enrolled students who can apply what they learn in class in open work hours in the afternoons and on Saturdays. After eighteen hours of work, students select the bike of their choice, and after six more hours of fixing it up, can take it home. Other students and their families can purchase the brightly painted bikes and bike helmets at the well-equipped basement facility.

In a final exam for the course, students were asked whether the things they learned could help save the world. Ravi Lambert responded, "When we fix bikes we are helping the earth, ourselves, and we're putting more wrinkles in our brains. Plus we're helping the environment. This is good because now we're the future, and we can make a difference when we grow older."[18]

Sustainability is a significant issue in innovative programming, and observers in the early years often questioned if IS218's success could be maintained if founding principal, Mark Karnovsky, were to leave. In 1995, Karnovsky left, and a new principal, Betty Rosa, was selected by the Community District Superintendent in consultation with the school and CAS staff. The transition appears to have been very successful. A formal evaluation of the CAS schools is currently being conducted by Fordham University. Preliminary results suggest major improvements in attendance, impressive reductions in behavioral problems, and small increases in test scores.

Sioux City School District:
Woodrow Wilson Middle School

At one time, Woodrow Wilson Middle School in Sioux City, Iowa, was characterized by low student achievement, high truancy and absence rates, numerous police citations, and a high rate of suspensions for vandalism, fighting, and insubordination.[19] As a result of Iowa's Department of Human Resources's goal to reduce the number of youths requiring residential treatment services, the state's attention turned to enhancing local delinquency services and making them school based.

Over the past five years, in an old building that houses 750 mostly disadvantaged students under the guidance of principal Pete Hathaway, a new kind of middle school has been shaped to fit the developmental and social needs of the students. Two elements have been employed in this reformation: site-based management, which has expanded decision-making power throughout the staff, and collaboration with local agencies to bring in an array of support people and services.[20] The curriculum has been designed to create flexible instructional settings, and students are slotted into classes that suit their needs. Those who require extensive remediation receive instruction in a small group that is team-taught by a regular classroom teacher and a Title I or special education teacher. Interdisciplinary teams coordinate across the curriculum, with strong emphasis on yearly themes. For example, sixth graders might concentrate on spiders, stars, or cultural diversity, while seventh graders work in units on ancient Egypt, and eighth graders are immersed in World War II or Greek civilization. Team meetings are held daily to coordinate lesson plans.

In addition to what goes on in the classroom, a multitude of motivational and cultural activities take place in the school, such as a Minorities in Teaching Program, conflict management training, peer helpers, life-skills training, Values and Choices Program, career fairs, and more.

Five innovative programs that rely on community partners have been introduced during the five-year period. All focus on preventing delinquent behaviors among high-risk students:

- The OutReach program brings minority counselors from a local community agency into the school setting, where they are matched with high-risk minority students. On hand before, during, and after school, the counselors provide one-on-one attention, crisis intervention, and home visits.

- A police-liaison officer is stationed in the school as another kind of counselor, and also to conduct gang-resistance training for seventh graders.

- The juvenile probation officer has an office in the school building allowing daily contact with adjudicated students.

- The probation officer also supervises the College Mentorship Program, which matches at-risk youth with supportive college students, and the Tracking Program, which follows adjudicated youth into the classroom to assure academic achievement.

- The After-School Program is administered by a local community social agency, providing homework help and tutoring, recreation, group work, and dinner, from 3 P.M. until 8:30 P.M. daily, including Saturdays. Almost half of the Woodrow Wilson students stay for the extended hours or participate in other extracurricular activities.

Evidence of success includes substantial improvements in test scores, many more students on the honor roll, dramatically lower number of suspensions, and attendance rates pushed up to nearly 95 percent. Paul DeMuro after a site visit to the Woodrow Wilson School on behalf of the Annie Casey Foundation, observed

a spirit of cooperation and a can-do attitude . . . with little or no evidence of that paralyzing social service disease, turfism, . . . the school district staff and the [public] and private service agencies are willing and able to stretch their thinking and reconfigure their services . . . they can get their thinking and actions out of the traditional boxes.[21]

Missouri Caring Community Schools

One of the most sophisticated examples of community schools, this program includes many components, agencies, and administrative levels. An initiative of the Missouri Department of Mental Health, this effort brings together the St. Louis City Public Schools and the Danforth Foundation in a collaborative effort with the state departments of health, social services, and education.[22] A pilot program at the Walbridge Elementary School in St. Louis provided an array of intensive services to children and families of the neighborhood in a school-based center. Services include family counseling, case management, substance abuse counseling, student assistance, parenting education, before- and after-school activities, youth programs, health screening, and pre-employment skills. In recent years, Walbridge began to provide respite care for parents, allowing students to spend the night at the school twice a month. An evaluation of the program at Walbridge showed that the children who got the most intensive services showed more improvement in academic subjects and behavior than did other children in the school and in a comparison group. It also disclosed that the police saw the program as a powerful force for crime reduction in the community.

James Ewing, the principal of the Walbridge Elementary School, recounted one experience with this program.

> I remember a little tiny girl coming in late every day. One day, I questioned why, and she said her mother was still in bed. I just picked up the phone and called Caring Communities. They found out there was no food, no furniture. They stayed with her for weeks. The mother is doing better. She came out to an affair recently with her hair done.[23]

This program is now being replicated across Missouri as a result of new state legislation, which appropriated $24 million for sixty new sites. Five state agencies are allied in this endeavor along with a privately funded Family Investment Trust that facilitates communication between the state and communities. New sites will be encouraged to get more involved in school reform to complement the support services so that school performance levels will improve.

Other Examples

In addition to IS218, the Children's Aid Society operates three other schools in Washington Heights and is providing technical assistance to several other sites to implement their model. In *Full-Service Schools,* I described the Hanshaw Middle School in Modesta, California, to demonstrate how a school district could be the lead agency for creating a one-stop center. The Elizabeth Street Learning Center in Los Angeles incorporates all sorts of child- and family-strengthening programs, in an integrated K–12 campus. I have been told that the entire school system in Farrell, Pennsylvania, is the nation's only cradle-to-grave model (incorporates infant care and senior citizen activities using fifty-seven different outside resources), but I have not been to visit the site to confirm this claim. The Turner School in Philadelphia, described in the previous chapter, demonstrates how universities can influence the development of community schools.

Common Elements in Community Schools

I have observed several key elements that seem to be present in all of these schools:

- plenty of individual attention

- a heavy emphasis on parental involvement and services for parents

- the availability of health centers and family resource rooms

- after-school activities

- cultural and community activities

- extended hours—open evenings, weekends, and summers

- respect and high expectations for students

Some, but not all, community schools are built around the concept of restructuring education to be responsive to the students' needs. Others focus more heavily on the provision of human services.

Yet each of these community schools is striving (in different ways) to become a village hub, with joint efforts from school and community agencies to create as rich an environment as possible for the children and their families. Each version of community schools packages the components in different ways, moving along a continuum from simple to complex administrative arrangements. Relocation of a contract service from one site (a public health or social service department or police officer) to another (a school building) is much less complicated than the creation of a new type of community school, where the educational system and the support interventions are completely integrated and operated collaboratively by several agencies.

DO FULL-SERVICE COMMUNITY SCHOOLS WORK?

While support for the concept of full-service schools is strong, even the most ardent advocates—myself included—want to be assured that centralizing services in restructured schools will make a difference in the lives of the children and their families. Evaluation results are spotty, which is not surprising given the early stages of program development and the difficulties inherent in program research, especially of complex projects that have many different components.

Along with Claire Brindis and David Kaplan, I recently reviewed the research on school-based clinics.[24] Several states (Florida, Kentucky, California) are beginning to produce reports on more comprehensive programs.[25] Individual researchers around the country have published papers with some positive results,[26] and several government publications have included summaries of preliminary research findings.[27] Let me summarize the major findings from these sources of information.

We start with school-based health centers. These programs have been successfully implemented in the communities and schools with the greatest needs, are enrolling high percentages of the student body, and are involving many parents. And the highest-risk students, with the greatest number of problems and no other source of medical care or no medical insurance, are using school clinics most frequently. More than a million students are receiving free, primary health care that is convenient, confidential, and caring. In centers with mental health personnel, substantial numbers of students and their families are gaining access to psychosocial counseling. The demand is overwhelming, especially for mental health services, substance abuse treatment, and dentistry.

Use of emergency rooms has declined in a few areas with school clinics, and hospitalization rates have decreased in others. This suggests that locating services in schools is cost effective, cutting down on the more expensive kinds of medical care. Because minor ailments such as headaches, menstrual cramps, and accidents on school property can be treated in school, absences and excuses to go home have decreased. School-based clinics have also demonstrated the capacity to respond to emergencies—for example, immunization campaigns and TB screening.

Scattered evidence suggests that a few school-based clinics have had an impact on teens of delaying the initiation of sexual intercourse (abstinence), upgrading the quality of contraceptive use, and lowering pregnancy rates, but only in the limited number of programs that offer comprehensive family-planning services and condom distribution. Large numbers of students are being diagnosed and treated for sexually transmitted diseases. In some schools, clinic users have been shown to have lower substance use, better school attendance, and lower dropout rates. Having a clinic in a school has no proven effect on nonenrollees, and rates of problem behaviors in the schools overall have not changed significantly. Comprehensive school-based programs for pregnant and parenting teens have demonstrated earlier access to prenatal care and higher birth weights, lower repeat pregnancy rates, and better school attendance.

Students, parents, teachers, and school personnel report a high level of satisfaction with school clinics and particularly appreciate their accessibility, convenience, confidentiality, and caring attitudes. In family resource centers with health clinics, preventive medical care and treatment of minor illnesses are the major services sought and used. In some programs, school staff also receive health screening, nutrition, and other services. Family resource centers have proved their ability to help families improve their access to basic needs such as food, clothing, transportation, and child care.

Early reports from the more comprehensive community schools are encouraging.[28] Attendance, grades, and graduation rates are significantly higher than in comparable schools, and reading and math scores have shown some improvement. Disciplinary referrals and suspensions have declined. Students are eager to come to schools that are stimulating, nurturing, and respectful of cultural values. Parents frequently participate as classroom aides or advisory board members, in adult education classes and cultural events, and by using case managers and support services.

While clinics, resource centers, and community schools have many differences, the successful programs share certain common elements in their histories. In most instances, school and community leaders, along with parents, join together to create a shared vision for a new kind of institution. One of the most extensive processes was undertaken to plan New Beginnings, a collaboration among five major agencies to create a family resource center at the Hamilton Elementary School in San Diego. The two-year feasibility study encompassed family interviews, focus groups of agency workers, case management and agency use practices, and migration patterns. Although the program was well defined by the research, the implementation process was long, complex, and time-consuming.[29] Ellen Brickman, (Fordham University), researcher conducted a formative evaluation of the Children's Aid Society's first elementary Community School. She recommended that any future plan should include a clear statement of the goals—what services and programs will be delivered, in what quantities, and to whom.[30] Moreover, she suggested that the plan spell out provisions for alleviating overcrowding in the school and set priorities for when the initial capacity of the program was surpassed. One parent participant I talked to in Los Angeles reported:

> I never imagined that I would have to go to so many meetings. At first, I was afraid to say anything, but then when we began to talk about what the parents in my neighborhood really needed, I discovered that I had a lot of ideas to share. One idea I thought was great was to have suppers at the school to which we would all bring food, and everyone could join together to celebrate holidays.

In developing a plan for a community school, outside support services must be appropriate to what already exists in the school in the way of health services, social services, and counseling. I have observed the crucial role school principals play in the implementation and smooth operation of full-service schools. Aside from leading the school's restructuring, they also must make community partners feel at home as well as provide them with adequate space for services with ample security and maintenance. In a middle school in Bridgeport, Connecticut, the principal raved about how important it is to have access to a community agency team that comes in to provide counseling to her students.

> We couldn't get along without them. They are so helpful to our children, and even have the time to visit with their families. Since they have been working with us, many more parents are willing to come to the school. Together we have created many community-wide events, like getting dresses donated for students to wear to the prom. Both the girls and their mothers flocked in to select their outfits. It was quite a scene.

In addition to the principal, successful programs rely on a full-time coordinator or program director. All personnel are trained to be sensitive to issues related to youth development, cultural diversity, and community empowerment. Bilingual staff are essential. A designated space such as a clinic or a center in a school acts an anchor, or even a magnet, for bringing in other services from the community. Perhaps the most important effect of the full-service community school is the structuring of an organizational capacity to bring new resources into the confines of the traditional school building. The Children's Aid Society schools exemplify this capacity. Every time I visit, I find a new program, usually brought in by another community agency, to augment the roster of services and activities.

IMPLEMENTATION ISSUES

As experience has been gained around the country with the various models of full-service community schools, practitioners, researchers, and observers have identified a number of areas that have to be addressed in the development of these complex programs.

Governance

As would be expected, the more complex the model, the more demanding the administrative arrangements. The mounting rhetoric calls for sophisticated collaborative organizations, whereby school systems and community agencies leave behind their parochial loyalties and pitch in together to form a new kind of union.[31] In reality, most of the emerging models have one designated lead agency. In Modesta, California, it is the school system, which dispenses its Healthy Start grants to a variety of public and voluntary agencies through contractual relationships. In places like New Jersey, community agencies may be direct grantees and enter schools through a memorandum of agreement. But in neither case is governance changed.

The first evaluation of New Beginnings in San Diego—the multiagency program that operates a family resource center in Hamilton School—warns that it is "difficult to overestimate the amount of time collaboration takes." The participants discovered that it was easier to get agencies to make "deals" (sign contracts to relocate workers) than to achieve major changes in delivery systems. Staff turnover, family mobility, fiscal problems, and personality issues were cited as some of the barriers to change.

Turf

When a whole new staff working for an outside agency moves onto school property, many territorial concerns arise. What role does the school nurse play in the school-based clinic? Why not hire more school social workers if family counseling and case management are needed? Issues arise over confidentiality, space, releasing students from classes, and discipline. It takes time and energy and, particularly, skilled principals and program coordinators to work through appropriate policies and practices.

The early experience with Beacons in New York City showed that it was difficult for an outside agency not connected to the educational establishment to set up a program in a school.[32] In this case, large grants were given to community organizations, which took responsibility for the after-school hours, but they had little contact with what occurred to the students during the school day. It took several years for the school and community agency personnel to recognize that they were working with the same students and the same families, and that what happened in the classroom and what happened in the gym after school should be interrelated.

Discipline of troublesome students is frequently a bone of contention between the old school staff and new social work staff. One of the most dramatic turf episodes occurred in an inner-city school on a day the community agency youth workers were awaiting the visit of the mayor and Michael Jordan, the athlete, along with the media. As the time approached, the workers noticed a student was chained to the fence in front of the school. When the school principal was confronted, he denied responsibility, saying that the school custodian over whom he had no authority had done it. A call to the central office of the Board of Education got the boy released from the fence and the custodian fired. The next day, the youth workers were accosted by angry teachers who charged, "You sacrificed a lousy kid for a terrific custodian." Although this was an unpleasant episode, it opened up communication between the school and the community agency personnel. They initiated frequent joint meetings to share information about the students.

Provide or Refer

Some comprehensive programs focus on bringing all the services to one site, featuring "one-stop" approaches to family and youth programs. These efforts are driven by the desire to get rid of fragmentation—the patchwork quilt of unrelated programs with different eligibility requirements, multiple data systems, and reimbursement mechanisms. Other programs rely on "linkages," with the central agency serving as a referral point for sending the families and their children to whatever services they need within the community. Programs featuring referral linkages do not adequately address the problem of fragmentation. Rarely are the linkages formal, and the client, particularly if a teenager, is not likely to follow through on the referral unless the intervention includes transportation and careful follow-up. The Kentucky centers were originally designed as places for coordination, but experience showed that parents and youth came into the centers (usually a designated room) hoping to receive services on-site. It was reported that many of the principals in the schools with youth centers expected the coordinator to take over the supervision of troubled students.

Controversy

In some places, community groups and school boards have resisted the idea of using the school building for anything but educational purposes. In a few instances, small, well-organized opposition groups have created large controversies over school-based service proposals, focusing negatively on reproductive health services and mental health services. Experience throughout the country, however, has shown that resistance on the part of school boards and community agencies has dissipated rapidly with the availability of state and foundation grants for comprehensive school health, mental health, and social services. The extensive local-needs assessments and planning prior to program development have equipped parents and school personnel with the necessary data to convince decision makers and to educate the media about the importance of integrating services in the school.

Even now, concern is often expressed about overburdening schools with too many extraneous concerns. In the opinion of the Committee for Economic Development (CED), "Schools are not social service institutions; they should not be asked to solve all our nation's social ills and cultural conflicts."[33] Nevertheless, CED supports the placement of social services in schools that are delivered through schools but that under no circumstances are funded by educational systems.

School-Based Versus Community-Based

Questions have also been raised about placing the locus of full-service programs in schools in communities that distrust the educational establishment.[34] Some community leaders have little confidence that the quality-education part of the full-service vision will ever materialize. Human resource planners have proposed an alternative model that places services in buildings run by community-based organizations in which families feel comfortable and are assured larger roles in decision making. Centro Sister Isolino Ferre and Quantum Opportunities Program, described in the previous chapter, are examples of such community-based programs. The service integration theory still holds, but the locus of services is placed firmly in the neighborhood and under local control.

Questions have also been raised about the viability of using full-service schools as sites for dealing with young people who no longer attend school. Some of the existing school-based centers do serve out-of-school youth as well as siblings and parents of current students, but others do not. For two major youth-serving organizations in New York City (El Puente and the Door), the transformation into full-service schools started with the community organizations that added basic educational components to their rosters of services and obtained certification as part of the public school system. This community youth center–school model offers an approach for working with school dropouts who are often youth agency clients. The disaffected youth are drawn back into the school system through the efforts of trusted youth service agency staff.

The resolution of this potential conflict between school establishment and community-based groups must take place community by community. I strongly favor schools as sites for comprehensive programs because they are publicly supported institutions and should be utilized by the whole community. The children are physically there already, at least at the outset, and anything we can do to further the children's interest in obtaining the best possible education should be supported.

A MODEL FOR THE FUTURE

In the planning stages of any full-service community school, the different roles and fiscal responsibilities of the various participants must be clear. The school maintains control of the academic program, and the outside agencies operate and finance everything else. The full-service community school is a home-grown product with many variants, developed at the local level by committed individuals who come together from diverse parts of the community to build more responsive institutions. We don't even know how many schools now have established partnerships with human services agencies, but the number is clearly growing. Relatively small investments by state governments and foundations have enabled innovative leaders to use existing resources to relocate personnel and to devise more integrated—and more responsive—delivery systems. In May 1997, the first Community School Summit brought together all the "players" mentioned above to try to gain national visibility and, perhaps, significant federal legislation for this emerging field.

In reviewing this chapter, I am aware that I have written it from my own point of view, the health and human services side of the community school equation. Yet I believe that unless the quality education side is as fully developed, these new kinds of schools will not be any more successful than the traditional ones. In the next chapter, I move on to consider the state of the art of school restructuring and reform.

Candace diCarlo, Photographer, Courtesy of the Turner School

6

SCHOOL REFORM

*Much facilitation of healthy child development must occur in schools.
Research and experience have illuminated a few key concepts. . . .
Developmentally appropriate education, in which the content and process of
learning meshes with the interests and capacities of the child; schools and
classes of small units, created on a human scale; sustained individual
attention in the context of a supportive group; students learning to cooperate
in class with an eye on future work and decent human relations; stimulation
of curiosity and thinking skills; linkage of education and health—each must
nourish the other.*

—David Hamburg, Today's Children

My conviction that the new wave of community schools has the potential for producing greater impacts on the lives of the youth and their families than other school-reform efforts is quite presumptuous from someone who is an outsider to the educational establishment. So in order to inform myself, and you, I have tried to find out what is going on in educational reform and to determine where educational restructuring fits into the Safe Passage movement. For this review, I have relied heavily on several sources—*Education Week, Phi Delta Kappan*, reports from the American Educational Research Association and other organizations—and I have visited various schools around the country.

We must admit that we all think of ourselves as authorities on education—after all, we all went to school, have had children in school, and pay school taxes. Certainly, we have been trying to improve the quality of our schools for as long as we have had public education. But it seems we can never catch up with the needs. The late Albert Shanker, the long-time and sometimes contentious president of the American Federation of Teachers, took a dour view of the situation. In a column subtitled "Lots of Bull but No Beef," he stated:

> If people made fortunes with their schemes for reforming the schools, we'd have a healthy crop of school reform millionaires. Year after year, new proposals appear . . . but sooner or later, they disappear, leaving the school substantially unchanged.[1]

It is true that the educational establishment has gone through a long progression of theoretical phases—from the basics to progressive education to Sputnik to open classrooms to alternative schools to pull-out remediation. Now, in the late 1990s, the talk is about academic standards, school choice, charters, computers, and uniforms. And, in fact, we are making some headway, with local-level implementations of carefully designed demonstration projects, conceived and directed by respected professors and replicated by committed principals, teachers, and other school personnel.

In this complex field of education, we have to distinguish between programs that are designed to prevent school failure and dropping out among selected high-risk students and those that focus on systemic changes to upgrade the quality of the education for all students—quality schooling is fundamental to the assurance of Safe Passage, for no one can make it in this country without a high degree of literacy and numeracy. While effective schools can be measured by their test scores, it is important to remember that much more than cognitive ability is influenced by school experiences. We have seen how many high-risk youngsters lack real school engagement; they are far behind their peers, have low aspirations, are frequently absent, and feel little connection to their teachers or the buildings they are forced to sit in until they can break out. Thus, an important outcome for effective schools is the promotion of healthy life styles and the prevention of high-risk behaviors—children who are engaged in school activities are much less likely to get into trouble with drugs, sex, or violence.

In this chapter I will give some examples of programs aimed at high-risk students and then take a look at the growing experience with school restructuring designs.

SCHOOL PROGRAMS AIMED AT HIGH-RISK STUDENTS

This nation has accumulated a wealth of experience with school failure and dropout-prevention programs. Each of the programs we visited in chapter 4 was aimed at high-risk populations and sought to enhance educational outcomes. Most of the work on full-service community schools in chapter 5 is directed toward improved school achievement and attendance. Those schools and community-based programs are comprehensive, in the sense that they put together many different components to intensify the effect. But here I want to discuss several programs that have only one or two components specifically aimed at certain school-related behaviors. These components include:

- individual one-on-one attention, case management, counseling
- intensive educational remediation through peer tutors, adult tutors, mentors, computers
- developmentally appropriate curricula in classroom
- small groups, warm, supportive environments
- incentives
- early intervention with parent education, home visiting, and preschool educational experiences[2]

I selected these programs because I have been tracking most of them for more than a decade to study their effectiveness and history of replication.[3] Replication is an important issue here since the test of a program is its sustainability, both in its original form and later when others try to reproduce it. It should be understood, however, that many other programs would fit into this discussion because they are aimed at preventing school failure or dropout, and they have some evidence of success.

Valued Youth Partnership

This program was initiated in San Antonio, Texas, to train high-risk, middle school, Hispanic students to become tutors and counselors for younger children in elementary school. Called *cross-age tutoring*, this component focuses on creating a sense of responsibility and accomplishment among the more vulnerable students. After two years, only 1 percent of tutors had dropped out of middle school, far fewer than the 12 percent of comparison students. Valued Youth Partnership students achieved higher reading grades, and observers attributed the success of the program to "high expectations on the part of the participants, students feeling that they belong, and the ability of a campus to adapt the model."[4]

The Valued Youth Partnership is currently being replicated in fifty-two sites, mostly in Texas through the Intercultural Development Research Association (IDRA) in San Antonio. In 1990, the Coca-Cola Foundation selected the program for nationwide replication, and it was recognized by the U.S. Department of Education for inclusion in the National Diffusion Network.

Cities-in-Schools (CIS)

The brainchild of William Milliken, this dynamic Washington-based agency claims to run the nation's largest dropout-prevention network. CIS operates a national organization with independent local affiliates who follow the CIS process—social service providers are relocated into schools to team up with teachers to address the needs of high-risk youths for individual attention. Specifically, CIS identifies local leaders who can form partnerships and bring resources such as case managers and social workers into schools, or who can sponsor alternative schools or other approaches to school dropout prevention. CIS programs have resulted in improved attendance and promotion rates and better academic performance among participants. In addition, access to intensive case management has helped to keep high-risk youths in school.[5]

Cities-in-Schools programs have been organized in 243 communities in twenty-six states and serve close to 120,000 students annually.[6] To meet the demand for replication and monitoring, CIS has created six regional offices to support training and technical assistance, and twelve states have fully operational programs. Through a partnership among the U.S. Department of Justice, CIS, and Burger King Corporation, sixteen CIS/Burger King Academies (alternative schools) have been opened, and ten Department of Defense partnership academies were projected to open in 1996. CIS is in the process of changing its name to Communities-in-Schools.

The School Transition Environment Project (STEP)

This school-based program was developed by Robert Felner, then at the University of Illinois, to ease the way for high-risk youth into high school. Felner and his colleagues were trying to modify or remove those conditions of risk in the environment that make children more vulnerable to difficulties and, at the same time, foster changes in educational situations that would increase the probability that the students would acquire the competencies and strengths that would help them make it.[7] In their freshman year, selected students are assigned to specially trained teachers within a designated unit for all their studies, guidance, and counseling. This "school-within-a-school" relies heavily on the homeroom teacher, who also acts as advisor, advocate, and liaison with family and school. A five-year follow-up of the original ninth graders showed a 24 percent dropout rate among participants, compared to 43 percent in a control group (this was clearly a high-risk population).[8] The study also documented positive effects on student achievement and attendance. In a later study of lower-risk students, STEP students reported that they had more positive school experiences, reflected in better student adjustment and better performance in terms of grades and attendance.

The Transition Project has been replicated and evaluated in at least five schools, and concepts from this work have been incorporated into the Carnegie Corporation's Turning Points initiative to reform middle schools (see below).

The Quantum Opportunity Program (QOP)

In our discussion of one replication of this program in chapter 4, we saw how QOP is a very successful and well-evaluated educational enhancement program usually located in community-based agencies rather than school buildings. It provides intensive, after-school, sequenced education, development, and service activities over the four years of high school to small groups of disadvantaged teens.[9] The program also gives students stipends to encourage continuing education. Based on earlier demonstrations in four cities, QOP is now being replicated in seven sites under the auspices of the Department of Labor and the Ford Foundation.

Liberty Partnerships

One important component of educational enhancement is the offer of incentives—either stipends, as is done in the QOP program, or college scholarships. New York state has initiated the Liberty Partnerships to stimulate universities to get involved with high-risk high school students and to help them gain admission to college.[10] For example, one intensive Cooperative Group Work summer program for at-risk African American females documented significant increases in math skills in the following school year.[11] According to the researchers, the program's cooperative learning and peer-tutor approach were effective learning strategies for these students.

Another Liberty intervention arranged for free, six-week, "mainstream" SAT coaching for high-risk urban eleventh grade students.[12] The course was delivered in the school building by specialist trainers who were sensitive to the needs of disadvantaged youth and tutors who were available between sessions. The participants ended up with higher SAT scores than nonparticipants, with an average of 700, indicating the possibility of entrance into "mainstream" colleges. Michael Bazigos, the researcher, attributed the success not only to the coaching but also to the "counselor cajoling and badgering." The New York State Liberty Partnerships program continues to fund fifty-eight sites in the state, involving 16,000 students.

Parents as Teachers (PAT)

This program is often cited as the model for early intervention. It provides parents with information and support in their children's early years through scheduled home visits by certified parent educators, screening, and referral. Started in one district in Missouri in 1981, the program has since been implemented in every school district in that state. Studies have shown that the children of parents who participate in PAT have much higher achievement and language ability levels by age 3, by kindergarten, and by third grade, than do nonparticipants.[13] PAT parents improved their coping skills and reported reduced family stress, particularly among families with children who had been identified as having developmental delays and among those who had previously demonstrated poor parent-child communication.

Parents as Teachers has experienced tremendous growth in recent years. According to the Parents as Teachers National Center in St. Louis, more than 1,600 PAT programs are currently in operation in forty-three states and around the world.[14] Some twenty-two evaluations in eleven states and one foreign country are in the works. New initiatives for teen parents are underway.

Working from the Outside

The six examples above demonstrate that targeted programs featuring one or more well-designed components can impact the achievement levels and attendance patterns of participants. In a sense, these are all prevention programs, aimed at helping youngsters and their parents to get on the right track. While one is school-based and the other community-based, the Transition Project and QOP are formulated on similar theories—to create small, cloistered environments, with large amounts of support from trained adults and intensive cognitive training that is relevant to each student.

You may have noticed that these programs address only one group of students, typically those selected because they are doing poorly in school or exhibit behavioral problems. Most of these efforts originated outside of the school system: Valued Youth Partnerships and CIS are nonprofit organizations, Liberty and PAT are state programs—they do not involve the entire school system. The school restructuring experience is a more complicated story.

SCHOOL RESTRUCTURING EFFORTS

It is difficult to portray all that is going on in school reform efforts. Educational improvement is on the top of the agenda of each and every politician and administrator, but no two strategies are alike. I want to focus here on several significant developments that are taking place that could have major impacts on the Safe Passage movement. New American Schools encompasses seven important school restructuring designs and involves many of the leaders of school reform movements; and the Turning Points initiative translates research about middle schools into carefully planned action.

New American Schools

In 1989, President George Bush convened the first ever U.S. education summit that actively involved all the governors, including William Clinton. One proposal that emerged called for a private, nonprofit corporation that would create "break-the-mold school designs for the 21st century." Fulfilling that charge, the New American Schools Development Corporation (NAS) was formed by business and foundation leaders in 1991, and over the past six years it has documented important experiences, mostly positive, that have improved America's schools.[15] NAS has expanded its partnerships to include states, school districts, the RAND Corporation, and the Education Commission of the States.

NAS's history will give you an idea of just how many educators are out there who think they know how to restructure schools. In 1992, when NAS called for proposals, they received 685 applications. Some eleven design teams were selected "whose ideas will serve as blueprints for reinventing America's schools for the next generation of children."[16] Winning teams included many of the authorities we will meet below (Sizer, Comer, Slavin) along with Mark Tucker's National Alliance for Restructuring Education, which promised to produce 243 "breaking-the-mold" schools by 1995; William Bennett's Modern Red School House in seven systems; and Audrey Cohen's College of Human Services, which would work in thirty schools around the country.

At the time of the first awards, *Education Week's* Lynn Olsen commented on how many ideas the teams had in common—what one observer referred to as "the new conventional wisdom."[17] Most of the proposals stressed the use of multiage classrooms; the promotion of individual attention through the use of advisors and smaller groupings of students; cooperative learning; greater flexibility in teaching and extended days; and increasing coordination between education, health, and social service providers. Skepticism was expressed about the value of the NAS enterprise, however, especially from those who had spent months preparing proposals that then were rejected in favor of what they perceived as "the educational establishment."

Initially, NAS experienced rough sailing, not only because the $200 million annual business contribution never came through, but also because many of the proposals were hard to implement within the three-year period allotted.[18] Questions were raised about the feasibility of program exposure through national seminars and meetings. By 1995, the budget, largely based on foundation and business contributions, had peaked at $36 million, and in 1996 it was down to about $17 million.[19]

The field has narrowed down to seven "design teams," made up of representatives of the original groups who spent the first two years of the project proving that their interventions would make changes in the outcomes for the students. A study of the demonstration projects by RAND researchers identified three factors that influenced progress toward achieving the goals of transforming schools: team readiness/capability, type of design, and the implementation strategy used in the early phases.[20] The capacities for change of the local school sites was an important element. All school staff had to buy into the new design and be part of the continuing governance, and all staff had to have access to retraining and concrete models. The design had to match the needs of the school:

for example, high schools that prided themselves on electives were not open to a core curriculum. An on-site facilitator was an essential component of the day-to-day implementation. And a great deal of time was required to develop vision, change curricula, and institute new practices. The least complex, most highly developed models achieved the greatest success.

The knowledge accrued from the demonstration phase has been used to define the requirements that NAS become strong technical assistance organization that can communicate its vision and work intensively with schools to implement well-documented models. By September of 1996, 500 schools located in twenty-five states had been selected to implement the work of the seven design teams, with each school picking the most appropriate model for it—based on the theory that "one size does not fit all."

The NAS experience does not come as a revelation to old-time school watchers. Stanley Pogrow, a professor at the University of Alabama, pointed out, "It is far more difficult to figure out how to implement theory than it is to generate it. . . . Thus it makes no sense to expect practitioners to develop their own techniques for implementing a complex reform idea. . . . In medicine, if individual practitioners invent their own procedures, we call it malpractice."[21]

New American Schools Designs

Below are the seven designs to show the range of thinking about how to change schools to make them effective and responsive.[22]

Atlas Communities This approach centers on pathways, or clusters of schools (elementary, middle, high school) that link together. Teachers collaborate with parents and administrators to form learning communities that are based on locally defined criteria.

Audrey Cohen College Each grade focuses on a "purpose"—for example, the whole fourth grade concentrates on working for good health by planning, carrying out, and evaluating actions that build knowledge and skills to benefit the community and the world. (I saw one of these schools in Memphis, and it was bubbling over with invention and creativity—the students were very busy and excited about what they were doing. The classroom walls and even the ceilings were covered with exciting and colorful materials that the students had made to illustrate the theme of the current project.)

Co-Nect Schools create and manage their own high-tech equipment, using technology for teaching, learning, professional development, and school management. Students are placed in small cross-disciplinary clusters.

Expeditionary Learning Outward Bound This approach relies on intense, long-term studies inside and outside of the classroom. Students stay with teacher teams for more than a year.

Modern Red Schoolhouse More traditional than some of the other designs, this one follows a rigorous curriculum, uses frequent assessments, focuses on teacher development, and involves the community.

National Alliance for Restructuring Education This group's goal is to make changes all the way from the classroom to the state educational system through partnerships of schools, districts, states, and national organizations. Five task forces focus on standards, learning environment, management, community services, and public involvement.

Roots and Wings This elementary school design builds on Success for All, which is one of the most successful and best evaluated school reform programs. Developed by Robert Slavin and colleagues at the Center for Research on Effective Schooling for Disadvantaged Students, at Johns Hopkins University, it is a comprehensive, school-based intervention that starts at age 4 with preschool, heavily emphasizes one-on-one teaching through individual plans, utilizes family support teams, and works closely with teachers in the classrooms. Slavin believes that one must "relentlessly stick with every child until that child is succeeding." Extensive research has proved the effectiveness of this approach.[23]

Rebecca Herman and Sam Stringfield, who advised the Department of Education regarding ten programs that were designed to help disadvantaged children in school, reported:

> Of the programs [reviewed], Success for All has the strongest external research base. . . . The key elements—regrouping, assessment, individualization, remediation—are systematic. The structure of the program, rather than the personalities implementing it, are designed to maximize the probability of academic success. . . . The most at-risk students showed the most improvement. . . . Success for All reduces (grade) retention and special education assignments and increases attendance.[24]

Success for All has been implemented in 140 elementary schools in fifty-six districts in twenty states.[25] Successful replication experience suggests that the program can work in diverse circumstances and does not rely on a particular school structure or principal.

Turning Points

Until recently, scant attention was paid to the sorry state of middle schools. Happily, however, that situation has changed. In an unusual example of using research to inform action, the Carnegie Corporation conducted an intensive survey of the status of middle schools and issued *Turning Points: Preparing American Youth for the 21st Century.*[28] The study found "a volatile mismatch between the organization and curriculum of middle grade schools and the intellectual and emotional needs of young adolescents."[29] This report laid out important principles for schools to follow if they wanted to transform themselves into holistic, integrated models of education for 10 to 15 year olds. The foundation then supported fifteen states and their local school districts to implement the recommendations, and at the same time launched a national evaluation under the direction of Robert Felner, now at the National Center for Public Education, University of Rhode Island.[30]

The proposed process for reforming middle schools is organized around several important concepts, which are adopted and implemented by participating schools.

- Large middle grade schools should be divided into smaller communities for learning that foster relationships between adults and students.

- All students should meet with success in acquiring a core of common knowledge and skills.

- Teachers and principals should be empowered to make the key decisions necessary to transform middle grade schools.

- Teachers should be specifically prepared to teach young adolescents.

- Schools should promote good health; the education and health of young adolescents are inextricably linked.

- Families should be engaged with school staff in enhancing their children's education, and schools should be connected with their communities.

For evaluation purposes, schools were classified by the level of implementation. High implementation was defined as having team units with no more than 120 students and a teacher student ratio of under 1 to 25; frequent "advisory" sessions between students and teacher advisors, with one teacher serving no more than twenty-two students; allowing teachers four to five planning periods per week; and paying attention to issues related to adolescent development. Those schools that implemented the entire "package" were found to have significantly better outcomes than schools that only partially implemented the program and those that made very few changes. The schools with high implementation began to transform themselves into "small communities for learning." Most importantly, observers found that

> reforms implemented independently of one another are likely to produce little or no significant rise in achievement, especially for disadvantaged youth. Not until a critical mass of reforms is in place and operating together in an integrated manner do significant positive changes occur.[31]

The Turning Points initiative is a dynamic process that will continue to yield valuable information as other schools enter the network of innovators, and as states begin to implement systemic changes that allow for smaller class sizes, schools-within-schools, intensive teacher preparation and in-service training, and other components that have been identified as part of the school reform package.

Accelerated Schools Project

Developed by Henry Levin of Stanford University in 1986, this approach was initially directed at elementary schools to make them function better by enriching students rather than discouraging them. By the latest count, more than 1,000 schools across the country have implemented this concept, many of them middle and junior high schools. The three principles of Accelerated Schools are: unity of purpose whereby all members of the school community share a common set of goals; empowerment of every member to participate in decision-making processes, implementation, and accountability; and building on the unique strengths of every participant.[26] These principles are turned into actions under the guidance of a trained coach from outside the system, who helps the staff follow a defined process for changing the climate of the school through thoughtful innovation. Everyone works together to transform classrooms into powerful learning environments responsive to the needs of every child. It takes about six years to transform a conventional school into an accelerated one.

A National Center for the Accelerated Schools Project integrates resources from ten regional centers and over 200 certified trainers. Many research studies have been conducted on participating schools and show significant improvements in achievement outcomes and attendance, substantial decreases in tracking, curtailment of suspensions and disciplinary measures, and greatly enhanced parent involvement.[27]

Other School Restructuring Efforts

Some of the most significant cutting-edge programs in the area of school achievement have been carefully evaluated and found not to work as well as might be expected. For these, the original demonstration model produced successful outcomes, but subsequent replications could not match them. Some program replications have been found to work in certain school systems but not others. In some places, when the evaluation showed that the program did not have the desired effects, the program developers altered the design, typically adding more components, greater intensity, and attention to staff training. These programs are all important, however, and should not be ignored because of mixed results.

THE SCHOOL DEVELOPMENT PROGRAM (SDP)

Created by James Comer of the Yale Child Study Center, and tested in the New Haven Schools in the early 1980s, this program mobilizes the whole "village" to help children grow. Specifically, SDP attempts to transfer mental health approaches to schools where "change agents" are created by strengthening and redefining the relationships among principals, teachers, support staff, parents, and students.[32] The formation of three teams is basic to the School Development Program:

- School Planning and Management Team. Parents, teachers, administrators, support staff, and students coordinate all school activities. The team develops and monitors a comprehensive school plan including academic, social, staff development, and public relations goals.

- Mental Health Team. School psychologists and other support personnel integrate and provide direct services to children, advise school staff, and parents, and access resources in the community. For example, one team set up a Discovery Room for giving children hands-on experiences, and another initiated the practice of keeping teachers with the same class over two years to promote continuity.

- Parent Participation Program. A parent is hired to work in each classroom on a part-time basis. In addition to serving as representatives to the Advisory Council, parents are encouraged to volunteer as teacher aides, to act as librarians, to run newsletters, and to organize social activities.

A number of evaluations of SDP have been conducted. Earlier studies conducted by both Comer and outside evaluators showed increases in student achievement in SDP schools, compared to similar schools, higher averages in math and better grades in reading and math.[33] All of these schools were observed to have full implementation of the model, with access to a well-trained facilitator. A recent study of SDP in ten sites, conducted by the Yale Child Study Center, showed that SDP had a positive impact on student behavior and achievement, especially at grades 3, 4, and 5.[34] An intensive study of the implementation of the Comer model in six elementary schools in Hartford, Connecticut, was less encouraging. Researchers Neufield and LaBue concluded that the process had not been implemented:

> Despite the desires, efforts and successes [of selected teachers, staff and administrators], the SDP has made little difference to children in any of the schools and is unlikely to move forward in ways that might significantly benefit children without considerable restructuring of the effort at the central office, the schools, and between central office and the schools.[35]

James Comer and colleagues believe that the success of the SDP depends on a full-time program facilitator designated by the school superintendent to work in the district, one school at a time. The School Development Program is now operating in over 600 schools in twenty states, and in other nations.[36] In 1990, the Rockefeller Foundation launched a major five-year effort to support training in the Comer Process and to stimulate replications through the auspices of the National Urban League. Several states, including New Jersey, announced plans to directly administer the development of the model in urban schools. The concepts supporting SDP have been integrated into school language—many systems refer to themselves as "undergoing Comerization."

THE COALITION OF ESSENTIAL SCHOOLS (CES)

Founded by Theodore Sizer at Brown University in 1984, this school reform movement promotes a teacher-run, student-centered school with a strong intellectual focus designed around nine educational principles. In 1988, the Coalition entered into a partnership with the Education Commission of the States to launch a joint reform effort known as "Re:Learning" to encourage states to create a policy environment receptive to CES ideas.

This approach is difficult to evaluate since it is more of a philosophy than a program—Herman and Springfield cite only two studies of CES.[37] One found lower achievement levels after the program was implemented in eleven Chicago schools, an effect attributed to poor implementation of the model and high student-to-faculty ratios.[38] Another study reported preliminary results of a long-term study of ten diverse CES schools with inadequate comparison groups. Most of the schools reported higher graduation rates, better attendance, and lower dropout rates.[39]

Central Park East, founded by Deborah Meier, has received substantial attention for many years as *the* successful CES model. This innovative school offers a common core curriculum in the humanities and sciences. Students are organized into small advisory groups that meet daily and receive consistent attention from their advisor. Examination is by portfolio (a collection of student work), and graduation requires demonstration of mastery in each intellectual area, such as language, mathematics, science, and social science. Weekly community service is a requirement. The school has extended hours for help with homework, foreign languages, and computers.

An unpublished evaluation conducted by David Bensman tracked earlier graduates from the first cohort of CPE students and found four years later that they had high rates of educational and personal success.[40] Some 95 percent of students interviewed had graduated from high school or gotten a GED, and 70 percent were in college; only 39 percent of similar East Harlem students had completed high school. Building on that study, Paul Tainsh produced an analysis to show that Central Park East graduates would in the long run produce a high social benefit through earnings because of their improved educational outcomes.[41]

I visited Central Park East early in its evolution. I will never forget an encounter with two 12-year-old boys who were sitting quietly in a classroom seriously engaged in sewing. They told me they were working on their togas as part of the cross-disciplinary study of the Roman Empire, the subject for the semester. This scene was truly moving, the intensity and seriousness of these young boys, in a child-centered setting where all the staff seemed deeply committed to creating an integrated learning environment.

Since 1990, the principles of the Coalition of Essential Schools have been widely subscribed to in the school reform movement. At least 916 schools are "members" of the Coalition, and a recent annual CES meeting was attended by more than 3,500 participants. The national movement has been stimulated by huge grants from the Annenberg Foundation; in New York alone, a Center for Collaborative Education has been set up to network with at least twenty-five schools interested in implementing the CES process.

Pamela Nesselrodt and Eugene Schaffer observed the replication process of five CES member schools and found that none had fully implemented the program.[42] Schools were reluctant to delete "nonessential courses," and teachers were not prepared to change their roles in the classroom. The researchers concluded:

The full implementation of the CES program requires radical reform in not only a school's curriculum and instruction but also in its staffing, scheduling, and management. It calls either for opening a brand new school with a staff dedicated to the principles and methodologies of the program or gradually changing an existing one. Either way, it calls for many hours of planning and staff development. Since CES offers little guidance in the implementation of its principles and emphasizes that each school will implement them in a manner appropriate for its student body, schools must each begin from ground zero in breathing life into the "vision" provided by the program originators.[43]

An earlier study of implementation in eight CES schools documented similar difficulties, particularly the heightening of tensions among faculty factions, differing interpretations of the coalition's ideas, parental opposition, and unexpected costs.[44] None of these critiques came as news to Theodore Sizer, who told *Education Week*, "It's easier to come up with a plan, and it's harder to get the powers to be to go along with that plan."[45]

LESSONS LEARNED FROM SCHOOL REFORM INITIATIVES

Herman and Stringfield's report for the Department of Education on ten promising programs for educating disadvantaged students concluded that "a more mature field of promising programs exists in the 1990s than at any previous point in our history"; that positive changes are possible in most schools; but that "none of these programs can be made teacher-proof, school-proof, or district-proof."[46] In addition to the Coalition, Comer, and Success for All, they reviewed schools' experience with Mortimer Adler's Paideia Proposal (didactic teaching, coaching, and small group seminars), Reading Recovery (diagnostic survey, tutoring, teacher training), METRA (tutoring by older students or aides), and computer-assisted instruction. They also looked at schoolwide Title 1 (a publicly funded program for remediation for disadvantaged students) and extended day and year programs. In reviewing the research, Success for All appeared to come the closest to the ideal.

According to the National Education Commission on Time and Learning, "Times have changed, and the nation's schools must change with them."[47] Using the provocative title, *Prisoners of Time*, the commission portrayed the uniform six-hour school day, 180 days per year, as a "design flaw" that must be remedied through creative reinvention. The Commission identified forty interesting (but largely unevaluated) schools and programs that employed some or all of the following approaches: using school time differently, in longer blocks; employing computer technology; extending the school day and year; providing time for professional development; and providing support services for children or families.

School reform or restructuring is a much more complex task than the implementation of a single component program like cross-age tutoring. And the more demanding the model, the more difficult to get all the involved parties to agree to the process. Systems changes—altering curriculum, transforming relationships with teachers or administrators, lengthening hours—are difficult to achieve. The mounting experience with the New American Schools and Turning Points, with the Comer and Coalition schools, demonstrates just how demanding these challenges are. Obviously, the older the students, the harder it is to produce positive outcomes. Elementary schools that try to replicate model programs such as Success for All and Accelerated Schools may be more amenable to change than high schools that are trying to implement Comer or Sizer principles. And younger children tend to be easier to work with than older ones (and teachers of younger children more flexible than teachers of older ones?).

Looking back over the program models with the strongest evaluations and the most successful outcomes, certain components seem to be associated with effective programs in addition to those mentioned above. What seem to be needed in the classroom are:

- changing classroom techniques to encompass cooperative learning and team teaching
- extensive teacher preparation and training
- higher expectations for students
- smaller class sizes

And in the whole school:

- teachers involved in planning and decision making
- schools-within-schools, houses, academies
- on-site facilitators or coaches from outside to work with school staff on restructuring issues
- a shift toward the use of mental health professionals in teams
- partnerships among schools, community agencies, businesses—all kinds of collaborative arrangements
- extension of hours the school is open
- parental involvement on school committees, in classrooms

It is not very often that practitioners get advice from foundation officers, but in the case of middle school reform, four of them have issued a "Manifesto for Middle-Grades Reform."[48] Joan Lipsitz (of Lilly, now retired), Hayes Mizell (of Edna McConnell Clark), Anthony Jackson (of Carnegie), and Leah Meyer Austin (of Kellogg), based on their collective experience and compelling research data, believe that sustainable school reform is achievable. Schools can be changed to become developmentally responsive to the needs of adolescents, can enhance achievement, and can overcome barriers created by the past treatment of minority and poor children. But, as they point out, "School improvement cannot be achieved on the run, distractedly, shallowly, or piecemeal."[49]

Schools that have successfully implemented Turning Points and other reforms appear to have access to ongoing technical assistance and networks of colleagues with whom to share experiences. Professional development receives high priority. Participants appreciate the importance of accountability and can use data for assessments and planning. Superintendents provide strong leadership for change and designate a coordinator or team leader.

Lipsitz and colleagues have also identified barriers to school reform. They believe that the intensity and focus can be lost in an "almost Pavlovian response" to the end of foundation support. Reformers then abandon ship and turn to the next initiative. Even without loss of support, turnover in leadership, especially at the superintendent level, can lead to a "hemorrhagic depletion of systemic and institutional memory."[50] In some communities, school leaders lack an understanding of what middle school reform is all about. They think that "one size fits all" rather then recognizing the challenge of adapting schools to meet different developmental and community needs. A major obstacle to reform is the political infighting among school boards, superintendents, unions, and the public. In summary:

> Reform requires behavioral change that is extremely difficult for everyone. . . . If school reform fails, it will not be because it was midguided. It will be because the effort—and not just of the school, districts, and states, but also of the foundations—was not sufficiently comprehensive, intense, or long-lasting to sustain the schools' focus on creating academically excellent centers of teaching and learning. . . . school reform is not for the literal, the timid, or the undecided. To be successful, it must be rooted in powerfully held, shared values that define and determine the entire school-improvement enterprise . . . echoing the golden rule: educate others' children as we would have others educate ours.[51]

School Reform and Full-Service Community Schools

You may wonder why this discussion of school reform is separate from the previous chapter on full-service community schools, when the components of successful programs look remarkably similar. The reason is that the two movements are being driven by very separate engines. The push for educational improvement is coming largely from the educational establishment, prodded by politicians and a concerned general public, who associate school achievement with the national quality of life. The push for community schools is coming from a much less visible group, a mix of health and social service providers and innovative university professors, who recognize that support services have to be joined with quality education if disadvantaged children are going to make it.

I was struck by this bifurcation of movements when I attended a conference featuring the New American Schools. Almost all of the energy (and research) seemed to be directed toward what was going on in the classroom, with little attention paid to the after-school hours or the need for support services. Of course, every design model is different, and each replication takes on its own ambience. But the experience with Turning Points suggests that schools entering into the restructuring process are so busy with teacher edification and curriculum matters that they rarely get around to implementing the principle of promoting health through school auspices. The emerging community school movement must rely on the school reformers to come up with the methods for producing quality education. And in my view, as I implied in the beginning of this chapter, school reform in disadvantaged communities will not be successful without opening up the school building for longer hours and incorporating an array of child and family services.

As school systems are exposed to the various school reform models discussed above, they are selected as if from a Chinese restaurant take-out menu—some from column A and some from column B. Memphis, a testing ground for the New American Schools initiative, has all seven of the NAS designs in operation. The Atlas model incorporates pieces of both the Coalition of Essential Schools and the School Development Model. The Comer School Development Model has been "married" to Zigler's Schools of the 21st Century (they are both located at Yale) to produce CoZi schools, programs for children from birth to age 12. CoZi schools, if properly implemented, would put together the most advanced thinking about both quality education and support services and result in restructured full-service community schools.

ISSUES FOR THE FUTURE

Implementation of the National Goals

One important development in the education field has been the promulgation of eight National Goals, formalized into law by the passage of *Goals 2000: Educate America Act of 1994*. The goals call for children to be ready to learn when they start school; higher graduation and achievement rates, especially in math and science; more teacher education and professional development; adult literacy and parental participation; and safe and drug-free schools.

A National Education Goals Panel issues annual reports to chart progress in achieving the goals. The 1995 report documented "modest" success since 1990: better prenatal care and more children being read to as steps toward being ready to learn; and some increases in grades 4 and 8 in math achievement (none in reading).[52] However, the report shows growing gaps in adult literacy and an increase in substance abuse among students along with other misbehaviors. In response to the slow pace of this effort, the panel has emphasized the concept of parental participation. They believe that if the National Education Goals are to be achieved, families, schools, and communities must be brought together to create stronger partnerships.

Charter Schools

The latest educational reform movement is growing around the concept of charter schools. Half of all states have recently passed legislation allowing individuals in a community to come together and apply for a charter to set up a new school or to redesign an existing one. The charter may come from the state department of education or from the local school board (every state is different), but all of the charter schools use public funds, allocated to them on a per-pupil basis, and are governed by their own body, not by the school board. Most states have limited the number of charters (California has 100 slots) as well as the size of the school (400 to 600 students), and require open admissions for all such schools. Only eight of the twenty-five states with charter school laws require that teachers be certified. Both the National Education Association and the American Federation of Teachers have endorsed the concept of charter schools, but urge greater attention to employee rights, academic standards, and account-ability. During the 1996 presidential campaign, President Clinton championed charter schools and pushed successfully for the inclusion of funds ($51 million) in the FY 1997 budget to help states and communities get started (see chapter 13 for further discussion of funding).

Advocates for charter schools—parents along with school reformers—believe that the autonomy, deregulation, and flexibility inherent in this model will create better learning environments for children.[53] Opponents fear that the movement toward charter schools is another end-run around public education and will only weaken the current system. They cite examples of reforms that are already taking place in traditional school systems— such as those already cited—as the path to follow.

My interest in charter schools has been stimulated as a result of my research on full-service community schools. In my travels around the country, I meet terrific people struggling to put together the pieces of comprehensive program-ming, but they are often frustrated by what they perceive as the intransigence of the educational bureaucracy. Often the thought is expressed, "Wouldn't it be great just to start from scratch?" Charter schools appear on the surface to offer that opportunity. Yet I have this nagging feeling that unless the whole system loosens up and allows greater autonomy and flexibility, creating islands of creativity will have little impact. It is not fair to the people struggling within the system to set up outside camps to "goad" and "threaten" those who choose to remain in it. I have heard advocates for charter schools express sentiments such as "this is a power tool to blast through the system" and "it will create friction without blowing the system up." What happens to the students in the noncharter schools as the charters siphon off money and talent, and engender more controversy? Charters could undermine the school- and community-based efforts that are already underway around the country.

Universities are jumping on this bandwagon. The Harvard University Project on Schooling and Children has launched the Innovative Schools Initiative (ISI) to study and support innovations in the organization, management, and gover-nance of schools. The group plans to identity successful models and support these reform efforts by offering professional education to teams of school de-signers, leaders, and board members. Director Katherine Merseth asserted, "It's really quite exciting to be able to create a school from scratch, exactly the way you want it. The charter school bargain of increased accountability in return for greater autonomy offers a terrific opportunity to introduce innovation into public schooling."[54]

Will School Reform Assure Safe Passage?

Obviously, nothing is settled in the educational domain. Exemplary programs are proliferating along with interventions based on "half-baked" ideas. Entrepreneurs are rapidly moving into the education scene, claiming that they can run schools better as private businesses than can public education entities. Major battles are being fought over the implementation of national standards in specific subject areas. No one can say for sure whether standards will raise quality and achievement or discourage creativity and flexibility. It is hard for parents to keep up with all the jargon. Although lofty goals of parent participation are much in evidence, most of the reform initiatives are still under the control of professionals. School boards and teachers' unions maintain their authority over school systems, but both power bases are being challenged.

Are schools assuring Safe Passage? Some definitely are, and some definitely are not; for the remainder, the outcomes are unclear. I believe that an increasing number of city schools in communities with serious commitments to assisting disadvantaged children are both centers of educational enrichment and safe havens. I know that many suburban schools are very stimulating and challenging places. Experience around the country, however, points toward very slow progress in broad educational reform, with strong resistance against any kind of standardization or outside regulation.

Film still from movie "Girls Town"
Phyllis Belkin, Photographer, courtesy of October Films

7

COPING WITH SEX, DRUGS, AND VIOLENCE

We need to look at the problems our children face like we look at a leaky bucket. If the bucket has six holes in it and we plug only five, we will still have a leaky bucket. To make a difference we have to collaborate. We have got to develop a comprehensive program to take care of the multiplicity of problems children face.

—Jocelyn Elders, M.D., *"Protecting the Nation's Future"*

Quality education is clearly a prerequisite for assuring Safe Passage to America's children. But when it comes to the prevention of high-risk behaviors, we have to move out of the education field and look at three other fields that specifically focus on sex, drugs, and violence. In this country, we have a vast assortment of "categorical" programs, programs that are supported by designated funding and that focus on changing targeted behaviors. (In chapter 13, I describe the maze of federal and state programs that keep this fragmented prevention enterprise afloat.)

In the late 1980s, I examined ninety-five different categorical prevention programs in three fields—substance abuse, teen pregnancy, and delinquency—and published the results in *Adolescents at Risk: Prevalence and Prevention*.[1] The point of that study was to demonstrate that selected programs "work." I found a number of programs that were successful at preventing specific behaviors; more importantly, the components that made up the effective programs were similar across prevention fields.

In 1995, we spent many hours trying to track down those programs to determine their status: Were they still operating? Had they been further evaluated? Had they been replicated? What more could we learn from them? Had new programs emerged?[2] Most of the original programs (eighty-three) could be located. Of these sixty-six were still in operation, forty-seven were being replicated, and thirty-one had conducted new research. Among the seventeen programs that were no longer operating, more than half of their originators were still in the prevention field and had designed new initiatives based on previous experience. Since 1990, a number of new programs have emerged, and more recent evaluations of established programs have been conducted.

In this chapter, I review a few selected evaluated programs in the three fields—delinquency, substance abuse, and teen pregnancy—and take a look at some programs in a relatively new field, AIDS/HIV prevention. All of these evaluation results were reported since 1990, although some of the programs were initiated prior to that time. In describing the evaluation results from the various interventions, you will see an emphasis on behavioral changes—for example, a decrease in cigarette smoking or a delay in the initiation of sexual intercourse. Many programs focus on increasing knowledge (such as understanding the negative effects of smoking) or changing attitudes (such as the acceptability of unprotected sexual intercourse). Changes in knowledge or attitudes, however, do not necessarily predict changes in behaviors. A teenager can know that a behavior may lead to problems, may think that it is a bad idea, but nevertheless do it. Therefore, we must be sure that the programs can give evidence of behavioral changes before we believe that they really work.

To determine whether a program really works, you have to examine the methodology of evaluation research. Scientists call for random assignment, meaning that subjects are put into experimental and control groups randomly rather than by self-selection. But this is not usually feasible when evaluating social programs—practitioners cannot refuse to accept a student or a patient or a client because of the research design. One way around this dilemma is to compare classrooms or schools with and without programs. Another is to compare participants with nonparticipants. Many programs rely on pre- and post-testing to show the changes in the participants, with no comparison group. My approach to evaluation research is to focus on the programs with the best available documentation so I can at least get a rough measure of whether they helped or hindered the clientele.

This chapter presents only a small sampling of contemporary youth programs in the fields of delinquency, substance abuse, and teen pregnancy prevention. Every day, new programs are brought to my attention, too many to describe. What I haven't even touched on here are school-to-work interventions,[3] mentoring,[4] intergenerational programs,[5] community service initiatives,[6] reports from major youth organizations such as the 4H, and comprehensive community-based efforts. Just remember, 85,000 public schools, 25,000 private schools, and more than 17,000 community-based youth agencies operate in this country, and all produce programs and activities, most of which are directly or indirectly involved with ensuring Safe Passage.[7]

You may find this chapter a bit repetitive, with themes reiterated in each field. I could have edited out the redundancies (which would have pleased my editor), but I chose to leave in the particulars for those who are interested. For readers do not require such details, I have included a short summary of "what works" following each field description.

PREVENTING DELINQUENCY AND CRIME

Although youth violence is perceived by most Americans as a major contemporary issue, efforts to prevent delinquency have been going on for a long time. Gangs were a problem even at the turn of the century, and crime waves flooded the headlines of the 1920s and 1930s.

Many theories have been put forward about how to deal with youth crimes. Early on, the idea of a genetic disposition toward crime fostered attempts to wipe out "crime families." Later, youth crime was seen as a form of psychopathology that should be treated by intensive therapy. Closer to our time, delinquency has been viewed as a product of family dysfunction and poor schools and impoverished neighborhood environments, all of which require significant improvements before we can expect the behaviors of youth to change.

Until recently, few prevention programs could prove a direct effect on delinquency in terms of reduced arrest rates, truancy, or vandalism. One reason for the lack of success may have been that the programs were targeted too narrowly at actions such as gang membership or petty theft, not at the underlying causes. It may be that prevention of delinquency can be accomplished more readily by reducing risk factors such as school failure, and increasing protective factors such as building closer relationships to the family.

We were able to identify several excellent programs that have strong evaluations and numerous replications. These programs actually do focus on promoting general social skills, school attendance, or family functioning, program concepts that we will find repeated in fields other than delinquency prevention.

Examples of Successful Programs

BOYS AND GIRLS CLUBS

This large national youth organization implemented SMART (Self-Management and Resistance Training) Moves in housing projects where new clubs were located. The program included group counseling on decision making about drugs and sex along with other recreational and educational club activities. A team of researchers from Columbia University, led by Steven Schinke, conducted evaluations at fifteen study sites and compared housing developments with sites implementing SMART Moves and those with no programs. A 13 percent reduction in arrest rates was shown in housing projects with clubs; drug use and drug trafficking were also lower.[8] Other evaluations of SMART Moves determined that the program worked better with older youths than younger ones, that participants preferred receiving this type of intervention in a club setting rather than in a school,[9] and that adding additional sessions improved the results in terms of reducing substance use and sexual activity.[10] The Boys and Girls Clubs have replicated SMART Moves in many clubhouses across the country, adding more sessions and greater peer involvement to strengthen the program. With a grant from the U.S. Department of Justice for gang prevention activities, Boys and Girls Clubs have expanded their outreach in housing projects.

CHILDREN AT RISK

The Center on Addiction and Substance Abuse (CASA), a think tank headed by Joseph Califano, head of the U.S. Department of Health and Human Services during the Carter administration, designed this program.[11] With support from numerous government agencies and private foundations, CASA selected five cities in which to launch an intensive delinquency-prevention program addressed at promoting ties between vulnerable teens and mainstream social institutions such as family, school, and community. Components include case management, family services, education services, after-school and summer activities, mentoring, stipends as incentives, community policing along with tutoring and home visiting, and enforcement of community policies such as drug-free zones.

Evaluation results at the end of the first year were promising: program participants had fewer contacts with police than youth in a comparison group, fewer contacts with the juvenile court, and were more likely to be promoted to the next grade.[12] At the end of the two-year program, the results were less encouraging, showing fewer reductions in risky behaviors. But by the time of the follow-up a year later, the program participants were doing significantly better than the control group. They had lower drug use and less contact with the law. Adele Harrell at the Urban Institute particularly noted the importance of case management with these very troubled young people.[13] The program had great difficulty involving the families of the participants, and in times of crisis (which were frequent) were not able to get adequate responses from the child welfare system.

CENTROS SISTER ISOLINO FERRE

One examplary program, described in chapter 4, is the unique settlement house in Caimito, Puerto Rico, that includes a Koban police station among its many offerings.[14] The Koban, modeled after an innovative Japanese program, houses three police officers who work in conjunction with the staff of the Centro to deliver youth-serving activities. A recent evaluation found that crime rates in Caimito had fallen 26 percent as a result of the location of the Koban in the Centro.[15]

DORCHESTER YOUTH COLLABORATIVE

This program has been operating since 1970 in a high-risk neighborhood in Boston as a safe haven and alternative to the dangerous street life. Youth Prevention Clubs offer structured activities including sports, arts, and multiethnic performance groups, production of videos through a Center for Urban Expression, and community outreach using a neighborhood coordinator. A strong collaboration with the police department provides counseling and support by specially selected officers who hang out at the youth center and get to know the members. "Near peers," young people two to six years older than the program youth, are trained to act as mentors and advocates. Police reported a 27 percent decrease in crime in the target area compared to a 14 percent reduction in the city as a whole (1990–1993).[16]

POSITIVE ADOLESCENT CHOICES TRAINING (PACT)

Developed by Rodney Hammond in conjunction with the Dayton, Ohio schools, PACT has been cited as a "unique, broad-based, violence prevention approach developed specifically for African American youth."[17] This program uses cognitive-behavioral group training to address issues of self-control, anger-management techniques, and negotiation skills. It is administered to small groups of high-risk boys by trained, doctoral-level, clinical psychology students. Specially prepared videos are used extensively. A preliminary outcome study of middle school students who received twenty hour-long sessions showed that, after three years, 18 percent of the students with training had been referred to juvenile court compared to 49 percent of those who lacked the training. Betty Yung and Hammond have published a program guide to PACT that gives detailed instructions on the components of the intervention, how to manage groups, and how to involve parents.[18]

PRIMARY MENTAL HEALTH PROJECT (PMHP)

An early intervention program targeted on elementary school children focuses on shaping social behavior. PMHP was first developed by Emory Cowen and colleagues at the University of Rochester in 1957, and has produced well-documented results over many decades.[19] The original program used highly trained community associates in elementary classrooms to provide intensive individual attention to high-risk children. The most recent research continues to show that children who received PMHP services had significantly fewer problems and were more socially competent than comparable children. In 1991, California initiated the Primary Intervention Program (PIP), modeled after PMHP, now considered the most extensively evaluated school mental health project around. PIP uses trained child aides, who are backed up by mental health practitioners, to work with high-risk children individually or in small groups in specially equipped playrooms at the schools. These services are provided through a cooperative effort between the school districts and the county mental health departments.

California has built an ongoing evaluation into their program. The 1995 results, based on data from 185 California school districts, reported positive changes in school adjustment and social behavior among two-thirds of the students, confirming previous evidence of success. The Primary Mental Health Project has been replicated in as many as 600 schools, particularly in California and New York.[20]

Current Thinking About Delinquency Prevention

The delinquency-prevention field appears to be split between individual, targeted approaches and collective, community-wide ones. The individual tactics, directed at preventing conduct disorders and promoting social competence, overlap with the field of mental health. The collective, group approaches, directed at preventing violence and promoting healthy youth development, appear to call for the same strategies as in every other field: integrated and comprehensive educational, employment, and health programs. The Children at Risk Project exemplifies the new wave of programming in its integration of a whole package of components with a strong emphasis on individual attention.

The National Research Council, in conjunction with the Kennedy School of Government, recently put forward their recommendations about how to deal with violence at the local level.[21] In addition to many policy recommendations, the report highlighted program facets that should sound familiar by now:

- family resource centers with "one-stop shopping"
- early intervention with home visits
- alternative schools, gang programs, and mental health services
- "full-service schools" that offer extended hours, safe havens, peer mediation programs, a K–12 curriculum on nonviolent conflict resolution, recreation such as midnight basketball, tutoring, and day care

The conference also called for initiatives to help children participate in the legitimate economy, such as I Have a Dream, which promises young people a college education if they succeed in high school; and Youth Build, which pays young people to train in construction and housing rehabilitation. These recommendations go way beyond the field of delinquency prevention and in fact encompass a comprehensive school-community approach to developing a healthy climate for family and youth development.

In the mid-1990s, a broad consortium of youth advocates lobbied Congress (unsuccessfully) to expand the prevention aspects of the crime bill. The Midnight Basketball League received a lot of attention at that time. Advocates pointed out that criminal involvement was greatly diminished when the Chicago Housing Authority instituted basketball from 10 P.M. until 2 A.M. along with life management workshops, motivational seminars, counseling support services, and employment training. Conservatives in Congress were skeptical and ridiculed the effort as further evidence of liberal "pork barreling." A thoughtful piece by Richard Mendel of the American Youth Policy Forum, titled "Prevention or Pork?," itemized in great detail the many documented programs that have either directly or indirectly helped to reduce delinquency rates. Mendel's list covers all categories of prevention, not just programs associated with delinquency prevention. As he points out, "To date, nowhere in American have all these pieces been pulled together in one community. . . . Nowhere has the impact of well-defined youth-oriented crime prevention programs been fully realized. Prevention's potential remains untapped."[22]

Delbert Elliott, the director of the Center for the Study and Prevention of Violence at the University of Colorado, also delineates between individual and neighborhood/community levels of approach.[23] At the individual level, he recommends Head Start, parent effectiveness training, behavioral skills training, family group homes, and employment programs, but warns that such interventions have been proven to have only short-term effects. To make real differences in the lives of young people, Elliot proposes bringing the principal institutions of the community together into sustained and integrated efforts at single sites—for example, through family support centers, community development corporations, and school-based clinics.

Although limited by a relatively small budget, the Office of Juvenile Justice and Delinquency Prevention (OJJDP) at the U.S. Department of Justice has promoted the replication of effective prevention programs. This office recently issued a guide for communities wishing to pursue a comprehensive strategy for prevention and treatment.[24] This review describes twenty-five effective and promising interventions, nine of them early intervention programs and sixteen for adolescence. Rather than focusing directly on delinquent behaviors such as truancy, OJJDP looked for programs that could compensate for the risk factors for delinquency, such as lack of family support or poor cognitive skills. Many of the programs cited as well-evaluated resulted in improved educational outcomes produced by lower class sizes, cooperative learning, tutoring, and youth employment. Programs that showed behavioral improvements followed family therapy, parent training, and classroom behavioral management techniques.

The Centers for Disease Control and Prevention (CDC) has recently launched a major effort in violence prevention by supporting the implementation of fifteen promising programs along with long-term evaluations.[25] These projects encompass a range of familiar strategies, such as social and conflict-resolution skills training, or individual and family counseling, but a few break new ground. Supporting Adolescents with Guidance and Employment (SAGE) targets African American male adolescents with an intensive Rites of Passage mentoring program, summer employment, and entrepreneurial experience in running a small business. PeaceBuilders is an elementary school-wide program to change the school climate and promote prosocial behavior through parent education, community involvement, and mass media tie-ins. The Boston Violence Prevention Project, based in the emergency department of a large hospital, offers consultation and counseling to adolescents who have been victims of assault. So far, these programs have gathered only baseline data, and it will be a few years before we can determine which interventions work best. But it is encouraging to know that these efforts are underway to shape our understanding and intelligence.

As to the future of federally supported crime prevention programs, we can get a hint from President Clinton's proposed 1998 budget, in which he called for grants to communities to fund after-school programs (probably like the Beacons), local antitruancy programs, youth courts, and probation officers.[26]

A final source for views on how to prevent delinquency is the Milton Eisenhower Foundation, a nonprofit agency that promotes programs that work to prevent violence in high-risk communities. The Centros Sister Isolino Ferre and the Dorchester Youth Collaborative, mentioned previously, are two successful efforts with which the foundation has been involved. As a member of the board of this organization, I have had the opportunity to hear firsthand about the "cutting edge" in working with high-risk youth through community-based organizations. Lynn Curtis, president of the Eisenhower Foundation, has repeatedly emphasized, "To a considerable extent and based on scientific evidence . . . it makes sense to create a national private and public sector policy that stops doing what doesn't work and that uses the money to help replicate what does work, at a scale equal to the dimensions of the problem."[27] Acting on this belief, the foundation has organized a large-scale *Communicating What Works* program that teaches inner-city organizational leaders to gain greater visibility and media attention.

WHAT WORKS BEST IN DELINQUENCY PREVENTION?

Individual Level

- Promote early intervention, addressed to both children and parents.

- Address risk factors.

- Train parents of young children and back it up with home visits; teach parents to problem solve with their children.

- Train youth in social and problem-solving skills.

- Produce curricula that are culturally and socially relevant.

- Add booster sessions to curriculum-based programs.

- Use trained specialists for one-on-one interventions and case management: family workers, community associates, school aides.

- Involve youth in program planning.

Community/Neighborhood Level

- Design holistic programs to ensure availability of multiple components.

- Mix education, social support, cultural and recreation programs.

- Create a one-stop, integrated approach.

- Use school sites for intensive physical and mental health interventions.

- Utilize community-based youth organizations and housing projects as sites for after-school programs.

- Train community police to expand the scope of outreach into the community.

SUBSTANCE-ABUSE PREVENTION

Substance-abuse prevention is a major industry in the United States. A huge array of school and community programs have been promulgated by local, state, and national coalitions. Over several decades, cadres of university professors have generated reams of theory about prevention, which they have translated into classroom-based curricula. The latest approach concentrates on the social and psychological factors underlying substance use and attempts to alter teen norms about the acceptability of drug use and to teach young people how to deal with peer influences.

My impression of this field is that it is very "mushy." Although it has been proven repeatedly that the implementation of a classroom-based prevention curriculum only impacts on usage rates to a limited degree and has little effect on high-risk youth, other forms of prevention programs have been slow to emerge.

Programs That Work

LIFE SKILLS TRAINING

This school-based curriculum, created by Gilbert Botvin at the Cornell University Medical Center, is the most thoroughly documented effort in the substance-abuse-prevention field. Botvin pioneered the concepts of teaching peer-pressure resistance and coping skills by using techniques such as role playing, feedback, and homework. At least seven evaluation articles have appeared since 1990, and a recent follow-up study of twelfth graders in fifty-six schools shows significantly lower substance use rates among the experimental group several years after the intervention in junior high.[29] Botvin and his colleagues attribute the success of this program to a high standard of fidelity to the program design. The teachers were well-trained and supervised, the high "dosage" of fifteen sessions in the initial seventh-grade year was followed by fifteen booster sessions in the next two grades, and increasing general personal competence was emphasized as well as resistance skills. Although early research was based on mostly White populations, Botvin has more recently demonstrated the effectiveness of his approach with African American and Hispanic students in targeting cigarette smoking.[30] Life Skills Training has been widely replicated, and training is available from the Cornell group.

PROJECT NORTHLAND

A community-wide program to prevent alcohol use, developed by Cheryl Perry and colleagues at the University of Minnesota, was started at twenty-four school districts and twenty-eight communities in that state.[31] Starting with sixth graders in 1991, the program included multilevel, multiyear carefully designed interventions over a three-year period (through eighth grade). Activities included: The Slick Tracy Home Team Program, activity books designed for students and their families to work on together; the formation of community-wide task forces to address policy issues; Amazing Alternatives curriculum and program that included parents and students in alcohol-free alternative activities; peer involvement; teen theater; and exposure of teens to community action experiences. The task forces were successful in passing local ordinances restricting alcohol sales. Outcome evaluation indicated lower alcohol and tobacco use, particularly among those who were nonusers at the outset, and increased resistance and communication skills on the part of the students.

MIDWESTERN PREVENTION PROJECT

Designed and implemented by Mary Ann Pentz and colleagues from the University of Southern California, this effort has received considerable attention as an important model for a multicomponent school/community intervention. The original program in Kansas City, called STAR, involved schools, parents, and community leaders, and paid attention to health policies and the mass media. Pentz has summarized recent findings on long-term outcomes as "20–40 percent reduction in monthly and daily tobacco, alcohol, and marijuana use through a 5 year follow-up," and also found positive effects on parental use.[32]

This experiment in Kansas City officially terminated in 1991. Local schools continued with a revised model that has not been as effective as the original theory-based comprehensive approach. Pentz has continued to build on this experience and is developing broad-based models that target at younger ages, with the creation of more prosocial schools that have high expectations for students, and components that promote better bonding between students and parents.[33]

BIG BROTHERS/BIG SISTERS

Although not considered a substance-abuse-prevention program, a recent evaluation by Public/Private Ventures (P/PV), a youth development and research agency, found that its major impact was in that area.[34] Based on a study sample from eight agencies, almost 1,000 youth were followed over eighteen months and compared to control groups. Youths who were matched to mentors were much less likely to start using illegal drugs or alcohol, and this was particularly true among minorities. School behavior improved, as did relationships with families. Gary Walker, president of P/PV, observed that this program did not provide direct antidrug counseling, but it did provide a relationship with a responsible and supportive adult on a continuing and intensive basis.

SEATTLE SOCIAL DEVELOPMENT PROJECT

Based on the work of David Hawkins, Richard Catalano, and colleagues at the University of Washington in Seattle, this program is often presented as a potential model for dropout and delinquency prevention as well as substance use. Its holistic approach addresses the risk factors for these problems by offering parent training and school restructuring techniques in grades one through six. Parent workshops are provided each year with developmentally appropriate material, such as child management skills in the earlier years and prevention of drug use in the later years. The student is encouraged through social-skills training to become actively involved in the classroom and to receive consistent positive reinforcement from both family and school. Teachers are trained in proactive classroom management, interactive teaching, and cooperative learning.

Research on the cumulative effects of the program on students as they entered fifth grade showed significantly more family communication, a greater attachment to school, and lowered delinquency and drug abuse.[35] At the end of sixth grade, positive effects were shown in skills, attachment, and bonding, and some reductions in smoking and alcohol use among girls.[36] Among boys, the intervention had positive effects on both social competencies and academic skills, and they were less likely to report delinquent behaviors, but their use of substances was not significantly different than in a control group. The researchers attribute the positive outcomes to the modification of classroom practices by the teachers rather than to the family management training (few parents participated). The Social Development Model is currently being replicated in two school districts in the state of Washington under the direction of Richard Catalano.[37]

Current Thinking About Substance-Abuse Prevention

Substance-abuse prevention is a field that is loaded with catalogues, reports, and compendiums of programs that "work." After all, the dissemination and sales of classroom-based curricula is a big business. My own experience with this field has been frustrating. A couple of years ago, I was invited to sit in with the major experts in substance-abuse prevention to advise the then-"drug czar" about what to do. I spoke my piece, as usual, about how classroom-based curricula were good but not sufficient, and how if you want to reach high-risk youth, you have to launch more intensive, targeted programs (like Quantum Opportunities or Children at Risk). My remarks went over like a lead balloon, and I noticed that they were significantly abbreviated in the conference report.

But as you can see from my examples, broader approaches are emerging from the field. Both the numbers of different programs and the reports that describe them have proliferated significantly. Much of this activity has been stimulated by the Center for Substance Abuse Prevention (CSAP) (in the U.S. Department of Health and Human Services (DHHS)), a federal agency that came into existence in the late 1980s with a strong commitment to move beyond curricula and to develop broader community-wide initiatives.

We can gain some insights into the orientation of CSAP by looking at selected projects from their High-Risk Youth Demonstration Grant Programs.[38] They have awarded grants to programs in each of five areas.

- *Individual* approaches feature social and life-skills training, individual or group therapy, Student Assistance (a program that places trained social workers in schools to conduct intensive counseling with students and families), tutoring, and mentoring.

- *Family* programs include family therapy, family-skills training, play therapy, parent training, and family involvement.

- *School-based* approaches include reforming teachers' methods and cooperative learning, strong school policies on the use of substances, using advocates to enhance school bonding, and training school personnel.

- *Peer group* programs involve clubs, working on perceptions of peer norms, peer-resistance training, and the like.

- *Community-level* efforts include cultural enhancement programs, community service experience, rites of passage, drug-free youth groups (Boys and Girls Clubs), safe havens, changes in social policy, and involving the religious community.

A new nonprofit organization, Drug Strategies, recently published a compendium of forty-seven drug-prevention curricula, of which ten had been evaluated and only six were proved to have any effect on drug, alcohol, or tobacco use. Each curriculum was scored on key elements such as helping students recognize pressures from peers and the media; practicing social skills; using interactive teaching techniques; involving the family and the community; and providing for teacher training. The guide concludes that "prevention is most effective when school lessons are reinforced by a clear, consistent social message that [substance] use is harmful, unacceptable and illegal."[40]

The U.S. General Accounting Office made an effort to analyze drug-use-prevention programs for 10 to 13 year olds in the early 1990s.[41] Out of a field of 700 suggested programs, they found 226 that met reasonable criteria such as comprehensiveness and longevity, and then conducted intensive site visits of ten programs. They concluded that the lack of evaluation placed limits on their ability to draw conclusions but identified six factors as important in the design of potentially successful community-based prevention programs:

- a comprehensive noncategorical focus

- an indirect approach to drug-abuse prevention (for example, alternative activities such as education and recreation)

- the goal of empowering youth

- a participatory, interactive approach (such as group counseling)

- culturally sensitive staff

- highly structured activities

In the fall of 1996, drug abuse—especially marijuana use—was on the rise again, a phenomenon that became a major issue in the 1996 presidential campaign.[42] Of course, each side accused the other of allowing this to happen. Dole said Clinton was a poor role model who had stopped supporting drug intervention after he took office. Dole proposed a national campaign based on the slogan "Just Don't Do It." Clinton blamed Dole for budget cuts in drug intervention, and proposed regulation of cigarette advertising and a broad media campaign along with more school-based prevention programs.

And, of course, everybody blames parents. The new hypothesis is that the parents of today's teenagers used drugs in the 1960s and therefore are less likely to try to moderate the behavior of their children. Surveys show that parents and teenagers talk about drugs less frequently than in the past, mirroring other indicators of the increasing number of youth who are growing up without strong authoritative parental guidance.

A lesson to be learned from all of this is that the delivery of prevention and health promotion messages has to be a continuous process. New children enter the vulnerable teenage years every day. The job is never done. In the late 1980s and early 1990s, the government launched a major prevention initiative located in the Center for Substance Abuse Prevention (CSAP). CSAP was well-designed, organized on sound theory to confront risk and protective factors, and even well-funded at the start. But currently it is under serious attack along with other social programs and has just barely survived a round of budget cutting. A new five-part drug strategy announced at a White House briefing in February 1997 did not even mention CSAP. The only prevention effort that received attention was a major $350 million media campaign, of which the government would pay half, and the rest would be raised from the private sector. Apparently, "Just Say No" is back "in" with the administration. We can only hope that advocates will convince Congress that the comprehensive school and community approaches developed in recent years also need support.

WHAT COMPONENTS WORK BEST IN PREVENTION OF SUBSTANCE ABUSE?

Individual Level

- Help children bond to family and school through parent and teacher training.

- Involve parents in prevention activities.

- Train and supervise mentors to provide sustained attention.

- Have training in social skills enhanced by adding sessions on coping and problem-solving skills and by greater "dosage"—more sessions in each year and booster sessions in subsequent years.

- Replicate evaluated classroom curricula in schools with fidelity to the original models ensured by meticulous teacher training.

- Pay attention to risk factors, and shift the emphasis away from substance use toward general competency and determinants of high-risk behaviors.

Community/Neighborhood Level

- Broaden the scope of programs by adding community interventions to school programs.

- Act to change the school and community climate regarding the acceptibility of substance use.

- Reduce access to cigarettes and alcohol.

TEEN PREGNANCY PREVENTION

My background is in the field of teen pregnancy prevention. From 1968 to 1981, as the research director and a research fellow at the Alan Guttmacher Institute, I published documentation of the rise in the teen pregnancy rate and numerous articles about what should be done about it. Our prescription at that time was more and better sex education and access to contraceptive services, backed up by the availability of abortion services. By the early 1980s, when I became an independent researcher supported by foundations, I had come to believe that the problem of teen pregnancy would never "go away" until it was treated as a symptom of larger problems related to poverty and race. I believed then, as I do now, that the solution lies in changing the life course for young people, giving disadvantaged youth other options in life, incentives to bypass early parenthood.

An experience that has stuck in my mind over many years took place at a meeting in Florida about pregnancy prevention. A panel of teenagers was brought up on the stage to tell us their stories. One very pregnant 14 year old girl explained, "I was just leaning on a fence, and this dude came over, stuck his thing in me, and had an 'organism.' " I was overwhelmed by the thought that out of such a casual act a new life would emerge, a child would be born to a mother with no clue about how to raise it or even where it came from. One would have had to reach this young woman early on to stimulate her cognitive skills, raise her expectations, and teach her about social competency.

The field of teen pregnancy prevention has received renewed attention in recent years. Many, including President Clinton, view prevention of teen parenthood as an important ingredient in the reduction of the welfare caseload. Although controversy is rife, most people agree that the provision of sex education, contraceptive services, and life-options approaches are all vital. (No such consensus exists, however, on the use of abortion as a means to terminate unplanned pregnancies.) My review of programs identified a number of successful programs that have now been evaluated and are being replicated.

Programs That Work

TEEN OUTREACH PROGRAM (TOP)

Originally sponsored by the Association of Junior Leagues, TOP combines volunteer community-work assignments for high school students with weekly school-based discussion groups of values, decision making, and career options. It has been continuously evaluated since 1984 by Susan Philliber of Philliber Associates and Joseph Allen of the University of Virginia.[43] The most recent research confirms that this approach is very successful. Using random assignment, the researchers showed lower rates of school failure, dropout, and pregnancy among students in the program.[44] The Teen Outreach Program has been widely replicated around the country, and the program model is currently being marketed and disseminated through a nonprofit organization, Cornerstone Consulting Group.[45]

ADOLESCENT PREGNANCY PREVENTION PROGRAM

Sponsored by the Children's Aid Society (CAS), this is a multicomponent, community-based creation of Michael Carrera and colleagues. The seven prevention components consist of: on-site medical and health services, including contraceptive counseling; performing arts workshops; skills training in individual sports such as squash and tennis; academic assessment and homework tutoring; a college admission program, whereby every successful participant is guaranteed a place at Hunter College with all costs subsidized; family life and sex education; and a job club and career awareness program.

Philliber Associates has recently produced very preliminary research findings based on data compiled from participants at six New York City sites during the 1993–1994 program year.[46] The findings suggest that participants had better educational outcomes, lower levels of sexual involvement, better use of condoms, and lower pregnancy rates than national averages and New York City rates. The Adolescent Pregnancy Prevention Program has its own training institute in New York City, directed by Michael Carrera and Patricia Dempsey. Practitioners receive hands-on instruction in the model at that site. At least eight replications are currently operating in New York City, and ten others are in cities around the country.[47]

Michael Carrera is often cited as "America's Most Accomplished Sex Educator," reflecting his great popularity as a motivator of youth workers and an advocate for the rights of young people. He recently advised:

> Avoid fragmentation—have as many activities as possible under one roof. It may be a fact that there is this great service across town . . . but [the other program] may not share the same crucial philosophy that you do. The more a program is fragmented, the more kids that get lost. . . . If this were your own kid, what would you want to happen?[48]

PREVENTING ADOLESCENT PREGNANCY (PAP)

During the research phase of this multicomponent program designed by the Girls Inc., four age-appropriate interventions were implemented at four demonstration sites, addressing parent-daughter communication, assertiveness training, career planning, and access to birth control. Research conducted by Heather Johnson Nicholson and colleagues at Girls Inc. showed reduced sexual activity by girls at the treatment sites compared to control sites.[49] Better use of birth control and lower pregnancy rates were related to "dosage," the number of sessions attended in the various programs. In two programs, length of participation was crucial to program effectiveness. PAP is now being disseminated by Girls Inc. through their program replication process. In 1994, this program was being offered in seventy-five cities.[50] A grant from the Centers for Disease Control has enabled Girls Inc. to offer training to practitioners around the country.

I HAVE A FUTURE

This comprehensive pregnancy prevention program, developed by Henry Foster of Meharry College, received more than its share of publicity when hearings were conducted regarding Dr. Foster's appointment to be surgeon general. This life-options approach offers after-school enrichment programs, health services, training in Nguzo Saga principles of African American prosocial behavior, and mentoring to children who live in public housing projects.[51] Preliminary research has documented significant reductions in pregnancies among active program participants.[52]

SCHOOL/COMMUNITY PROGRAM FOR
SEXUAL RISK REDUCTION AMONG TEENS

This multicomponent program was created by Murray Vincent and colleagues at the University of South Carolina. It included community education, the creation of a sex education curriculum, teacher training, parent involvment, and a school nurse who provided contraceptive services. The original research showed lower pregnancy rates in the target area, but the rates returned to high levels after the school nurse was eliminated.[53] An independent analysis of the program, conducted by Helen Koo and colleagues at Research Triangle Institute, confirmed the original research "that the more concentrated and organized intervention . . . with its unique combination of intensive, community-wide health education and proactive contraceptive services—was responsible for the marked decline in the area's adolescent pregnancy rates in the mid 1980s."[54]

The Kansas Health Foundation is supporting a major replication and evaluation of the School/Community Model in three Kansas sites under the direction of Adrienne Paine-Andrews at the University of Kansas (Vincent is a consultant). The replications are being conducted with great attention to the lessons learned in South Carolina in regard to parent and community involvement, strong program elements, and careful planning and evaluation.[55] The project anticipates using various strategies, involving many different community sectors, and establishing local ownership by paying careful attention to known principles of "reinvention." According to Paine-Andrews, preliminary findings after two years show the development of new programs, policies, and practices. In 1994, the estimated annual teen pregnancy rates dropped by 20 percent in targeted counties.[56]

IN YOUR FACE PROGRAM

The Columbia University Center for Population and Family Health operates school-based, primary health clinics in five schools under the direction of Lorraine Tiezzi. One aspect of the pregnancy prevention work is the In Your Face Program, which uses group counseling to bring together students who are at high risk of early unprotected sex.[57] They are identified through a behavioral risk-assessment tool, a survey taken by all students at the beginning of the each year. Specially trained Hispanic health educators work intensively with students to develop ways, including abstinence, to prevent unwanted pregnancies. Workers escort the students to a hospital-based family planning clinic if they are sexually active and want contraception. Over a four-year period, the pregnancy rate decreased by 34 percent, and the number of students accepting contraception doubled as a result of this program.

REDUCING THE RISK

Although most students in the United States are exposed to some form of sex education in the classroom, most of the curricula have not been evaluated. And among those that have, the results are not very encouraging. One of the few with encouraging results is Reducing the Risk, a sexuality education curriculum at the high school level created by Richard Barth.[58] The sixteen-session curriculum aims to change student norms about unprotected sex, as well as to strengthen parent-child communication concerning abstinence and contraception. Evaluation of Reducing the Risk by Douglas Kirby and his colleagues showed that the program reduced the likelihood that students would become sexually active, although it had little effect on those who were already sexually experienced.[59]

Current Thinking

In 1995, the Institute of Medicine (IOM) studied the issue of unintended pregnancy and identified twenty-three programs that had been evaluated according to the IOM's criteria.[60] The IOM panel concluded from their review of the research on pregnancy prevention that success was limited and had to be measured in small increments (like months of delay in initiating sexual intercourse). They found strong support for pursuing two "messages" simultaneously—delaying intercourse and using contraceptives if sexually active. The panel found that three abstinence-only curricula that had been evaluated had no significant effects on relevant behaviors.

In 1995, DHHS commissioned Kristin Moore to conduct a thorough review of adolescent pregnancy prevention programs. The report summarizes seventy-nine interventions including some that are outdated and others not evaluated. Reducing the Risk is highlighted as a well-evaluated, successful prevention program that is theory-based and combines factual information with skill-building techniques. The report cites the importance of family planning clinics in the mix of programs, a facet that is often overlooked because there are so few evaluations of this type of delivery system. Moore concludes that although many teen pregnancy prevention programs have been implemented, almost none have been adequately evaluated: "Current interventions suffer from numerous deficits. Few are informed by a theory of adolescent behavior or based on a clear operational model. . . . programs tend to be pieced together with available funds, hunches, and high hopes . . . and tend to be small and short lived."

One new program of interest that aims to address this critique is the Annie

Casey Foundation's Plain Talk initiative. Based on the New Futures experiments (see chapter 9) and other experiences, the foundation hopes to create community settings in which youth, adults, and service providers can come together to design their own responses to the need for access to contraception among teenagers. The first two years' experience in six communities has shown that community residents are ready to play significant roles in this initiative as long as strong facilitators (project managers) are on hand to offer guidance.[61] Arriving at a community consensus on sensitive issues like sex and contraception is a time-consuming process. Making information available enhances the process, but data collection also requires the support of professional staff to complete the requisite community mapping effort. It will be interesting to track the results of this initiative because it encompasses so much of the new thinking about broader community-based programs: attempting to improve the lives of young people by reshaping key social institutions in their communities. (Two similar community-based initiatives, supported by the California Wellness Foundation and the Centers for Disease Control, are profiled in chapter 12.)

The Johnson and Johnson Foundation has entered into a partnership with NOAPPP (National Organization of Adolescent Pregnancy Prevention Programs) to set up the National Urban Adolescent Pregnancy Prevention Program.[62] Some twenty-one programs were selected out of 200 applicants to be considered for in-depth evaluation. The list gives evidence of the breadth of the emerging field, including as it does programs that feature school-based condom distribution; comprehensive, multifaceted collaborations; targeting teen clients who have just received a negative pregnancy test; rites of passage; employment and training; and others that have been mentioned here. Of course, it will be several years before any new evaluation efforts will be able to report the effects of these programs.

In mid-1996, President Clinton kicked off a National Campaign to Reduce Teenage Pregnancy and appointed Dr. Henry Foster as his (unpaid) senior advisor. The goal is to reduce teenage pregnancy by one-third by the year 2005. Proposed actions include taking a clear stand against teen pregnancy, enlisting the media in this cause, supporting state and local action, stimulating a national discussion on values, and strengthening the knowledge base about effective programming. At the same time, a new nonprofit organization has been formed, the National Campaign to Prevent Teen Pregnancy, supported by foundations to develop specific actions along the same lines. One of the Campaign's first products was a commissioned review of the research by Douglas Kirby, which concludes:

> there are no simple approaches that will markedly reduce adolescent pregnancy . . . [to be successful] they must have multiple components . . . involving one or more aspects of poverty, lack of opportunity, and family disfunction, as well as social disorganization more generally. Notably, studies of multi-component programs and youth development programs provide some evidence that they reduce pregnancy or birth rates.[63]

**WHICH COMPONENTS WORK BEST IN PREVENTION
OF TEENAGE PREGNANCY?**

Individual Level

- Train in social skills, and add more sessions (increase dosage).

- Make sure curricula are replicated to follow models.

- Work with teachers to ensure effectiveness of classroom-based programs.

- Offer group counseling that includes life-options approaches.

- Facilitate use of family planning services.

Community/Neighborhood Level

- Incorporate reproductive health care in school-based clinics.

- Combine multiple components that involve two or more program elements and increase the power of the intervention.

- Offer comprehensive programs aimed at school achievement, recreation, problem solving (not directly at teen pregnancy prevention).

- Provide community service experiences.

LESSONS FROM HIV PREVENTION

HIV prevention is the new categorical program on the block. In the early 1990s, CDC began to distribute substantial grants to state departments of education and city school systems for AIDS-prevention programs, with the U.S. Department of Education overseeing coordination and the U.S. Department of Health and Human Services supporting treatment. As a result of these and other efforts, a great deal has been written about how to prevent AIDS. It reads remarkably like all the other literature, except that the interventions are more targeted.

In reviewing recent reports on AIDS prevention, I was interested to find that several referred to my work. The Women's Network published a list of components of successful intervention programs from *Adolescents at Risk*, stating that "although HIV/AIDS were not among those examined, the lessons learned from the research about behavior change are applicable to [the HIV/AIDS] field as well. . . . Too many prevention programs, Dryfoos notes, address only the problem behavior and not the root cause of it."[65]

The Network then went on to recommend that each of the eleven components listed in *Adolescents at Risk* be part of a comprehensive HIV/AIDS prevention program (see the updated version of "what works" in chapter 8). According to the Women's Network, many current programs exist, but few include the critical components, and very little evaluation exists. They presented three models, one created by Mary Jane Rotheram-Borus for runaways in residential centers. This carefully evaluated program featured four components: thirty carefully designed information sessions, training in coping skills, access to health care and social services, and individual counseling sessions.[66] Participants reported increased condom use and decreased high-risk behavior compared to nonparticipants. A second model targeted gay and bisexual males and incorporated case management with peer group sessions. The third model was The Door, a comprehensive youth center in New York City, where all participants are required to undergo a physical exam, sexual health/awareness counseling, and an HIV personal-risk assessment. Confidential HIV testing and counseling are available in that facility. A DHHS commissioned review reports on a successful program targeted at African American adolescents who are at high risk of HIV infection, which consists of weekly group meetings that include intense training in competency skills, social support, and empowerment.[67]

The congressionally based Select Committee on Children, Youth, and Families, just before its demise, published *A Decade of Denial: Teens and AIDS in America*, summarizing the extant research up until 1992 in this emerging field.[68] And in 1993, the *Journal of Adolescent Health* devoted an issue to HIV/AIDS program development.[69] One can generate a familiar list of components of effective HIV/AIDS-prevention programs from the experience of these expert panels: early intervention; persistent messages delivered through multiple channels; comprehensive approaches, addressing a range of behaviors and concerns, not just HIV; and inclusion of social skills training.

These experts stress the importance of dosage, maintaining that youths must participate in all of the sessions of a preventive curriculum. Scare messages do not work and sometimes have the opposite effect of that planned. Parents should be involved from the earliest stages of program planning. The experience cited with successful school-based HIV prevention programs suggests several important components:

- inclusion of specific information about the dangers of drug use, including steroids, and the consequences of unprotected sex

- thorough treatment of the protective value of abstinence, condoms, and spermicides

- use of role models and people with AIDs

- attention to consciousness raising for the entire school community about AIDS issues and the importance of prevention

- backup from community-wide coalitions

The HIV/AIDs-prevention literature is much more explicit about targeting high-risk youth than are teen pregnancy prevention approaches. Street youth, dropouts, drug users, gay youth, and specific ethnic groups with high incidence of HIV positivity (such as Hispanics) are among those for whom special interventions are being implemented. These programs generally include intensive outreach by trained, credible, street workers (often ex-drug addicts), direct access to health and social services, condom distribution, needle distribution, availability of HIV tests, and drug treatment. Practitioners are advised to create simple messages and to deliver them through many different programs within a short period of time. Emphasis is given to correct condom use and safe sex practices.

Douglas Kirby has been tracking the effectiveness of sex education programs for some years and in 1994 reviewed twenty-three studies of sexuality and HIV education programs in schools.[70] He found two specific curricula that significantly delayed the onset of sexual intercourse—Postponing Sexual Involvement and Reducing the Risk—and two others that increased the use of contraception—AIDS Prevention for Adolescents in School and Interpersonal Skills Training, a curriculum devised by Steven Schinke. Kirby also reviewed the findings on school-based health centers and school condom-distribution programs. While he found the research on both inconclusive, he reported that, as of 1993, 375 schools in the United States had condom distribution programs, some of which are used by large numbers of students and are potentially an important delivery mechanism.

The latest prevention approach to be fostered by the CDC, the Prevention Marketing Initiative (PMI), is based on social marketing principles. A large-scale media campaign has been launched to promote safe sex among 18 to 25 year olds, using public service announcements and an AIDS Hotline and Clearinghouse. An emerging consensus on both teen pregnancy prevention and HIV/AIDS prevention calls for a range of interventions, put together into comprehensive, community-wide efforts.

COMMON THEMES

These summaries of the three major prevention fields—delinquency, substance abuse, and teen pregnancy—reveal many similarities. Out of thousands of programs currently operating in these diverse areas, only a few have been adequately evaluated. Yet, in each field, a few robust and effective programs have emerged that can be used in designing Safe Passage strategies. One message comes through loud and clear for those who are interested in influencing adolescents: *Multiple components have to be put together to strengthen the impact.* Single-component efforts such as classroom curriculum or individual counseling are useful but probably not sufficient for changing the environment in which the high-risk behaviors are taking place. Every report in every field ends with a call for more comprehensive, less fragmented, better integrated family, school, and community initiatives.

Most of the reports cited above also deal with policy issues. Violence prevention requires restrictions on the sale, purchase, and transfer of guns. Substance-abuse prevention calls for the enforcement of laws on sales and taxes on cigarettes and alcohol. Teen pregnancy and HIV prevention depend on the availability of condoms and other forms of birth control. These kinds of community strategies must be included in any serious discussion of prevention.

PART III

ELEMENTS OF SUCCESS

8

WHAT WORKS, AND WHY?

He's really smart but he doesn't want anyone to know it. He's afraid they'll call him a nerd. So he acts out a lot, roams the halls, talks back to his teachers. I told him the next time he was given a disciplinary removal, I'd spend a week sitting in class with him, making sure he didn't mess around. I had to show him I'm serious about his education.

—Leon Dickerson, Choice Team Coordinator

We are now going to look at what works to help young people overcome the barriers to Safe Passage. This chapter summarizes all that we have learned about program components and compiles those factors that successful programs appear to have in common. I have organized the factors at four different levels: individual, family, school, and community.

If we are to design an effective and comprehensive "package" of services, what pieces should we include? Admittedly, youth development people do not know all the answers. So in this chapter, I also lay out a number of unresolved issues and ambiguities relating to how these programs are implemented and how they may be replicated. Remember that I said the test of a program design was whether it could be reproduced by someone other than the program designer. While we must understand the components of successful programs, we also need to know how to expand the network of excellence—and widely replicate what works.

SUCCESS FACTORS AT THE INDIVIDUAL LEVEL

Early Intervention

Everybody knows intuitively that early intervention is a must. In this book, I have presented further evidence of the long-term effectiveness of early intervention on social behavior and school achievement. The Parents as Teachers program and the Primary Mental Health Model are two examples of services—along with many other programs, such as Head Start—that have demonstrated the importance of preschool interventions. Schools of the 21st Century incorporate these components and extend the approach back to birth and forward to age 12.

Questions have been raised about the efficacy of early intervention if the program simply ends when the child enters school. A review of early childhood programs by Dale Farran substantiates the importance of extending support beyond preschool; "Improvement in the educational program provided for low-income children in the first 4 years of elementary school [is] more effective than simply providing 1 year of preschool."[1]

Based on the results of classroom-based interventions designed to change behaviors, programs are moving down to earlier grades on the theory that once behavior sets in, it is far more difficult to change. Yet you must believe that it is not impossible to change the life scripts of older children. Many of the programs described here do just that—for example, effective community schools at the middle school level can change the course for students along with improving the outlook for their families. Having made a pitch for early intervention, I would be unhappy if that statement were construed as an argument against programs for middle and high school age youth. We should be wary of setting up a competition for resources between different age groups or different kinds of target populations. Consistent attention is necessary at every level. Programs must be age appropriate and based on a sound understanding of youth development.

One-on-One Attention: Creative Shepherding

The critical importance of individual attention as a means of helping young people achieve Safe Passage is verified in a variety of programs: use of trained specialists, child aides, case managers, cross-age tutors, teacher advisors. We observed in the Quantum Opportunities Program how the counselors wrapped themselves (literally and figuratively) around the participants. The Children at Risk Program relies heavily on case managers to help young people cope with family problems and deal with the social welfare system. Recall the words from Robert Slavin that one had to "relentlessly stick with every child until that child is succeeding."

Marion Pines, a pioneer in dropout prevention, summed up her experience:

> We have learned that no single system can adequately address complex and interrelated challenges. What we are learning is that continuity of effort makes a difference. Dropping in and dropping out of a kid's life does not work. A sustained and caring adult contact makes a tremendous difference.[2]

The documented success of the Big Brothers/Big Sisters program has given a big boost to mentoring as an intervention, but the research shows that the volunteer mentors must be carefully screened, well-matched to the client, and regularly supervised by paid staff in order for the program to work. From my years of research and observation, I am convinced that young people have to be attached to a caring adult. Without that attachment and bonding, most of these young people will never make it.

One experience in my own life always comes to mind when I think about this subject. About a decade ago, I went to Nepal with my son Paul, and we arranged our own private trek in the lower Himalayas accompanied by several Sherpas, indigenous people who serve as guides for climbers. It was pretty steep and rocky, and I know that I couldn't have made it up the mountain without the support and encouragement of my Sherpa. And that is exactly what is needed by these at-risk children. Joe Klein's characterization in *Newsweek* of Leon Dickerson (see quote at beginning of chapter) is revealing: "His official title [at a program called Choice] is team coordinator but a more accurate job description might be shepherd."[3]

Developmentally Appropriate

The most effective programs relate to teenagers according to where the young people are "at," instead of where the professional staff think they ought to be. For example, youth workers have to be very careful how they approach the virtues of abstinence when dealing with a group of sexually active teens. As one youth worker told me, "I try to tell it like it is but not overdo it."

Youth Empowerment

Certain phrases emerge from visits with youth workers around the country. Many feel that what they are doing is "empowering youth," giving them the skills and motivation they need to make it. Others talk about having high expectations for their young people. El Puente has a very strong youth leadership ethos: Students are expected to get involved in solving community problems now and in the future. You can see the growing involvement of young people in the planning, design, and implementation of programs. Ernest McMillan, director of the comprehensive Fifth Ward Enrichment Program in the Houston inner city, recounts:

> . . . the realities of living in a war zone and actively listening to the various expressions of the youth [who] serve as guides to the program's development. We have consciously tried to shift from operating as a riverfront hospice that plucks the victim from the swift currents to moving upstream and interceding in the battle itself, recruiting youth to become partners in the fight.[4]

As practitioners describe it, they are listening to the voices of youth and how they see their world. But we must be wary here of empty phrases. Evoking the language of empowerment does not always mean that power is shared. It may just indicate familiarity with politically correct language rather than the intention to allow young people really to make decisions for themselves.

SUCCESS FACTORS AT THE FAMILY LEVEL

Parental Involvement

Extensive experience with family programs verifies the importance of frequent home visiting by a trained practitioner as the best method of securing family involvement and offering parent effectiveness training. Parents of high-risk youth will come to schools and community centers if what they are offered is useful and nonthreatening. Community schools have proved that virtually all the parents will come to a community festival celebrating an ethnic event. Many parents will eventually take advantage of educational courses in English as a Second Language, computers, job preparation, and aerobics. Parents will enthusiastically sign up to volunteer or work part-time in schools as teachers' aides or community advocates.

Experience in family resource centers reveals the growing demand for crisis intervention and attention to immediate basic needs, such as food, clothes, shelter, and basic health care. A designated space within a school where parents can hang out and talk to each other over coffee and refreshments is heavily utilized. (Chapter 10 continues the discussion of parental involvement.)

Reaching Across Generations

In recent years, much more attention is being directed toward involving senior citizens in youth development programs. Grandparents are being encouraged to participate when parents are not available. Programs that use senior citizens as mentors and tutors have been around for a while, but the new wave of more innovative efforts encourages retired professionals to work as medical consultants, scientific advisors, and other professional endeavors. Referred to as the "other national service program," the federally supported SeniorCorps utilizes the services of more than 60,000 volunteers.[5]

SUCCESS FACTORS AT THE SCHOOL LEVEL

Educational Achievement

As I have stated repeatedly, the enhancement of educational achievement, measured by grades, promotion, and graduation rates, has become a desirable objective of just about every kind of prevention program. School achievement as a goal is often combined with others such as reduction in substance abuse or unprotected sex (although fair methods for measurement of achievement is still a controversial issue).

Many approaches to improving achievement and retention in schools have been documented here and elsewhere.[6] The evidence that cooperative learning techniques are effective continues to grow. The importance of smaller schools, smaller class sizes, and heterogeneous grouping has generally been confirmed. The reorganization of middle schools into small, intimate, thematic academies or houses is apparently productive, creating more stimulating environments and engaged students. Successful classroom behavioral management techniques have been devised and tested. More schools are moving toward extended days and extended years. One observes a rash of experimental schools arriving on the scene that are alternatives, magnets, charters, "visions," or community schools. No two are alike, but they all seem to have in common a consistent attention to ensuring that each student progresses and learns. Many are devising more challenging curricula that contemporary students will find relevant and will broaden their educational options and career horizons.

It is difficult to imagine that any other kind of prevention program will be successful if it doesn't address the acquisition of basic cognitive skills. None of these other components will ensure Safe Passage if the young person is not fully literate and ready to enter the labor force. In my evolving doctrine (it is always evolving), schools become more and more central to the movement to rescue the children. But to be effective, schools must drastically alter the way they operate, incorporating the growing knowledge about youth development and successful interventions.

Effective Principals

The people factor is paramount in the success of programs for assuring Safe Passage. Although many categories of personnel could be cited (nurse practitioners, community aides, classroom teachers), one group carries significant responsibility for the most productive programs. School principals serve as the entry point for the development of comprehensive school-based approaches. According to Don Davies, a leader in school-community partnerships, effective principals have "grasped the meaning of shared responsibilities for children's learning and well-being. They have learned that the school alone simply can't do the job . . . that partnership means reciprocity."[7]

School-based but not School-operated

Although schools are the sites for many of the programs we have visited, a number are operated by community agencies. In the case of school-based health or mental health clinics, outside practitioners come into the schools to offer direct services. For instance, the Beacons bring community-based agencies into the schools, allowing the buildings to remain open for extended hours, even weekends and summers.

On-site Facilitators

The implementation of complex programs that reorganize schools or establish multicomponent programs is often difficult. Even to ensure successful replication of classroom-based prevention curricula, outside facilitators are needed to train school personnel. For some of the more sophisticated school reorganization projects, such as Success for All or Accelerated Schools, facilitators or coaches may remain on-site for extended periods of time. Apparently, having access to consistent and skilled advisors helps teachers and youth workers to change their modes of operation and to resolve conflicts that can arise in these situations.

Social Skills Training

The role of social influences on changing youth behaviors has been thoroughly explored in recent years and incorporated into prevention programs. More research support has been allocated for testing classroom curricula than for testing the impacts of mentoring or case management or alternative sports and recreational activities. As a result of the strength of the evaluations, I believe that behavioral social skills curricula can have positive effects. Programs such as Life Skills Training can teach social competency, decision making, how to deal with aggressive feelings, and other social relationships. But research also confirms the need to build into these programs additional sessions, booster sessions in subsequent years, and more substantive material in the curriculum that relates to social competency and the family. The key concept here is increased dosage— greater intensity and sustainability.

Recent experience with new curricula show that the messenger may be as powerful as the message. People With AIDS (PWAs) have been more effective than classroom teachers in persuading students to change their sexual behavior. And practicing behavioral skills—using role play to deal with unwanted sexual encounters or with trying to obtain condoms—is a powerful component of prevention programs. Evidence is mounting, that curricula alone do not influence the behaviors of high-risk youth, but they can be very important components of comprehensive programs.

Group Counseling

Effective prevention curricula are based on a sound interpretation of the psychosocial issues related to adolescent development. Many of the participants gain important insights into their lives as a result of these courses. But students don't have the opportunity to talk about their troubles. Group counseling is another approach that is being successfully used in schools and community agencies to deal with problems. You are probably familiar with Children of Alcoholics, or COA groups, that concentrate on issues in such families. Groups have also been organized around suicidal inclinations, grief, asthma control, sexuality, gay and lesbian issues, parents, drug and alcohol use, violence, and just about every subject that comes up in the lives of teenagers. For some teenagers, it is helpful for them to know that other young people share their anguish and have found solutions.

The In Your Face program initiated in the Columbia University School-Based Clinics is a good example of organized group counseling that has met with success. The program targets high-risk students, involves them continuously with group and individual interventions, and helps them confront their problems with sexual issues.

Community Service

The concept of community service has taken hold in the youth development field. Several of the most successful programs, such as Teen Outreach and Quantum, require participants to spend time working in community agencies, childcare centers, and retirement homes. Community schools such as Turner incorporate community placements into the curriculum—students in the Community Health Academy regularly work in a hospital assisting the dieticians and the floor nurses. Programs like El Puente are designed around the concept of community involvement and teaching young people that they are responsible for building the communities of the future.

SUCCESS FACTORS AT THE COMMUNITY LEVEL

Location in the Community

Having stated that almost any program can be run in a school setting, it is equally important to realize that almost any program, including educational interventions, can take place in a community agency. As time goes on, the distinction becomes less clear between types of sites. For example, El Puente started as a community center and became a school, but it is indisputably community based with strong roots in its Hispanic neighborhood. Quantum Opportunities Program is strongly based in the community in order to remediate for the low quality of the schools in the neighborhood. The national youth organizations— Boys and Girls Clubs, Girls Inc., and the Urban League—maintain sites in store fronts, malls, housing projects, and churches, places that are accessible to young people at all hours and that are not associated with school; many high-risk youngsters have an aversion to classrooms because of negative experiences in the past.

Community Outreach

In the poverty programs of the 1960s and 1970s, street outreach work was a highly visible activity, employing thousands of indigenous people to reach out to their neighbors with all kinds of messages about health promotion and poverty reduction. During the 1980s, this component seemed to disappear, only to reemerge recently. Today, an approach that uses street workers and trained community aides to conduct health promotion and disease prevention, or teach conflict resolution and nonviolent behaviors, is being used successfully in HIV- and violence-prevention programs. It is one sure channel for reaching high-risk youth.

Because so many of the neediest young people live in inner cities, much more attention is being paid to working at the street level. To do this, the youth workers have to be able to relate to indigenous youth and gang members, and they have to be able to communicate ideas about prevention in ways that are both understandable and acceptable.

Cultural Responsiveness

These days, many programs derive their strengths from cultural or racial identity. Quantum and El Puente each strive to surround young people with successful role models and expose them to experiences where they can learn about their own cultural traditions. Parents, too, trust programs that can communicate with them in their own languages and respect their culture.

Community Police

Several programs involve local police in innovative arrangements. The Koban, described in Caimito and replicated in several U.S. cities, translates the Japanese model to our country. Specially trained police officers live in the settlement house and are available to work with youth advocates as a team. Community policing efforts are expanding, using police officers as case managers, youth advocates, and recreation leaders. Specially trained police officers and probation personnel have offices in schools, giving them direct daily access to troubled youngsters.

Safe Havens

When participants are asked what they like about many of the programs described here, they say, "It's safe." They feel protected by the people who operate the facility, protected from the dangers of street life and, in some instances, protected from abusive families and disinterested schools. Not only do some of the programs offer a sense of physical safety, the youth who hang out there know that they can rely on the staff to help them with threatening problems. The young people particularly appreciate being in settings where the adults are nonjudgmental.

Incentives and Entrepreneurial Approaches

Financial incentives have been built into successful programs in a variety of ways. The classic model of I Have a Dream offers students a college scholarship if they complete high school. Quantum pays stipends for completion of each task. Valued Youth pays high-risk older students to teach younger students.

Many programs teach participants to set up small businesses. The Turner school in Philadelphia has a health food market and an after-school snack store run by students. There, children learn how to purchase items wholesale, prepare them for purchase, wait on customers, and handle money. By next year, a garden will be established at the school to grow produce for the store.

The Children's Aid Society's Teen Prevention Programs all offer some form of small business experience, either selling foods at sports events or, as in one replication in Akron, running a used clothing store. The Entrepreneurial Academy at IS218 teaches business skills at the middle school level and operates a school store. That school also has a project that recycles bicycles and sells them. On the first day of school, every "entrepreneurial" student is presented with a briefcase that includes an appointment book, watch, small calculator, and other tools of business efficiency.

Multiagency Multicomponent

I have highlighted the call for programs with multiple components that rely on partnerships between schools and community agencies in both the review of existing programs and in summaries of recommendations for future programs. This broader approach is backed up by a theoretical shift in program rationale that is moving us away from focusing on specific behaviors—sex, drugs, and violence—to a more holistic view of teenagers. The new view indicates programming through multiple channels to alter the life of the participant. Children at Risk, Fifth Ward Achievement, Quantum, Children's Aid Society's Teen Pregnancy Prevention Program, and many other efforts have put together packages of activities to wrap around young people.

One rationale for comprehensiveness is the importance of integrating services and creating one-stop centers. Another is that comprehensive centers can provide "controversial" services in broad settings. Counseling on contraception is offered as one voluntary component in a school-based clinic. Mental health treatment is made available in the context of a youth service center featuring recreational facilities. Parents can obtain drug and alcohol treatment in family resource centers that highlight child care and parent education.

Comprehensiveness means more than providing a bunch of services under one roof. To be effective, the different components need to be integrated so that the client perceives the program as "seamless." For example, a student in a full-service community school should view the supportive environment as a whole—what goes on in the classroom has to be consistent with what goes on in the school clinic and in the after-school program.

Food

Experienced youth workers know that young people need a lot of caloric sustenance along with the caring. Many programs offer after-school snacks (pizza and hamburgers are favorites). Extended-day schools serve breakfast, lunch, snacks, and, in a few places, dinner.

Residential Care

One approach to dealing with high-risk youth that we have not touched upon previously is residential care, in which identified troublemakers of all sorts or habitual runaways are removed from their homes and placed in group settings. They generally live in small "houses" with "houseparents," are taught social skills, and are provided educational programs as well as treatment for any physical or mental health problems. While the older models of group homes were therapeutic, more recent homes have been opened as safe havens for molested youth or those who are otherwise homeless. A study by the U.S. General Accounting Office found many interesting models but little evaluation.[8] That agency concluded that these programs had potential and identified characteristics of the most promising efforts (these should be familiar to you by now): individual attention, caring adults, comprehensive services, social and coping skills training, family involvement, and safe havens. A distinctive part of residential care was that the successful homes introduced routines into the otherwise chaotic lives of the children and enforced discipline. Arrangements were made for these young people after they left residential care to ensure that they had intensive and consistent follow-up from a staff member.

I believe we will hear much more about residential care in the future because, given the option, many of today's rootless youth would choose a safe haven with regular meals, an orderly environment, and caring people over the anarchy of the streets. The most controversial aspect may be the cost, estimated by the GAO at over $40,000 per participant per year.

Intensive and Long-term Involvement in a Program

Many of the programs that have been singled out as exemplary require almost daily attendance by the clients and students over a number of years. This intensity is an important factor in helping young people acquire sufficient skills and change their self-concepts.

POLICY ISSUES

Many difficult policy questions emerge from this review of programs. Some advocates for youth believe that interventions should start at the policy level, and all practitioners agree that you cannot discuss prevention without attention to policies. But I don't believe that there is a lot of agreement about the resolution of these issues at any level, in communities, states, or the nation.

Policies in the substance abuse field have recently received considerable attention. If we look at alcohol abuse, enforcement of drunken driving laws has significantly reduced fatal accidents. Both alcohol and cigarette consumption by youth have been shown to decrease when taxation raised the prices. Hopefully, eliminating cigarette advertising aimed at youth (such as the Joe Camel campaign) will diminish usage. Recent FDA regulations make the sale of tobacco products to anyone under 18 a federal violation.

Violence prevention begins with gun control, clearly a controversial subject. Other policies in the delinquency field affect how juveniles are dealt with in the justice system. The trend is toward more punitive policies, such as treating adjudicated juveniles as adults. Curfews have been proposed as one method for lowering street crime among teenagers although as many crimes are committed by juveniles in the afternoon as at night.

Those who consider the media to be a negative influence on young people's lives have recommended greater controls over the content of television and movies, particularly in the areas of violence and sex. Efforts are underway to control the Internet.

Many policies that relate to pregnancy prevention among adolescents have generated controversy. Barriers to the provision of birth control inhibit the use of contraception. School-based reproductive health programs are only effective when comprehensive services are available, starting with high-quality sexuality education and including on-site distribution of condoms and other birth-control methods, as well as referral for abortion in the case of unwanted pregnancies. Strong support for abstention programs is being articulated despite the lack of evidence that they are effective.

Many policy issues are implicit in the discussion of educational achievement. Such practices as expulsion, suspension, tracking, and grade retention can discourage high-risk students from continuing in school. The debate is in full swing about whether the implementation of national standards will improve educational achievement across the board. Policies are now being set forth to create safe havens and drug-free environments in schools that may employ body or weapons searches and locker checks.

Family policy obviously affects children. No one knows how profound the impact of welfare reform will be, although it is likely that more children will be poor and hungry, especially if they are immigrants. Policies that create more job opportunities and child care spaces are clearly an issue here.

We cannot contemplate creating a Safe Passage Movement for all children in this country without careful consideration of the implications of policies of all kinds. The pendulum swings between tolerance and control affect the lives of many perplexed teenagers at every policy shift.

IMPLEMENTATION ISSUES

While visiting a variety of programs revealed a significant batch of common factors in successful efforts, it also pointed up some common unresolved issues. This section includes broad questions about targeting programs, and replicating and staffing them. I also bring up the subject of mass media—their influence on youth, both negative and positive, and its place in youth development programs.

Targeting Behaviors

Some programs are based on the theory that specific behaviors such as cigarette smoking or early unprotected sexual intercourse must be targeted. The intervention has to be designed with a strong message focusing on that act in order to get the participant to concentrate on it. Other programs are based on the theory that one should try to alter more universal behaviors and work on areas such as decision making and dealing with peer influences. Still other approaches address broader social needs such as education, employment, and housing, predicated on the assumption that until basic needs are met, young people are not amenable to behavioral change.

Targeting High-Risk Youth

Youth experts do not agree on whether programs should be universal or targeted. Some practitioners argue that singling out certain young people and putting them in special programs will make them feel stigmatized. Instead, they say, we should try to create stronger communities and schools that respond to the principles of youth development. Others assert that the main problem is an inequitable distribution of resources. Advantaged youth have enough resources to maintain their advantage and, therefore, we have to use extra resources to launch programs that are targeted at those who need them.

A distinction has to be made between targeting and segregating. Targeting as a social policy has validity if it addresses the equity question. For example, state attempts to equalize educational funding gaps between inner cities and suburbs are of increasing importance around the country. Policies that segregate children by defined criteria may be counterproductive. For example, special education classes for students with behavioral problems have led to the isolation of mainly disadvantaged children, who then fall farther and farther behind.

Adequacy of Replication

The faithful replication of successful program models often referred to as fidelity is a major issue. I have seen many instances of inadequate replication, attributed not only to lack of funds but also to inadequate preparation and lack of involvement by staff (particularly teachers), as well as to nonsupportive administrative personnel. At one replication of a well-known program, I heard all the theory and rhetoric of the founding "guru," but observed a disorganized staff and disorderly participants. An evaluation showed only limited effects on measures of self-esteem and no effects on school or behavioral measures. I have seen two different sites that were trying to replicate programs that included computer-based curricula, but they had been waiting more than a year to obtain the technology and therefore could not implement the program model in its entirety.

Several studies demonstrate the importance of technical assistance in creating a second generation of programs. Almost all of the success stories have technical assistance built in, in the form of university or think-tank–based teams that come into schools or community agencies and facilitate program implementation. The continuing work of the New American Schools initiative will concentrate heavily on providing on-site consultation to school restructuring efforts.

Cookie Cutters Versus Anarchy

How often I have heard community advocates proclaim, "Just give us the funds, we'll know what to do with it." Yet, as we have seen, excellent program models can founder in the absence of structured replication. I believe that practitioners at the local level require considerable guidance in organizing and implementing programs. Michelle Cahill, a youth development expert who has shepherded the New York City Beacons since their initiation, reports, "You can't just hand out materials for new program ideas and expect that the program will work."[9] She attributes the successful replication of the Teen Outreach program in twenty Beacon schools to the high level of training provided by the program distributers.

The experience of the Kentucky Family and Youth Service Centers is revealing on this point. According to evaluator Robert Illback, "Each program represents a 'field experiment' in which coordinators are selected, given broad guidelines, and 'turned loose' to meet identified needs however they can."[10] The result, according to observers, is a set of innovative, complex, and largely untested approaches, with wide variations and the absence of viable controls. In this case, the conceptual model underlying the program structure is still in the process of evolution.

Charismatic Leaders

You have been introduced to a number of dynamic individuals who deserve much of the credit for creating and operating youth programs and running schools. Program visits reveal just how compelling these people are—you definitely can pick up good and bad vibes from on-site observations. In the final chapter I will return to this subject, because these leaders are fundamental to the Safe Passage Movement. But recognition that individuals are important also suggests a major question: Can a program run without these folks? What would happen if they left? Are they replaceable?

The challenge for the youth development field is to document the models and create the training opportunities that will produce new leaders. The successful experience of Public/Private Ventures with the replication of the Summer Training and Employment Program (STEP) in more than 100 communities is telling. Gary Walker and colleagues have observed, "The replication record of STEP should provide hope that operating effective social interventions is not a rare or mysterious talent, but more a matter of adequate resources, defined strategy and content, and guidance and ready assistance regarding concrete implementation issues and problems."[11]

Interdisciplinary Education

Many people who work with youth were trained in traditional roles. Teachers are graduates of educational establishments that have not changed their own curricula to adapt to contemporary needs. They rarely come into schools prepared to manage team teaching or to organize cooperative learning classrooms. Few school pupil personnel—counselors, psychologists, and social workers—have been trained to deal with issues such as sexual abuse and family substance abuse. Youth workers in community-based programs often are trained through in-service programs, but they are not prepared to work in collaborative arrangements with schools. Many of the successful programs we have looked at require personnel who have very strong interpersonal skills, can understand the issues arising in cross-disciplinary efforts, and are strongly committed to seeing results.

Universities and professional organizations that offer interdisciplanry training have come together to create a Network of Networks. As reported by Richard Brandon of the Human Services Policy Center at the University of Washington in Seattle, an initial meeting of major educators and trainers concluded that this new field of collaborative programs embodies an

> implicit model of change in the attitudes, skills, and orientations of individuals that lead them to foster changes in the institutions where they work, which in

turn leads to changes in the clients served by those institutions. This same model applies whether we are talking about university faculty changing the institutions which train professional students, and thereby affecting the way students practice when they leave the university; or we are talking about how students trained in collaborative practice transform the service institutions where they work, and affect the lives of children and families.[12]

A National Center on School and Community at New York City's Fordham University, directed by Carolyn Denham, acts as a clearinghouse for information on interprofessional education and community schools. Technical assistance and training for in-service or preservice education is coordinated by Hal Lawson and Katherine Hooper-Briar at University of Utah in Salt Lake City. The Human Services Policy Center in Seattle brings together five graduate and professional programs at the university (education, public affairs, public health, nursing, and social work) that work collaboratively with numerous schools and community agencies in two nearby school districts. Students are exposed to both classroom-based and experiential learning.

Wheelock College in Boston is one of the few undergraduate schools that is creating an interdisciplinary program that prepares students to work in service delivery systems that will be preventive, supportive of family development, and appropriate for contemporary children:

> We aim to structure professional training in each of the three human service professions of teaching, social work, and child life . . . to both intellectually and experientially transcend current role definitions within those professions.[13]

Training

The Children's Aid Society, having set up a technical assistance center to help people create community schools, finds that the demand is overwhelming, especially for developing collaborative relationships between schools and community agencies. Other questions frequently raised include: How do the school principal and the support-services coordinator divide up their responsibilities? How can special education programs be integrated into community schools? How can evaluation be conducted so that it produces evidence of success but is not too intrusive or expensive?

One of the most interesting initiatives is in the preparation of police to work in community and youth projects. The program in Caimito has played host to hundreds of police officials, and the Milton Eisenhower Foundation has arranged for networking among other Koban replications in Columbia, South Carolina, Baltimore, and Washington, DC, and police departments around the country. This foundation also facilitates training for community-based organizations in management, evaluation, and communication techniques.

Every field has its own cadre of trainers. In teen pregnancy prevention, the area I know best, Advocates for Youth, Educational Development Corporation,

ETR Associates, SEICUS (Sexuality Information and Education Council of the United States), and various regional centers all provide technical assistance and training in prevention interventions.

Staff Turnover

Just when a program is finally up and running, the director gets a better job offer or the case manager moves across country. Staff turnover both in program development agencies and in youth-serving agencies and schools is a major deterrent to program implementation and replication. Pay scales are generally low in community-based organizations, and many staff are pressured by financial concerns to move to better-paying jobs if available. Principal and superintendent turnover creates a frequent barrier to program sustainability.

Unions

In my field visits, unions were sometimes cited as barriers to program development. This was particularly evident in regard to school reorganization programs, where tenure was an issue. Innovative principals found it difficult to put together a new team in situations where no staff changes were possible. In some communities, union rules make it hard to replace ineffective principals.

The National Education Association and the American Federation of Teachers (AFT) have sought to set the record straight on these issues by taking the leadership in many educational reform initiatives. The AFT recently endorsed the concept of charter schools, with the proviso that they preserve employee bargaining rights.[14] (Only eight of the twenty-five states with charter school laws require that teachers be certified.)

Time

The more complex program models may take five to seven years to implement. The need for extended time for planning and communication cannot be overestimated. Meetings can be the bane of any program developer's existence. Yet as more actors come on the scene from different agencies, with different perspectives on clients, more time is required to make joint decisions and to share information.

Many of the people providing that precious individual attention I keep talking about report that they work seventy to eighty hours a week, including weekends. Safe Passage requires just such an enormous commitment of time. No one expects to get paid for all the hours it takes.

Media: A Powerful Influence?

The extent to which media exposure can be used to promote positive behaviors is definitely an unresolved issue in program development. Although most people would agree that salacious and violent television shows are not good for children, it is unclear to what degree educational television and other forms of positive messages can exert a beneficial influence on behaviors.

Public television in New York City produces a show called *In the Mix*, where the material is presented by teenagers, about teenagers, in a style that teenagers say they want. The program covers a range of subjects—education, employment, AIDS, family and peer relationships, going on a date. Substantive sections are interspersed with music videos that teens select. The producer, Sue Gates, developed discussion guides to be used in schools and with community groups showing how to use the films as triggers for group discussions and socials skills exercises. Preliminary research shows that students and teachers find the *In The Mix* videos interesting and stimulating, but compiling evidence on behavioral impacts is almost impossible to obtain. RMC Research Corporation staff joined a group of very high-risk students watching the segment "Teens Talk Violence." They reported:

> Students watched the video with riveted attention . . . all wanted to talk about how violence figures in their lives . . . the session became a catharsis, helping them air their anxieties, fears, frustrations, and street smarts at an specially stressful point in time. The principal was astounded at students' reactions, pointing out that this was probably the first time that they were interested in doing better in life and learning new things.[15]

Many people believe that public service messages can influence behavior. Partnership for Drug Free America has been placing full-page ads and media spots for years, yet no research has documented that the ads are effective. EN-ABL, a teen-pregnancy-prevention approach used in California, had a large media component using billboards, ads, and television, but it had no effect. Youth were aware of the campaign, but they did not abstain from sex (see chapter 9). Maryland also launched a media campaign to prevent pregnancy that was initially deemed a success when the rates declined, yet shortly thereafter the rates rose, suggesting that ads may not have influenced the rates one way or the other. Now, a new national initiative focusing on preventing teen pregnancy has announced its intentions of using media as the centerpiece of the strategy. President Clinton also plans to feature media spots in new smoking-prevention initiatives. We have no reason to believe that these new ventures will succeed any better than those cited here.

Advocates for Youth has long been involved in working with media producers to integrate positive youth development messages into soap operas and sit-coms. Awards are given annually for those programs that present sexual issues with honesty and integrity. Networks are under a lot of pressure from parent and youth advocate groups to clean up the airways and act responsibly.

In my view, the most effective potential role of media for changing youth behaviors is to use films as triggers for group discussions. This requires well-thought-out videos as well as trained group discussion leaders who can use the materials to help teenagers learn valuable life lessons and deal with their feelings.

WHAT DRIVES REPLICATION

We have acquired a great deal of knowledge about effective programming, and a number of models and designs are now available to schools and communities that want to improve the outcomes for youth. In fact, many of the programs cited in these pages are being replicated. The subject of replication is fundamental to the question of "going to scale." It is not enough to be able to pinpoint a bunch of demonstration projects around the country. We have to gear up, community by community, to make sure that institutions change how they function and incorporate this knowledge.

In studying these various prevention fields, I have tried to ascertain the status of replication. What programs are being reproduced on a large scale, and what are the elements that determine wide replication? A number of factors are suggested by this review, which I will discuss along with actual examples from the previous chapters.

In late 1995, when we surveyed the programs included in *Adolescents at Risk*, we found that about 70 percent of the programs that were still going had been replicated, some in rather significant numbers.[16] For example, Parents as Teachers is operating in 1,600 sites, the Primary Mental Health Project is now running in more than 600 sites, and the Comer Social Development Model is being organized in at least 500 schools. Other programs that were found to be effective are being reproduced in one or two places near the original site, such as the Adolescent Diversion Project out of Michigan State University in Lansing. The much-heralded and carefully evaluated Midwestern Prevention Program is not being replicated outside of Kansas City and Indianapolis, where the experiments took place. And only 55 percent of the programs that were currently being replicated had been evaluated since 1990. School-based curricula, used most frequently in the teen pregnancy and substance-abuse prevention fields, were the most likely to be replicated in the absence of evaluation.

Some of the following discussion about replication is based on the results of that survey, embellished by my own observations over the years. Whether a program is replicated is based on many determinants: No one program replication encompasses all of these elements, but most include several.

Evidence of Success

Strong evaluation and clear documentation of good results do establish a program's reputation. And, of course, publication of evaluation findings in a peer-reviewed journal or book is "de rigueur." The most famous example (which I have not mentioned previously) is High Scope/Perry Preschool, a two-year early intervention in Ypsilanti, Michigan, that tracked participants and a matched control group over several decades, and has consistently shown long-term positive effects on intellectual performance, dropout rates, pregnancy rates, and delinquency rates. That program experience occurred in the 1970s yet it continues to be cited to gain support for preschool programs such as Head Start.

A number of programs have been described here that have established reputations and documented evidence of success. Success for All, The Teen Outreach Program, Life Skills Training, and the School Transition Environment Project are all programs that are being replicated across the country. Each was developed in a different specialized field.

Charisma of the Leader

I mentioned that charismatic leaders are often identified as key elements in successful programs. They also are a determinant of whether their programs get replicated. Qualities such as eloquence, evidence of commitment, being personable, and conveying a sense of authority give programs an aura. James Comer of the School Development Program is an excellent example of a gentleman who speaks with both authority and humanity and has enormous credibility as a mental health specialist and a people motivater. Theodore Sizer, mastermind of the Coalition for Essential Schools, another very attractive and convincing individual, created his own institution within Brown University that fosters replication of his model. Michael Carrera is the guru of the teen pregnancy prevention field, an eloquent spokesperson who has garnered considerable support to teach others how to set up his multicomponent program around the country.

You may have noticed that the individuals cited here are all men. With the exception of Deborah Meier, Michelle Cahill, and Karen Pittman, few of the well-known youth development leaders are women, although many of the hands-on program people are.

Legislation

Several programs have successfully moved from being demonstration projects to becoming models for state or federal initiatives. Parents as Teachers in Missouri is the best example; not only has it been fully supported in its home state, it is also being replicated across the country. The Primary Mental Health Project made the transition from being a university-generated demonstration to a statewide initiative in California. DARE, which started in the Los Angeles Police Department, was written into the federal Drug-Free Schools legislation, and the model of Cities-in-Schools receives support from both the U.S. Department of Justice and Department of Labor. The latter also supports Quantum and STEP replications around the country. The U.S. Office of Juvenile Justice also supports the Boys and Girls Clubs Targeted Outreach Program. It should not be surprising that some youth programs, like other large businesses, employ lobbyists who know their way around Washington and keep in close touch with congressional committees during budget talks.

Political Savvy

It is useful to involve prominent business leaders on the board of directors and to know the "right" people who can help raise funds. The Boston Compact, a school-business partnership, is a program that gained strength as a result of a better tie to the Mayor's Office. The New York City Beacons have maintained their funding by making visible to Mayor Guiliani that they have strong community-based support. Cities-in-Schools has worked at communicating with government agencies, which gives it high visibility at conferences and public hearings (though not in the academic research literature).

Attention to Training

I emphasized the importance of training as a component of good practice. Experience has shown that replication can take place in a much more orderly way if training is organized and presented directly by the program developers. Success for All grooms its own facilitators out of its center at Johns Hopkins. Cities-in-Schools has set up its own "university," a kind of training-franchise operation that practitioners pay to attend. The STEP program relies on resources from Public/Private Ventures to train new start-ups. Teen Outreach is being disseminated by Cornerstone Consulting Group through training programs, sales of curricula, and work with national organizations.

Foundation Blessings

A large grant stimulates rapid dissemination of program models. Foundations clearly make choices when they award their grants. The Rockefeller Foundation has a large Comer School Development Model initiative. The Coalition of Essential Schools has been supported by huge sums from the Annenberg family. ALERT, a substance-abuse-prevention program, is disseminated by the Best Foundation (Hilton money), and the replication of the School Community Program for Sexual Risk Reduction is being subsidized by the Kansas Health Foundation. As I have pointed out, a number of foundations are supporting various aspects of the development of full-service community schools.

Marketing the Program

Mail-order brochures abound, with advertisements for the various manuals, curricula, and videos needed by schools and community organizations to replicate programs. Here's Looking at You is heavily merchandised, as are most of the commercial substance-abuse-prevention programs. Catalogues from ETR Associates, Sunrise Publications, and many other companies arrive frequently with enormous inventories of items that are offered in the name of health education and promotion.

National Youth Organizations

National youth agencies have moved to the forefront of stimulating, innovative program development. As membership organizations with many local affiliates, they have the capacity to work with affiliate staff to assure rapid dissemination of program ideas. Many employ field staff, all hold frequent conferences and workshops, and all have excellent training and monitoring capabilities. Boys and Girls Clubs has widely disseminated SMART Moves, and Girls Inc. has made the Teen Pregnancy Prevention Program (as well as other program components) widely available to its own affiliates and to other organizations. 4H Clubs, located in thousands of communities, are set up to implement packaged components that are disseminated through state extension services and a national clearinghouse.

For the first time, national youth organizations are getting involved in serious evaluation efforts, responding to the charge in the Carnegie Corporation's *A Matter of Time*, which calls for youth agencies to document the effects of their programs.[17]

National Research Organizations

"Think tanks" have the ability to employ program developers, conduct research, disseminate their own publications, and offer technical assistance. The Oregon Social Learning Center in Eugene is a large operation, with many researchers working on family interventions. Public/Private Ventures not only created STEP, it also conducted the demonstration projects, revised the approach, and is currently overseeing a large-scale replication.

Nonprofit research organizations such as the Urban Institute, Child Trends, and P/PV play very important roles in generating the evaluation data on which the claims of success are made. For instance, the Urban Institute conducted the Children at Risk project's evaluation, and Quantum was evaluated by Andrew Hahn at Brandeis University.

Presentations

Giving papers and keynote addresses at conferences, annual professional meetings, and gatherings of practitioners gets the word out. Michael Carrera is a very popular speaker; David Hawkins, creator of the Seattle Social Development Model, is frequently involved in delinquency and substance-abuse prevention meetings; James Comer of the School Development Program is sought after for his compassionate mode of presentation. Presentations through the national media have become more commonplace, and feature stories on successful programs are being sought by networks. Philip Coltoff, the dynamic director of the Children's Aid Society, is often seen as a spokesperson for the youth development field; Karen Pittman, a pioneer in the youth development field, is another articulate commentator on both the U.S. and the international youth scene.

Intuitive Appeal

Certain programs are attractive to practitioners and the media because they are new, cutting edge, imaginative, dynamic, or otherwise exciting. But program fads are discernible. For example, incentives were popularized through Eugene Lang's I Have a Dream Initiative. Postponing Sexual Involvement was believed to be a model "saying no" effort. School-based clinics received a lot of publicity in the beginning as new and possibly controversial health settings for youth. New initiatives capture the attention of the press for a while, but then the media goes on to the next wave—right now it is boot camps. Practitioners are influenced by fads as well, especially when new sources of funding are tied to new program initiatives.

Responsive to Special Groups

Program models designed to address the needs of various populations are in demand by community-based organizations. The Fifth Ward Enrichment Project and the I Have a Future programs are both of great interest to African American agencies, as are Valued Youth Partnership and El Puente to Hispanic groups.

University Involvement

In the past, many of the successful programs grew out of university initiatives. But I believe that universities no longer dominate the replication of the models. More national youth organizations and nonprofit youth service agencies have moved to the forefront of youth development activities. With the exception of universities like the University of Pennsylvania and Fordham, which consciously made a decision to undertake community-based projects, universities do not generally have constituencies ready to implement programs. Although many of the important interventions are still based in university communities, they are more likely than in the past to be housed in special centers. Success for All, School Development, and the Coalition are educational programs that are now promoted through centers that have been spun off from university departments.

WHAT ABOUT THE EXCEPTIONS?

Why do some programs with high-quality evaluations and charismatic leaders not get replicated? The successful Midwestern Prevention Project developed by Mary Ann Pentz and colleagues at the University of Southern California included five components: school-based curricula, parent programs, community organization, social policy change, and mass media appeals. As far as Pentz knows, this project is not being replicated anywhere despite a great deal of exposure through conferences and publications. The program is believed to be just too complicated to implement without considerable financial support or sustained technical assistance.

So then why do some programs with negative evaluations, with findings that show that the program has limited effect, nevertheless get replicated? In some cases, the evaluation is used to change the model to improve the potential. In other cases, the evaluation is ignored, and the program is marketed with no change. The latter is most observable in the substance-abuse field, with huge sales of manuals and training time despite a lack of research supporting the validity of the programs.

One thing is sure: *Research findings alone definitely do not drive replication.* We will discuss this subject further in the next chapter, when we take a look at what *doesn't* work to ensure Safe Passage.

Lauren Chelec, Photographer

9

WHAT DOESN'T WORK, AND WHY?

Coming through the door at Anywhere High School, a visitor is struck by the legacy of more than two decades of school-based prevention wars. In the main office, a bulletin board announces the start of a new AIDS program, led by a teacher who taught classes in health and nutrition when those issues were highly visible. This year's "life issues" classes are required because they cover a new state-mandated unit on the prevention of sexually transmitted diseases. Up in the science wing, biology teachers are introducing the substance-abuse program. . . . There's only one dropout-prevention worker, where a couple of years ago there were four. He is planning meetings with the 100 or more students who have been absent more than 20 days, and is frustrated because they don't show up. Meanwhile, social studies teachers have begun teaching about violence in America, and the superintendent has scheduled a special meeting of the board of education to develop a plan to combat teenage pregnancy. . . . Fragmentation breeds breakdown, and the school emerges as a hodgepodge of social initiatives with little direction or effectiveness.

—Timothy Shriver and Roger Weissberg, Education Week

T he assertion that many programs for youth are successful must be accompanied by the acknowledgment that many others do not work. After careful evaluation, certain programs were unable to prove that they had achieved their objectives, and a few were even proved to have exacerbated the behaviors of high-risk youth. Then there are those that have all the attributes of effective approaches but that cannot claim that they work because they have not been evaluated.

Remember the cardinal rule of prevention: An effective program has to provide evidence that it has positively influenced behavior—lowered drug use, improved contraceptive use, increased school achievement. It is not sufficient to prove merely that knowledge has been gained or attitudes have been changed. In this chapter, I present examples of programs that do not work, and try to explain why they failed.

FAILURE TO PREVENT SUBSTANCE ABUSE

Studies of unsuccessful interventions permeate the history of substance-abuse prevention.[1] Many of the curricula that seemed successful right after the program ended showed no effects a couple of years later. Several well-known programs in the substance-abuse field have produced evaluations documenting failure.

Project Alert (Adolescent Learning Experiences in Resistance Training)

Created by Phyllis Ellickson and colleagues at the RAND Corporation, this eight-session curriculum is offered in the seventh grade, with three booster sessions in the eighth grade. It is based on the social influence model of prevention and emphasizes refusal skills. In a carefully designed evaluation, Project Alert showed some success in a ninth-grade follow-up, but by the end of twelfth grade the experimental group used substances more than the control group.[2] The researchers concluded that the program's effect on behavior stopped once the lessons stopped, although the knowledge gained from the program—understanding the consequences of using drugs—was maintained longer. They proposed increasing the number of sessions for greater effect.

Project Alert is being disseminated by the Best Foundation for Drug Free America, a nonprofit organization supported by the Conrad N. Hilton Foundation. In its advertising brochure, Alert is described as a "fully validated drug prevention program."[3] In response to the evaluation, the curriculum has been updated and booster sessions added. Best reports training 4,000 teachers in this approach in recent years.

DARE (Drug Abuse Resistance Education)

Probably the best-known substance-abuse prevention program in the country, DARE has been awarded 5 percent of the federal Drug-Free Schools grants passed through states to localities. Communities all over America have posted

DARE signs. The model, which relies on a trained, local police officer to teach a prescribed curriculum, is promulgated through a national nonprofit organization with regional, state, and local chapters. Many small evaluation studies have been conducted since 1990. In 1995, Christopher Ringwalt and colleagues at Research Triangle Institute reviewed (through a process known as meta-analysis) eight acceptable evaluation studies of the DARE elementary school curriculum.[4] They found that while DARE increased knowledge and social skills, compared to other programs it did not modify use of substances. It was more effective than old-style didactic programs but much less effective than the new-style social-skills programs such as Life Skills Training.

DARE continues to be replicated. The program has survived even in the current budget-cutting environment because of its popularity at the local level, a good example of replication stimulated by intuitive appeal (it makes sense to involve the local cops) and political savvy. At last count, it was operating in at least 8,000 schools. New York City and Washington, DC, have just signed up for the program.

The *New Republic* recently published a feature story with a revealing title "Don't You D.A.R.E." This article by Stephen Glass reads like an old-fashioned exposé, documenting the success of the national DARE organization—almost a billion-dollar industry—in repressing criticism and gaining federal support. Glass recounts stories of researchers being "DARED"—threatened with loss of tenure if they persist in publishing anti-DARE research—and quotes an unnamed researcher who told him, "DARE is the world's biggest pet rock. If it makes us feel good to spend money on nothing, that's okay, but everyone should know DARE does nothing." According to Glass,

> For the past five years, DARE has used tactics ranging from bullying journalists to manipulating the facts to mounting campaigns in order to intimidate government officials, stop news organizations, researchers and parents from criticizing the program.[5]

Glass's article certainly confirmed my own ambivalence about this program. A DARE officer assigned to a very needy middle school asked if he could speak to me confidentially. He confessed in private that his efforts in the classroom were not effective and appealed to me to supply him with evidence he could show to his police chief so that his time could be more usefully employed. He wanted to provide one-on-one counseling to high-risk students. As you can imagine, I was happy to comply.

I must admit that every time I tell someone that DARE does not have any effect on substance use rates, I am told, "My kid loves it." Our local DARE officer is impressive. He feels that he influences children to view police in a positive light, as friends and advocates.

HERE'S LOOKING AT YOU, 2000 (HLAY)

This is a K–12, school-based curriculum produced and distributed by the Comprehensive Health Education Foundation, a private organization. The initial approach included refusal and coping skills, as well as cooperative learning techniques. Six different evaluations were reviewed by John Swisher and his colleagues at Pennsylvania State University.[6] They found positive results regarding knowledge and attitudes; however, only one study reported reduced use of substances, and that study was conducted without a comparison group.[7] Significant changes in the curricula were noted, including the incorporation of lessons that addressed risk factors, and more focus on behavioral skills training and on mastery teaching techniques.

A request was made to the Comprehensive Health Education Foundation for additional evaluation. In a memo from Neal Starkman, who was identified as a "writer and developer," it was claimed that "HLAY has been evaluated . . . more often than probably any other comprehensive drug education curriculum," citing results that indicated changes in self-esteem, knowledge, and a decrease in use of chewing tobacco in grades 1–3. The memo also refers to "needs assessments" made in Wappinger Falls, New York, that showed decreases in actual substance use, but these results were not referenced, so I could not track them down. HLAY is being used in about 24 percent of school districts nationally.[8]

FAILURE TO PREVENT TEEN PREGNANCY

Like the other prevention domains, the teen-pregnancy-prevention field has seen many programs come and go. Over the years, a number of program models have been strongly promoted as solutions—among them, parent communication, male involvement, community outreach, peer theater, dollar-a-day incentives, and Just Say No. Most of them have fallen by the wayside, either because they were evaluated and found to have little effect, or more likely were never evaluated at all.

Some of the ideas come and go and come again, such as community outreach, once a cornerstone of inner-city family planning programs that employed indigenous home visitors to inform and motivate women to attend clinics. Community outreach is reemerging as an important component of AIDS prevention, in which recovered drug addicts and individuals with AIDS carry prevention messages to community people hanging out on street corners or in bars. And lately, attention is turning toward large-scale multicomponent programs.

EDUCATION NOW AND BABIES LATER (ENABL)

In 1992, the State of California launched this ambitious pregnancy-prevention campaign. Directed at youths aged 12 to 24, this program was designed and implemented by the California Department of Health Services, Office of Family Planning (OFP), with the goal of helping youths postpone sexual activity. The effort included many components—an educational curriculum (Postponing Sexual Involvement, or PSI), mass media support, and parental and community involvement. From 1992 to 1994, the OFP funded twenty-eight ENABL education projects, largely in local community agencies, to deliver PSI in schools and community settings. The curriculum they used consisted of five sessions, each about one hour long, led by either teachers or peers. Some programs also implemented PSI for Parents, generally given in one longer session, but attendance was poor.

The media campaign used print, television, and radio to raise public awareness of the issue, to inform the public about the campaign, and to enlist youth. Extensive training was made available for ENABL project staff and curriculum leaders. Evaluation was built into the effort from the beginning, and survey data from treatment and control groups were collected at various points in time.

Research showed that at the end of a three-month period after the intervention, PSI had a minimal effect on attitudes and knowledge, but by the end of a seventeen-month period, the intervention had absolutely no effect on those who were sexually inexperienced prior to the program.[9] Those who were exposed to PSI were no more likely to abstain from sexual intercourse than those who were not exposed: "Neither teen-led nor adult-led PSI groups were significantly less likely to initiate intercourse than their respective control groups."[10] This disappointing result held true when comparing males and females, race or ethnic groups, or age groups—no significant differences in abstention were found. This also held true for those who were already sexually active before the program: They did not lower their involvement in risky behaviors as a result of the intervention.

Kirby and his colleagues suggest some reasons for these findings. It is possible that the comparison groups also had access to sex education during the same period, invalidating the study. Also, this evaluation did not measure the effects of the statewide media campaign.

This implementation of Postponing Sexual Involvement differed markedly from the original program, which was tested in Atlanta in the 1980s. For instance, California's scheduling of the sessions and use of other than teen teachers were unlike the model. It is possible that the curriculum worked in the earlier instance because of the setting and the presence of the designer, Marion Howard. Kirby points out that the PSI curriculum does have limitations, given its short duration and lack of attention to skills building.

RESPECT—RESPONSIBLE EDUCATION ON SEXUALITY AND PREGNANCY FOR EVERY COMMUNITY'S TEENS

Very little research has been conducted on the impact of family planning programs on the prevention of teen pregnancy. Yet utilization of family planning clinics has been documented among more than a million teenagers every year. One reason for the dearth of research is the difficulty in following clinic users and finding appropriate comparison groups. One recent study focused on Philadelphia's RESPECT project, a consortium of nine health care agencies that offered new or enhanced educational outreach and services in defined neighborhoods.[11] The network clinics were monitored frequently by the funders (foundations), and staff received training and supervision from the Family Planning Council of Southeastern Pennsylvania. These efforts were bolstered by a media campaign with posters and public transport cards built around the theme "Pregnancy: It's Not for Me." The clinics served more than 10,000 new patients over the three years of the project.

Careful evaluation of this well-implemented program was conducted by a team from the University of Pennsylvania that included Frank Furstenberg, a prominent researcher. They collected two sets of data from a random sample of 14 to 18 year olds who lived in the clinic neighborhoods, and those in the city as a whole. The results showed very few significant differences. The proportion of the respondents who had ever been to any clinic actually declined in the neighborhood areas while changing very little in the entire city. Attitudes changed very little as well, except that support increased for the idea that birth control clinics should be located in schools. The RESPECT project did not foster increases in sexual activity nor did it appear to increase use of contraception significantly. Pregnancy rates varied only slightly.

The researchers suggested several explanations for these disappointing results: The clinic users may not have lived in the selected neighborhoods, which were characterized as very high mobility areas; the media campaign was citywide and did not focus only on the clinic areas; and, finally, the methodology might have been faulty. Based on this research, several alternative approaches were suggested including intensive public health campaigns and school-linked health centers.

FAILURE TO PREVENT DELINQUENCY

The most recent approach to delinquency prevention focuses on the reduction of violent behavior through the introduction of conflict-resolution programs in thousands of middle and high schools. Several years ago, one article in *Health Affairs* generated a flurry of discussion that illustrates the controversy in youth development circles over what works and what doesn't. Researcher Daniel Webster assessed the "unconvincing case for conflict-resolution programs," based on his review of three major prevention programs that showed few behavioral changes.[12] For example, the Violence Prevention Curriculum for Adolescents, created by Deborah Prothro-Stith, offers ten sessions on risks, coping with anger, and dealing with interpersonal conflict. A somewhat limited evaluation found the program resulted in few significant differences in attitudes or behaviors. The lack of program effect was attributed to inadequate implementation of the curriculum by classroom teachers and to targeting high school rather than middle school students. Another program was modeled on Viewpoints, a fifteen-session curriculum taught by a trauma nurse, an emergency medical technician, an attorney, and a former drug dealer. While some change in knowledge was shown following the intervention, the program appeared to have a negative impact on problem-solving abilities. The participants were more likely to respond in violent ways than the nonparticipants. The third program, Positive Adolescent Choices Training (PACT), gave intensive social skills training to small groups (see chapter 7). According to Webster, although the participants showed improvement in targeted skills and lowered suspension rates from school, the evaluation was severely limited by small sample size, short follow-up, lack of statistical tests, and poor controls.

Webster maintains that these programs do not work because they are based on faulty premises. He believes that more comprehensive targeted interventions are needed—for example, providing individualized attention to enhance students' academic performance, mentoring and after-school activities, and early intervention. Conflict-resolution programs, despite their lack of success, are being rapidly proliferated because they "provide political cover for politicians, bureaucrats, and school officials, and distract the public from the structural determinants of youth violence."[13]

Health Affairs received so many responses to the article that they published four of them and Webster's response in a special section of the journal.[14] William DeJong cited New York City's Resolving Conflict Creatively Program (RCCP)'s success at creating "peaceable schools" as a result of infusing conflict-resolution techniques into many aspects of the school experience.[15] Other respondents cited unpublished research and new evaluations that showed more favorable results. Renee Wilson-Brewer questioned the selection of only those three programs out of a field of more than 100. She also points out that the Violence Prevention Curriculum for Adolescents is just one of the components of the Boston Violence Prevention Program which encompasses the activities that Webster supports. Speaking for the National Network of Violence Prevention Practitioners, Wilson-Brewer writes, "Although we concede that there is not yet a great deal of evidence on the effectiveness of school-based conflict resolution programs, some data do exist . . . We recognize the need to combine curricula with other interventions."[16] She also emphasizes the need for long-term funding of program evaluations, which would certainly help resolve the conflicts over the validity of conflict-resolution programs.

Another report, this one from the Harlem Hospital Injury Prevention Program, which offered a course in community conflict resolution, suggested that the intervention may have actually promoted more aggressive behavior among very-high-risk students.[17] Seventh graders who were exposed to a one-semester course developed by Alternatives to Violence reported higher levels of anxiety and more acting out than other similar students. The researchers theorized that by seventh grade, students who have already been exposed to high levels of violence have well-developed defenses that allow them to cope, and the program disrupted this process.

You may be familiar with McGruff, the cartoon hound, created by the National Crime Prevention Council (NCPC) to warn children about the perils of crime. Funded at close to $3 million by the U.S. Department of Justice, this creature has close friends in Washington, including a full-time lobbyist. According to the *Legal Times*, "From accusations that the program has become a wasteful crime entitlement for an already well-fed dog, to charges that the animal is too middle class for his message to resonate with kids in the crack and violence-ravaged inner cities, McGruff is on the defensive."[18] A few years ago, an extensive study commissioned by the Department of Justice revealed that McGruff had widespread name and symbol recognition but it was not possible to measure its impact on crime.[19]

John Calhoun, the highly respected executive director of the NCPC, takes issue with these criticisms. He claims that the character has been highly effective with young children and has helped improve citizen-police relationships. More recent ads created pro bono by the Advertising Council use more community-based images and carry a "harder" message for high-risk neighborhoods. The funds for McGruff are earmarked for the National Crime Prevention Council (i.e., no competition). In addition, the group has licensing arrangements with fifteen for-profit companies around the country that sell McGruff "Take a Bite Out of Crime" books, pamphlets, key chains, posters, and even stuffed animals.

FAILURE TO PREVENT SCHOOL FAILURE

The annual meeting reports of the American Educational Research Association are full of papers (largely unpublished) that document failed experiments. As has been said repeatedly, evaluation is difficult. It is hard to produce scientific evidence that interventions can change behavior. It is even harder to design programs that adequately influence the deep-rooted, complex behaviors of young people. And most difficult of all is to implement programs that necessitate changes in the way that *adults*—teachers, administrators, practitioners—treat young people. It has been said that you have to change the way 10 adults act to achieve success with any 1 child.

One example of educational research with disappointing findings was a replication of a national dropout-prevention program in four schools, comparing small groups of participants with nonparticipants.[20] The curriculum was designed as a class in life-skills development, study-skills enhancement, employment readiness, and awareness. The evaluation took place after the first year of the program (ninth grade) and found mixed results. Although the students said the program promoted personal growth, its effects on attendance, course completion, and dropout rates were inconsistent (up in some, down in others). The researchers surmised that the program model was not strong enough to overcome the severe and demanding problems of these very-high-risk students. They suggested that, in addition to problem-solving skills, access to counseling and support services was probably necessary as part of a much more comprehensive dropout-prevention strategy.

Another example focused on a more intensive dropout-prevention program, where high-risk students met in small groups with a resource teacher, had access to a counselor, and received stipends for achievement.[21] At the end of a year, treatment students showed no significant differences in grades from control students. The staff concluded that the program was not sufficient to counterbalance the years of learned failure. They also called for greater intensity and comprehensiveness, with more teacher and family involvement. In the second year of the program, a home-school coordinator was added to the staff. One of the by-products of this research was the finding that the high-risk children did not show lower measures of self-esteem compared to other children.

The Summer Training and Employment Program (STEP) was designed and implemented in 1983 by Public/Private Ventures (P/PV) as a national demonstration project. High-risk 14–16 year olds were offered two summers of employment, life-skills classes, and educational remediation during both summer and winter. P/PV has now completed an eight-year follow-up study in the five original cities based on randomized treatment and control groups.[22] After the first summer of the program, STEP participants had improved achievement in reading and math. STEP treatment youth had test scores about half a grade higher than controls and showed substantial improvement in their knowledge of pregnancy prevention (a related goal of the project). These immediate improvements in test scores were also shown in replications around the country.

Long-term results, however, were discouraging: three or four years after the program in the five original sites, treatment and control youth had dropped out of school at the same rates, had the same poor labor-market performance, and the same pregnancy rates. In a "soul-searching" publication called *Anatomy of a Demonstration*, P/PV documented lessons learned from this experience: beware of quick fixes. Long-term results require both short-term programs and larger institutional changes.[23]

In recognition of the importance of strengthening programs for long-term effectiveness, P/PV advises packaging STEP with other interventions. The recommended four-summer sequence starts with STEP for 14–15 year olds and adds Summer PECE (Practical Education for Citizenship and Employment), a program that organizes youth into community-service teams, and Summer Internships for older youth with field placements with local businesses and government. STEP is currently being replicated in more than 150 sites in nineteen states. P/PV provides intensive technical assistance, training, and materials.

The extensive research on educational practices has not been presented in this book. However, it is important to highlight several components that practitioners believe stand in the way of successfully engaging children, particularly disadvantaged ones in school. Cynthia Brown, a long-time promoter of equity in education through her work for the Council of State Chief School Officers, presented a list of the "same ole things" that have been discredited by careful research that she hoped schools would no longer do. She highlighted hiring undereducated aides to work in classrooms; using pullout programs to extract students from their regular classrooms to do drill work on basic skills; holding one-shot teacher workshops; taking students on field trips with no educational rationale; and providing teachers with computers but no training on how to integrate the technology into their instructional practices.[24]

The Iowa Department of Education has released a unique inventory of policies and practices that negatively affect student performance.[25] In their experience, tracking and ability grouping characterize students as "losers" and lock them into inflexible channels. Retention (failing a grade) is discouraged because it causes a permanent negative effect on performance. Instead, they recommend establishing alternative programs with fewer students, and early intervention. The report also mentions insensitivity to gender issues that favors boys over girls (particularly in math and science), lack of planning for alternative education for dropouts, inflexibility about graduation requirements such as physical education, punishing truancy by suspension or lowered grades, and many other factors.

My own list of negative policies are those that foster tracking, suspension, retention, and expulsion. Isolating achievers from nonachievers is a practice that discourages the latter and may not in the long run help the former. At the risk of being labeled anti-intellectual, I must add one more point here—my belief that the education field is overloaded with useless research. It is shocking that some 5,500 individuals are listed as presenters at the 1997 AERA meeting, yet only a few of the sessions have the potential for contributing to our understanding of what we can do to improve educational outcomes. Three presentations selected at random from the program will give you an idea of what I object to— "Algorithmic and Heuristic Learning Sets and Their Relationship to Cognitive Structure," "Maintenance and Transfer of the Elaborative Interrogation Strategy in Early Adolescents," and "Building a Communitarian Policy of Educative Accountability Using a Critical-Pragmatic Epistemology." My apologies to the authors of those papers, which may indeed contain useful information that will guide us in the future. I suspect, however, that these presentations are based on doctoral theses—the requisite ticket out of the public school classroom and its difficult children and into the heady realm of higher education and arcane theory.

THE "SELF-ESTEEM" BUSINESS

Our discussion of youth development programs would be incomplete without mentioning "self-esteem." Promoting self-esteem is a big business. Advocates believe that enhancing student's self-esteem—learning to feel good about oneself—is the solution to most teenage problems, particularly school failure. More than 5,000 schools subscribe to the Power of Positive Students (POPS) based in Myrtle Beach, South Carolina, the largest self-esteem program in the country.[26] The program, which has costs of up to $2,000 per school, is based on teaching life skills and self-confident attitudes. A nurturing environment is fostered through self-esteem seminars and pep rallies. According to Mike Mitchell, the executive director of POPS, "88-92 percent of success is due to attitude." One proponent described her experience in New York City schools: "Students were asked to tackle tongue twisters and success elicited rousing applause from their peers. They were encouraged to write positive slogans on their school work, such as 'my reading is improving every day' and 'I am an artist.' "[27]

Critics of the self-esteem movement believe that self-regard and self-competency derive from actual achievement, not from mouthing nostrums about feeling good about oneself. One research finding frequently cited contrasts Japanese and American fifth graders. "Even though the American kids were bursting with high self-esteem, stating satisfaction with their math abilities, their math performances were excruciatingly bad. Only one of America's 20 participating schools could manage to eke out a score comparable to the lowest score among the 31 Japanese schools."[28] Richard Weissourd, describing the "feel-good trap," maintains:

> Programs to raise self-esteem . . . are not raising it. Self-esteem has little or no impact on academic achievement, or on drug use, violence, or any other serious problems. Violent criminals . . . often have high self-esteem. . . . The self-esteem movement's constant praising of children is a short cut, a desperate substitute for the inability of teachers and other adults to pay sufficient attention to any one child."[29]

My own bias against the promotion of self-esteem as a prevention program was strengthened when I found myself at an important teachers conference, sharing the podium with a leading advocate of self-esteem. He conducted an animated and dramatic performance, telling many personal stories about how he had succeeded in life. For his grand finale, he got all the teachers to stand up and hug each other. He received a standing ovation. After I presented my usual dry research and call to arms, the reception was lukewarm. The warmth of self-esteem prevailed over the frigid problems of high-risk youth. Once in Montana, where I shared my negative views of self-esteem enhancement as a prevention program, I was prodded to step down from the speaker's podium by the Billings Fifth Grade Self-Esteem Club, all of whom just happened to be in the audience.

FAILURE OF COMPREHENSIVE PROGRAMS

You must know by now that I have a bias toward comprehensive multicomponent programs, efforts that weave together several interventions to create an integrated package. Such an approach was carefully tracked in the implementation of comprehensive school-based prevention programs at four junior high schools in Washington, DC. Each program was operated by a different community-based agency and was supposed to provide ongoing support and youth development activities to disadvantaged students at the school sites. These programs failed to produce evidence of successful outcomes and a report revealed some of the problems encountered in implementation:

- Because other school-based programs had been launched and failed, school administrators, teachers, parents, and even students were skeptical about whether the new program was viable.

- Community members, who believed that the program had significant funding, had "ruffled feathers" because it did not generate jobs for them.

- One principal was uncooperative and would not give the program staff access to school records, such as immunization. Another just ignored the program completely.

- Programs had insufficient space in the school. In one overcrowded school, neither the principal nor the recreation department (one of the partners) wanted the program on the site, which was a room with no windows and little ventilation.

- Program implementation was delayed because the project director was dismissed and a new one not hired for four months. Staff turnover was high. One program went through four counselors in a year. That clinic director attributed the turnover to the pressure of working in a school setting, in one room with five other people. Students knocked on the door constantly, and staff had no place to get away for privacy. Another program director was fired and never replaced.

- The Mayor's Youth Initiatives Office did not deliver on its promise to help the program coordinate with public agencies (human services, housing, health). They demanded too much paperwork from the projects.[30]

And this is just a list of problems from one unsuccessful project. It is rare to find such documentation. I suspect that many worthy youth programs have to cope with situations like these.

New Futures, a major demonstration project in five cities, was launched by the Annie Casey Foundation in the mid-1980s. The carefully selected grantees were expected to develop comprehensive, collaborative multicomponent programs coordinated by nonprofit agencies, school districts, or youth commissions. An evaluation plan was put into place under the aegis of the Center for the Study of Social Policy in Washington, DC. Throughout an intensive five-year period, efforts in Dayton, OH, Little Rock, AR, Pittsburgh, PA, Savannah, GA, and Bridgeport, CT, were studied and analyzed.[31] The research was unable to document any significant improvements in dropout, pregnancy, or employment rates attributable to the program. Even the students with intensive case management did no better than others. According to Douglas Nelson of the Casey Foundation, the key lesson learned was that "in low-income communities, service system and institutional-change initiatives, by themselves, cannot transform poor educational, social, and health outcomes for vulnerable children."[32] The results of the New Futures initiatives were generally considered disappointing.

Despite the early negative reviews, the Chatham-Savannah Youth Futures

Authority, created by state legislation, has moved ahead to overcome some of the problems experienced in the other communities. The effort there involves a large number of collaborators—more than eighty community "stakeholders" participate in Savannah's ongoing planning process. Community agencies provide many services such as case management, after-school programs, health and mental health programs delivered in a family resource center, middle and high schools, company worksites, and churches. More recent evaluation results were presented at a Department of Education conference on school-linked services:

> Dropout and retention rates have decreased while failure and suspension rates have increased . . . however, many remedial interventions at the middle school level have been effective in helping the highest risk students, but expected long-term positive outcomes for these students have not been observed. Evaluating the success of the collaborative in terms of its capacity as an organizing mechanism for services has yielded positive results.

The Savannah group believes that this collaboration has reduced the duplication of services to a minimum, eliminated competition for resources, and raised consciousness among media and policy makers about the condition of children.

FAILURE TO INVOLVE PARENTS AND PEERS

Don Davies, director of the Center on Families, Communities, Schools, and Children's Learning at Northeastern University in Boston, suggests that we

> visit 10 schools randomly . . . and you will discover in nine of them that most teachers and administrators still hold parents at arm's length. You'll see many of the tried-and-true forms of parent involvement—an open house in the fall, two or three short parent conferences a year, parents attending student performances and sports events, some teachers calling parents when a child is misbehaving, an annual multicultural fair . . . but you'll observe few if any parents . . . actively involved in the school's efforts to make changes in curriculum, student rules, homework policies, or scheduling.[33]

A few programs have been mentioned in this book that have successfully involved parents—Parents as Teachers, Success for All, IS218, among others. Practitioners, however, generally report that they have a hard time getting parents to attend workshops or to participate in school restructuring efforts, particularly parents of older students. At the same time, parents report lack of responsiveness and communication on the part of school personnel. The Fifth Ward Improvement project reported a decline in the participation of their parental support group because they lacked a designated staff person who could arrange transportation to meetings, make home visits, and facilitate communication. David Hawkins attributed the positive outcomes resulting from the Social Development Model to the modification of classroom practices by the teachers rather than to family management training. Few parents participated.

Few of the models presented in this book feature same-age peers as mentors or counselors, a component frequently mentioned in the previous book. One example of the change in program models with regard to peer involvement can be seen in Life Skills Training. Although the program had previously incorporated the use of peer leaders, the more recent work concentrates entirely on teacher-led programs, with strong evidence of the importance of teacher training. Marion Howard found that in replications of Postponing Sexual Involvement, the peer leaders were inadequately recruited and trained. Very little has been added to the literature since 1990 concerning the use of same-age peer counselors. The very successful Valued Youth Partnership model uses much older, high-risk youth to tutor younger children, not same-age peers.

WHY PROGRAMS FAIL

Programs that fail often do not include many factors we have seen were integral parts of successful youth programs. In some cases, program leaders believe that they are on the right track, but their implementation is too weak to be effective. I have rarely visited a program when the host failed to say, "This is not a typical day." A small sample of what went wrong that day includes, "The janitor didn't clean up, the social worker is sick, the school principal who promised to show up to meet you was called to another meeting, and there are usually many more kids here."

Lack of Sufficient Resources

I have not dwelt on the issue of the money needed to support youth programs, but let us just agree that it is essential. No program can flourish without adequate support to pay for staff and facilities. However, some programs with sufficient support still are ineffective.

Poor Replication

We have previously looked at the issue of fidelity. Replication is often very difficult, particularly in the absence of adequate resources and training. The availability of manuals, guidebooks, curricula, and, most recently, videos and teleconferencing does not assure competent replication. Often the person who created the original successful model is no longer in the picture, and the replicator lacks that person's skill, commitment, or "know-how."

Poor Leadership

We have talked about charismatic leaders and strong principals. But some programs are run by people who do not seem to have the right personality for the job. One intensive case-management program that we visited in a very deprived inner city had a director who just plain turned us off. We observed her first at a small staff meeting with four community-based workers, and later at a large meeting with school staff. With her own staff, she seemed quite disinterested, offering little in the way of advice or leadership when confronted with the difficult problems these people were encountering. At the larger meeting, which she ran, she seemed to lack focus, allowing the session to run on and on and on, tying up the time of twenty busy people, including two school principals. Several distressing cases were presented—a family in which truancy was excessive, a suspected child-molesting stepfather, a special education student who needed a lot of support. When cases were presented, she did not direct the discussion along channels that might be helpful, but just allowed everyone to have his say, whether or not it was relevant. Perhaps these observations are biased by the fact that she paid little attention to us. In fact, repeated attempts to follow up with phone calls were unsuccessful; she never returned our calls.

I do not know whether this is just an instance of "bad vibes" or a poorly run program. Perhaps, if the program director had a made a big fuss over me, I might have thought the program was terrific. But I still would take issue with the practice as I observed it at the meetings.

Overselling

The experience with the disinterested leader took place in a site that was replicating a national program that had received a lot of publicity. The national organization had gained considerable media coverage when its demonstration models were first evaluated and found to have positive effects. A representative of the organization at the national headquarters arranged for us to visit a site that closely followed the model. In fact, a very unobtrusive staff member from the national group who was conducting a process evaluation accompanied us. In a subsequent discussion with her, she did not perceive the leader as disinterested, and said that that was her usual mode of behavior. No one at the national organization could tell us the details of how this program was organized nor how much it cost. Yet the president of the organization continues to be quoted in the media as a great authority on effective programming, based on this program model.

Overloading

Some programs take on a larger challenge than they can handle. After the doors open, the problems are overwhelming. As one school-based clinic practitioner told me, "The first day we were in business, a 14-year-old girl came in and told us that she was being sexually abused by her mother's boyfriend. She had never told anyone else in the school, but I guess she thought we were more equipped to deal with her situation confidentially." The clinic staff had to stop everything, work with the girl intensively, contact her mother, contact the authorities, and make sure that the man could no longer molest the girl. I have heard similar stories in every clinic I have visited. No one expects that the young people in schools will have so many problems, particularly with stress and depression.

Poor Theory

Many programs fail because they are just too simplistic and not adequately focused on the broad needs of young people. For quite some time, people have believed that if teenagers "Just Say No," teenage pregnancy will "go away." By now, the evidence has mounted that programs focused only on abstention have had very little impact on pregnancy rates. The reason these approaches have been so ineffective is that they are "developmentally inappropriate." Teenagers want to make their own decisions about their behaviors.

Another theory that seems to backfire is that teenagers can be frightened out of their behavioral modes. Exposing juvenile delinquents to hardened criminals has resulted in more, not less, acting out. Media-based interventions are grounded in the theory that teenagers model their behavior after what they see on television or at the movies. The research on the impact of media on violence and sexual behavior is equivocal.

A study of selected programs by Martha Burt and colleagues at the Urban Institute found that traditional services are likely to concentrate on only one category of behavior (sex or drugs or school failure). Their study goes on to say:

> Such programs usually focus on problems (rather than individuals as a whole) and tend to offer short-term interventions. Programs that try to solve problems quickly and then close the case are not geared toward preventive interventions and have little staying power . . . they do not always address the most pressing needs of their clients . . . [and] it is difficult to get other community agencies to fill in the gaps.[34]

Unrealistic Expectations

Some practitioners expect magic but as you can see, it is not easy to produce desired changes in the behaviors that programs target. And it is even harder to prove that the impacts are really there. The RESPECT project in Philadelphia is an excellent example of good theory, good intentions, and probably good practice that had virtually no effect—or at least, no proven effect—on the target population. I am certain that the practitioners were very disappointed at the results. Yet it would be wrong to conclude from that experience that enhanced family planning clinic services and community outreach should not be encouraged. It would be correct to conclude that it was an appropriate intervention, good but not sufficient, and that something else would be required to assure outcomes.

Programs fail because of people, facilities, policies, turf issues, and a myriad of other reasons. When you think about the number of barriers to implementation, it is all the more surprising that many programs are able to overcome these problems and produce successful outcomes.

PART IV

VISIONS AND STRATEGIES

Susie Fitzhugh, Photographer

10

SAFE PASSAGE PARENTS

Adolescents don't want you to disappear; they want you to be just around the corner when they need you.

—James Comer, "At the Crossroads"

We know what young people need to achieve Safe Passage in our risky society: supportive parents or another attached adult, strong cognitive skills, social competency, room to experiment, visible opportunities, exposure to the labor force, and a sense of safety. I have critiqued the "state of the art" of meeting these needs and visited many effective programs. And I have identified certain universal factors that contribute to the success of all kinds of programs: one-on-one attention, educational enhancement, social-skills training, parental involvement, community service, and incentives. Organizational arrangements that appear to foster good programming encompass comprehensive, one-stop, multicomponent efforts; use of community-outreach workers and community police; and location in schools and community settings. Examplary programs have been shown to be sensitive to cultural diversity and to listen to the voices of youth. They are based on appropriate theories and use proven practices.

I have also explored the barriers to implementing programs and looked at issues that need to be resolved. Of course, funding is a pervasive problem—both securing it and maintaining it. Other questions focus on targeting populations, working out turf struggles, and training staff.

Enough is known about youth programming to proceed with laying out an agenda for assuring Safe Passage. What should this country look like to the next group of young people who enter their adolescent years? To secure Safe Passage, they should live in households that are relatively stable and serene, with parents who can attend to their needs. They should go to schools that are creative and organized to meet the requirements for each individual to find a course of study that will be rewarding and challenging (and consistent with the labor-force needs of the future). They should live in communities where people work together to build a strong environment that is physically and psychologically safe and offers a wide array of opportunities for social development.

In this part of the book, I present my ideas about what parents, schools, communities, and the nation and its fifty states as a whole would have to do to make this Safe Passage picture a reality. One chapter is devoted to each sphere. This chapter focuses on effective parenting.

PARENTS: HOW CAN THEY ASSURE SAFE PASSAGE?

The goal for parents in this strategy is to help children form strong attachments to responsible adults so that the children can successfully move through adolescence into their own adulthoods. Of course, we need to think about what families can do to assist their own children, but that is not sufficient. Parents can play important roles in the lives of all children through their participation in school and community efforts. Although I am not an expert on parent-child relationships, I will share with you some ideas and concepts accumulated over the years from research and observation. For those parents who are seeking more personal advice, many excellent books are available.[1]

Authoritative Parenting

Not all research results pass the test of intuition. One body of research that does makes complete sense, however, distinguishes between types of parents defined as authoritative, authoritarian, or permissive.[2] This theoretical construct has been challenged, but the ideas behind it work for me.

Authoritative parents are the most likely to rear children who are successful in just about every area, including school. These parents create a structured environment for young people in which limits are clearly defined and articulated. The child is made to feel responsible for functioning well within the structure, and the parental role is to assist the child to do so. The parent is supportive but also allows leeway for the child to experiment and make mistakes. Above all, the child feels accepted and valued.

Authoritarian parents set up rigid rules for their children and expect them to obey under all circumstances. Permissive parents are "hands off" and back away from any form of discipline or structure. Of course, parenting practices vary from day to day. Consistency is difficult to maintain given the changeability of teenagers and the complexity of situations that arise in contemporary living.

It is easier to tell someone to be an authoritative parent than for them actually to accomplish that style. It is hard to establish boundaries and to balance rewards and appropriate discipline. Many difficult questions include when and where children can come and go, how much home responsibility such as child care or kitchen duty, should be assigned to young people how much parents should be involved with homework, when the television can be on, which friends are acceptable and which are not, and what length of hair and style of clothes are acceptable. Hugh Price, the president of the National Urban League, points out that this is the first generation of adults afraid for and afraid of their own children.

Engagement

Laurence Steinberg wrote a book called *Beyond the Classroom* that created quite a stir.[2] After years of studying thousands of students and their families, he concluded that the problem with schools was not so much a failure of school reform as it was a failure of parents to be involved. According to him, more than a quarter of all parents have "checked out of childrearing."[3] Many of the students reported that they could bring home grades of C or worse, and their parents were not concerned. One-third said their parents had no idea what they did in school and, even more parents, never visited the child's school. Yet parents seemed to think that they were more engaged than they appeared to be from their child's point of view.

Engagement in school means attending back-to-school nights, visiting with teachers in classrooms, and helping select teachers or courses each year. If a child is experiencing difficulty, parents have to find out how to work with the school to solve the problem. Increasingly, parents are being invited to join in new school reorganization efforts as members of planning committees. Most significantly, parents have to convey to children from the earliest years that doing well in school is their most important task.

I always had difficulty intervening in school situations. My son was a classic underachiever, at least that is what the school frequently said. Whenever trouble loomed, usually over assignments undone, I sided with the school—I could never bring myself to challenge that authoritarian system that I thought surely must know what it was doing. In retrospect (since my son seems to be quite well-educated now), I was too timid to suggest that he might have been in the wrong classroom with a teacher who was not equipped to deal with restless boys. I hesitated to help too much with the backlog of incomplete homework, thinking that I might "spoil" him. Living in a small community, we tended to know and to castigate parents as "pushy" if they interfered too much in their children's education.

What parents strive for is that happy medium: the authoritative mode of engaged parenting that sets the child on a path toward achievement, facilitates learning, but expects the child to move forward independently to every degree possible.

Single Parents Can Succeed

It is not the number of parents but the quality of parenting that makes a difference. One authoritative mother or father can bring up children more effectively than two parents who are not functioning well or who are not in step with each other. Hard as the responsibility is for a single parent, she or he can shape the strategy of childrearing without interference from anyone else. Of course, this scenario becomes complicated by the presence of grandparents, who must share the single parent's convictions about raising children. And, in the case of shared custody, which puts the child in the home of the other parent from time to time, it is especially important to set standards as part of the custody agreement. So many children today are expected to grow up in complex family configurations with serial relationships, multiple marriages, gay or lesbian parents, half-sisters and- brothers, and rotating grandparents. It is very important during these times of changing family structures that childrearing styles remain consistent and that the child be secure in knowing that he or she can always lean on at least one strong adult.

Consistency

One of the most difficult situations for a child is to get caught between parents who have different parenting styles. The child may turn to the more permissive parent for approval of questionable activities, such as staying out late, and set up a conflict with the less permissive parent who believes in early curfews. Although many practitioners have focused on the importance of parent-child communication, communication between parents is a necessary precondition to successful childrearing. The earlier parents can join together to think through their joint strategies and approaches, the greater the chances that these policies and practices will be implemented.

Role Models

Parents are, for better or worse, role models for their children. Adults who drink heavily or smoke have a difficult time establishing credibility when they try to discourage their children from using substances. Single parents who act out sexually without discretion have a negative impact on their teenagers' ability to conduct responsible sexual relationships. Attitudes toward jobs are first observed within the home, and in some communities, many children are growing up with very little exposure to adults with successful connections to the labor force.

Parents can introduce their children to admirable adults who can serve as role models, seeking out people with interesting occupations, diverse ethnic traditions, or a high level of community involvement. In the life stories of resilient people, you almost always find tributes to a parent or teacher, to a clergyman, neighbor, or cousin who strongly influenced the life course of the person when he or she was young.

Responsibility at Home

Young people should be encouraged to participate in family life through chores and defined responsibilities. Parents have to find an appropriate balance between demands and exploitation. The chores have to be appropriate and not interfere with school time or time with friends. Many children today are overburdened with after-school child-care responsibilities for younger siblings, covering for mothers who have jobs. Other children expect to be waited on hand and foot with no sense of responsibility for the welfare of the family. Routine chores related to cooking, housekeeping, and gardening can be scheduled for children from the earliest years, with a view toward exposure to new skills and the future demands of the labor force.

Help Youth Find Jobs

The research is ambiguous about whether working for pay while still in high school is beneficial or destructive.[4] Like other social phenomena, it depends on the degree to which work time takes over from other responsibilities. It appears that working more than twenty hours per week while enrolled in high school can have damaging effects on both school and social behavior, but working ten hours or less has not been seen to be deleterious. My own view is that a part-time job during the school year and full-time summer employment can be an enriching experience for youth, both in terms of gaining social competency skills and cash for incidentals.

As a child during the Depression, I started working outside the home at about age 12, at first motivated by the need for cash to buy peer-acceptable clothes that my parents did not consider essential. Beginning with babysitting, moving on to clerking in the local department store, then staffing the dry cleaners, I finally ended up as a companion to an elderly woman. Actually, the woman, who was around 50, was an alcoholic with a broken leg, and my job was to make gin and tonics for her all day long. This early exposure to alcoholism taught me a strong lesson in the consequences of drinking. That job ceased abruptly one afternoon when she rattled off a stream of invectives against the Jews. I could put up with her behavior but not her racist attitudes, so I told her that I would no longer work for her. All those experiences made me feel very grown-up and independent, and exposed me to different kinds of people and challenges.

Sometimes it is difficult for young people to find appropriate employment, in which case it is appropriate for parents to assist them through personal contacts. When I was the director of research at the Alan Guttmacher Institute, people from Hastings would call me all the time to find summer jobs for their teenage children. I even employed my own son for one project, just as my parents employed my friend Nancy and me to work in their dress factory when the schools closed down for lack of coal during World War II.

Every teenager does not need to obtain a paying job, however. Community-service experiences are very rewarding and often better learning opportunities than the typical McDonald's. Parents can help in finding volunteer placements for their children—for example, at the local senior citizen home or child care center. For young people with strong vocational or avocational interests, parents can guide them toward securing internships in health agencies, university research departments, libraries, police departments, or other specialized sites. Many schools now require that a limited number of hours be spent doing some form of community service.

Help Youth with Schoolwork

Households that foster learning are much more likely to produce achieving children. Homework help when offered in a constructive way is very important, as is creating a quiet environment where good study habits are promoted. Dianne Scott-Jones suggests that parents establish rules regarding homework, including a routine and schedule for studying and completion of assignments.[5] She also believes time on the telephone, television viewing, and visits with friends should be restricted in order to ensure sufficient time for school work. In her view, parents should check to make sure school assignments are completed and stimulate discussion with the child about the substance of the school work.

When young people have interests that take them out of the neighborhood, such as music lessons or specialized sports events, parents have to arrange for transportation or for someone else to escort the child. For working parents, or those without cars, this can be very difficult. Sometimes other parents will help out.

Like all aspects of parenthood, it is hard to find the right balance. I have observed parents who are so concerned about their children that they are too intrusive in their efforts to help, commandeering the child's life and living vicariously through their children.

Studies of individuals at the tops of their professions have shown that they came from child-centered, though not necessarily well-adjusted, families. As children, they received considerable attention from their parents. The parents served as models for a strong work ethic and high standards, encouraged productive use of time, and expected high-quality performance. Mihaly Csikszentmihalyi and colleagues conclude from their study of talented teens that "a home environment in which one is secure enough to feel cheerful and energetic, and challenged enough to become more goal directed, increases teenagers' chances of progressively refining their talents."[6]

Cultural Surroundings

Being read to at early ages is fundamental to the development of language and the ability to read. I once heard James Comer say that if children are not read to before they are 5, they will have great difficulty ever learning to read. The same principle applies to listening to music. Having access to books, art, and music strengthens children's cognitive abilities as well as their cultural appreciation as they mature. All of this enrichment is available through public libraries, but parents have to take the initiative, at least initially, to help their child obtain a card, choose the books, and return them on time. If children are taught to use the library early in life, it will be a major resource as they grow older.

Too much television, playing video games, and hanging out on the Internet are all major issues in many contemporary households. As we have seen, many teenagers spend most of their waking hours in front of a screen of one kind or another. Some parents have successfully regulated television hours, and others have managed to help their children become engaged in alternative cultural or recreational activities that are more rewarding. Selected television shows can serve as useful times for togetherness and triggering communication. During election season, the whole family might be encouraged to watch political debates and then have a debate of their own. Musical events on television or radio can be shared.

Conversation begins at home. If a child grows up with a lot of dialogue with parents as a matter of course, this practice may be found continue during the adolescent years. Games are also a powerful communication tool. Our family has always been addicted to charades, Scrabble, and Boggle. Charades is an excellent tool for turning a distant teenager into an engaging show-off as he acts out legitimately in front of the assembled family and friends.

Sports are another way of having fun with young people. Tossing a ball back and forth or into a hoop is a wonderful way to lessen tension and open communication channels. (This has become standard practice on television, family sit-coms.) Swimming or dancing together are other great joint activities.

Authoritative parents play with their children. Authoritarian ones bully them into joining competitive teams and then chastise them if they don't perform well. Permissive parents don't get involved in their children's sporting life at all.

Religious groups have built-in rites of passage, with Bar and Bas Mitzvahs, First Communions and Confirmations, and other coming-of-age ceremonies. Taken seriously, these are important family events that can serve as opportunities for communication between generations. Families can create their own rites, celebrating achievements or special events. Observation of holidays can draw together extended families and help teenagers appreciate their family history and roots.

Food is a universal component of togetherness. In our multicultural family, we have several annual events (Passover, Thanksgiving, Christmas) that require contributions of food from all participants. Traditions evolve with each new generation. The addition of our grandchildren has introduced us to the celebration of the Chinese New Year.

Birthdays are, of course, a most important date. Teenagers approach their birthdays with mixed feelings, reflecting their ambivalence toward taking on adult responsibilities and risks and leaving behind what for some of them seemed like carefree years. Birthdays open up special moments for parents to relate to their children. Families should try to create birthday celebrations without an overdependence on expensive gifts and parties, but that is so hard to avoid in our market economy.

Involvement in Social Issues

The welfare of each child in this country is dependent on the welfare of all the others. Parents must become leaders in advocating for strategies that build strong schools and communities for everyone. It is not just a matter of caring about your own child's education: All parents have to indicate their concern for that famous "village" that raises the children. One of the most important lessons that children can learn is commitment to social progress, and the best way to learn that lesson is to see parents as active participants.

Young people, consciously or unconsciously, mirror their parents' social attitudes. Young Republicans and Young Democrats most frequently report that they come from homes that are strongly affiliated with those political parties. The idea that children always rebel against their parents by adopting antithetical views is not borne out by public opinion polls or surveys. As Donald Roberts points out, "Considerable intergenerational continuity exists between most parents and their adolescent children in fundamental values concerning morality, marriage and sex, race, and religious and political orientations."[7] Peer and media influences are sizable, but parents, at least initially, have the strongest effects on young people's values and can play a significant role in shaping the values of the next generation.

One area in particular that parents must address is race relations. Children must be exposed to and learn to respect people who are different from them.

America in the twenty-first century will be increasingly multicultural and multiracial. Our society has little hope of avoiding racial and class controversy, or even warfare, unless the next generation is brought up to believe in the values of equal rights. As we have seen, the chances for Safe Passage are less certain for poor children of color than for others. Denying certain groups opportunities for success will not only diminish the quality of life for the disadvantaged groups, it will also undermine the whole society and lower the quality of life for everyone.

For the involved parent, this means taking specific steps to work together with young people on these issues. Church youth groups have been very effective at creating cross-cultural events and providing services to the needy, such as homeless families. Many schools have international exchanges that offer teenagers the chance to experience other cultures through either travel to another country or by hosting an exchange student for a year. These kinds of activities should be encouraged, but they are not sufficient to break through the racial walls that exist throughout the country.

Families should consider the neighborhood they live in. Are all the people the same, or do they represent the racial groups who live in the wider area? Parents should pay attention to the racial and social mix of the schools their children attend and play leadership roles in developing strategies for equal representation.

One critical issue that arises in making choices about where to live and what schools children should attend is often stated as: Can I sacrifice my children's educational opportunities to my own social beliefs? During the last presidential election, the fact that Chelsea Clinton attended an elite Washington school was used as an argument in favor of school vouchers for private and parochial schools. My own answer to this difficult question is, No, you cannot consciously send your child to a school with low educational standards and dangerous settings. But you can work very hard along with other community members to try to upgrade the quality of public education so that future generations do not have such difficult choices to make.

AND SOMETIMES PARENTS ARE NOT ENOUGH

A family could provide a warm, stimulating, constructive environment with all the "correct" components and still have unresponsive teenage children. Some adolescents feel the need to "turn off" their parents as part of the separation process. It is difficult for parents to distinguish between the normal rebellion that takes place during most youth development and extreme rejection.

Get Help

Many people find parenthood an overwhelming challenge. Fortunately, various forms of help are available in most communities. Parents can obtain "effectiveness" training, which addresses many of the issues already raised—for example, communication, discipline, and establishing structure. Courses are available from community organizations, Parent-Teacher Associations, mental health centers, Parents as Teachers, and other agencies. Organizing an informal group of parents from the neighborhood, housing project, or church can also be a useful way to share experiences and learn from others. At the very least, parents need to be reassured that they are not the only ones perplexed by all the complex issues surrounding their children's healthy development.

Parenting Is Like a Youth Program

The principles I have set out in this book for practitioners are not really different from those for parents. What works to produce effective programs also works to produce effective parents: early intervention, one-on-one attention, role modeling, high aspirations for educational achievement, teaching social competency, and exposure to the world of work. As with programs, no *one* component, no *single* effort by parents, will have as great an impact as a well-planned, multidimensional strategy that is thoroughly communicated to the family.

AFTERTHOUGHT: WHAT ABOUT SEX?

As I read over the final draft of this chapter, I realized that something important was missing: how parents should deal with the thorny and controversial issues surrounding sexual development. This is particularly significant in light of the fact that, for many years, my area of expertise has been the prevention of teenage pregnancy. I have given many lectures advocating open communication between you and your child about sex, making sure that your child can make responsible decisions about whether to do it and with whom, and being certain that when your teenager becomes sexually active that she or he knows where to go for birth control. When my son was growing up, I certainly communicated about reproduction in great detail. But I have to admit that the open communication stopped short when he became a teenager.

I was reminded of my own inability to deal with the situation when I found this on the Internet recently in a parenting chat room.

> I found a condom in my 14 year old son's drawer when I was putting away his socks. He doesn't have a steady girlfriend. I asked him about it and he said he just wanted to be prepared. This made me very uncomfortable. I think that 14 is too young to be "getting prepared" and I told him so. He got really angry and said I shouldn't have been snooping in his drawer in the first place. He also asked if I would rather have him get AIDS. Of course I don't want him to get AIDS, but I don't want him to start having sex yet either! My husband just laughed it off and said that our son was fantasizing. I want my husband to talk to my son but he says he's staying out of this one. Am I overreacting or is my husband underreacting?

All I can add to this discussion is to advise using the same parenting style in regard to sexual development as to adolescent development in general. The authoritative message is "learn to be responsible for yourself" instead of the authoritarian "just say no" or the permissive "just have fun." Communication of that message has to start early—not at the time of crisis. And parents need to agree on appropriate strategies. The same principles apply to other high risk behaviors—smoking and drinking, driving recklessly, skipping school, hanging out with unreliable peers—the list is scary.

Parenting in the twenty-first century will not be easy. Parents have multiple and complex roles to play in the Safe Passage Movement. They must find pathways for their own children to succeed and to be protected. Parents must also offer leadership in paving the way for all children, recognizing that the demands of the twenty-first century will require new approaches to solving human problems.

Debbie Kates, Photographer

11

SAFE PASSAGE SCHOOLS

Rachel's Ideas for What Would Make a Good School

1. Good teachers

2. Good children who can learn and work hard

3. Good rooms decorated with banners like "Welcome to School"

4. A good principal—if he or she lets things be fair

5. A "listening center" as well as a "reading center"

6. If you're feeling unhappy, you should be able to call your mom or dad and talk about it.

—Rachel Meltzer, Second Grader

W

e have visited some innovative and exciting schools that are responsive to today's youth and their families. You have heard about successful school restructuring experiences following carefully designed programs. Admittedly, these exemplary places are largely demonstration projects in the early stages of replication. Yet they are producing ample evidence that change is possible, that school systems can evolve into new kinds of institutions that will fit better with the requirements of the twenty-first century. Whether the changes occur depends a lot upon whether the American people articulate their demands for schools that work and are willing to provide the support for implementing well-designed school programs.

I do not mean to imply that it is only the educational establishment that is responsible for implementing these strategies. Neither am I promoting a "cookie cutter" approach to changing schools. If there is one strong lesson that comes out of these observations, it is that *one size does not fit all*. In fact, much of the conflict in the school reform movements centers on the tension between the demand for autonomy and the pressure for enforcing standards of achievement. One approach that is gaining popularity is to allow every school (not just every school district) to create an institution that is appropriate in that neighborhood and works well for those students and their teachers. The concept of charter schools is germane to the idea of shaping new kinds of schools, but it may dampen efforts to make systemic changes in public education that will impact equally on all high-risk children and their families.

As a framework for this chapter, I have spun out my thoughts about what one responsive Safe Passage school might look like. Many of the ideas were inspired by my visits to IS218, the Children's Aid Society school in New York; the Turner School in Philadelphia; and the Hanshaw School in Modesta, California, as well as by observations of other exemplary programs.[1] I really do think of these places as combining new educational concepts with old-fashioned settlement house values—or, as I put it before, the marriage of John Dewey and Jane Addams.

VISION OF A SAFE PASSAGE SCHOOL

This Safe Passage school is an inner-city middle school with 1,000 students in grades 6 to 8. The building is clean, well-lit, and has windows that work and a heating system that functions. It is open from 7 A.M. until 10 P.M. seven days a week, all year round. The walls are covered with bulletin boards that feature student work.

This school is constituted through the City Board of Education, which has allowed the principal and the teachers considerable leeway in designing the curriculum. A Safe Passage Support System offers all the services needed in the school and is operated under the direction of a full-time coordinator who must facilitate the participation of community agencies. The two efforts are integrated through the Safe Passage Consortium made up of representatives of the school staff, the parent association, local health department, local social service agency, probation office, community police, mental health agency, Urban League, and youth organizations (Girls Inc., Boys and Girls Clubs). Students are also members of the consortium. The principal and the coordinator have joint responsibility for the school, with the turf divided between educational initiatives and support services. Their offices are contiguous.

The educational program divides the school into five separate houses (academies, magnets) of 200 students each. Eight teachers and a director are responsible for each house. The same students stay together for three years. Houses are named Arts, Business, Science and Math, Health Careers, and Classics. In addition to teaching staff, experts (paid and volunteer) in these subject areas are brought in from the community to work in the various disciplines. The curriculum for each house is designed by the teachers in conjunction with consultants. Basic core courses must be covered (English, math, social sciences, physical sciences), but they are shaped to fit within the specialized house themes. Although the official school day runs from 9 A.M. until 3 P.M., classes may run for several hours within a flexible schedule.

In addition to forty house teachers, twenty guides—counselor-mentors—are assigned to houses to act as case managers for students with problems and to oversee the welfare of the others. Thus, each house has four full-time guides. This school does not organize its pupil personnel services following the traditional mode. All the psychosocial services, including guidance counseling, psychological testing, and social work fall under the domain of the Safe Passage Support System.

Prior to entry into this school, all children are given a Safe Passage Assessment by a teacher-guide team. The parent is not present at that time, but if possible is invited to the school for a separate interview. The youth interview and survey protocol serve several functions. The school finds out about the child's interests and skills, information necessary for assisting the student to decide which house to enter. The survey protocol also includes questions about problems so that staff is informed about what issues must be addressed after the student enters the school. The interview ascertains who is the responsible adult in the family to whom the child is attached, and if no family member is identified, the school informs the guide who is assigned to the child. The guide must make a home visit and, if necessary, act as case manager or find a suitable adult to take this responsibility.

Support services are designed to meet the needs of the children and their families. The Safe Passage Assessment includes a health-screening section as well as questions about drugs, sex, alcohol, depression, access to weapons, nutrition, and exercise. The parent interview targets what support services are needed. The Safe Passage Assessment is the first basic document in the Safe Passage Record that is set up for each student, which tracks events over the three years of enrollment. All the components of the school have computerized forms that are entered into the record, including achievement scores, attendance at school, use of services, family involvement, and participation in after-school activities. At the end of each school year, students write a self-evaluation, which is used as a tool for planning the next year's program and future educational plans.

During the summer prior to the first year of the Safe Passage School, the principal, teachers, and other staff, along with the coordinator and key support workers, spend many hours designing the curriculum and organizing the school. During the school year, house teachers meet for several hours weekly to work on the curriculum, adding new materials and developing special projects for students. Weekly meetings are also held for all school and support workers to share information and spark new ideas.

A special curriculum is used that addresses the new morbidities (sex, drugs, and violence) and uses the latest techniques in teaching social skills. This health-promotion curriculum is taught by the support staff (not by teachers) on Wednesday afternoons while the teaching staff have their planning sessions. Some of the Wednesday afternoon sessions are used for special group counseling, for which the students are placed into groups according to their particular needs—for example, family relations, bereavement, depression, sexual issues, substance abuse, and conflict resolution. The guides staff these sessions along with volunteers.

Universities constitute one source of volunteers. Each house is connected to a university, usually through one related department such as arts, sciences, medicine, or business. University faculty are encouraged to assist with curriculum development, and university students assist teachers in the school. They organize after-school activities and schoolwide events. The universities are encouraged to invite the middle school students to their campuses to see what college life has to offer and to establish connections for the future.

The support services envisioned for this Safe Passage School include a family resource center; health, mental health, and dental care center; after-school learning center; after-school recreation; and evening activities for parents and other community members. The family resource center houses offices for the guides as well as additional staff who can assist parents with problems concerning welfare, housing, immigration, justice, or employment. Space is available in the family resource center for parents to sit and have refreshments. Parent education books and videos are available, along with a directory of community resources and announcements of cultural and recreational events in the area. The Parent Association also has space in the resource center to use for recruiting and training parent volunteers to act as classroom aides and to help out with school functions.

The guides and other family workers are outstationed from community agencies, including the Department of Social Services, the Community Action Agency, and the Community Mental Health Center. Some of the guides are graduate students who commit for a year of internship. Five of the guides are from AmeriCorps, the federally sponsored program that assigns people to programs for disadvantaged youth. A specially trained community police officer is assigned to the family resource center to help families and their children deal with the justice system, but also to act as a family or child advocate through the center.

The health and mental health center provides primary health care, dental health, and mental health counseling to the students and their families. It is staffed by two full-time nurse practitioners, a medical assistant, four social workers, and two health educators. This center is associated with a local community health center that is a managed-care organization. The school guidance counselor and school psychologist are also located in this center. Additional part-time staff include a pediatrician, dentist, dental assistant, psychiatrist, and other specialists available for consultations. The health center has a back-up arrangement with the local hospital for emergency care and hospitalization.

The school opens at 7 A.M. for breakfast, homework help, and recreation. The after-school program is open to all the students and offers school-related programs such as homework help, more advanced classes, computer work, or training in English as a Second Language (ESL). The gymnasium is open for sports, and board games are put out for those who want to learn and play chess, Scrabble, and Monopoly. Art workshops are available, as is instruction in music and dance. All of these activities are staffed by outstationed workers from other agencies as well as volunteers.

One corner of the school is furnished with a few couches and comfortable chairs where students can just "chill out," sit around, and talk quietly. The student council is responsible for the upkeep of this corner and for enforcing behavioral standards to maintain quiet and calm.

In the evening, parents and other community members attend classes in aerobics, computers, ESL, business skills, cooking, cultural subjects, and other classes suggested by the Consortium. The parents organize frequent food events that bring whole families in for celebratory dinners.

Across the street from the school in what was a vacant lot is the Safe Passage Garden and Park. This area has been transformed by the students, the staff, and the parents, working together to create a minifarm for growing fresh produce and flowers, and an urban park with a little playground for neighborhood toddlers. Every student at Safe Passage has a job in the school, garden, park, or community. The students operate a play group after school for toddlers where they receive training in child development. The Business House operates the Safe Passage Store where the produce is sold, as well as other products that the students believe to be commercially viable. Art works from the Arts House are also on sale here.

Many, many people are in the Safe Passage School every day. Table 11.1 summarizes what the staffing and organization look like. The principal works closely with the academic staff to stimulate the development of a challenging curriculum and an intellectual school climate. The coordinator works with the support staff and volunteers to ensure high-quality services and, under the di-

---

TABLE 11.1   Organization of a Safe Passage School

School System	Community Agencies
People supported by the city Board of Education	People supported by funds from United Way or local foundations, or contributed by participating agencies

---

Principal	**Safe Passage Coordinator**
Assistant principal	20 guides
5 House Directors	5 from AmeriCorps
40 Teachers	15 relocated from local agencies, or
Consultants (including some volunteers)	graduate school interns
Librarian	Family resource center coordinator
Custodial staff	Health, mental health, dental center staff: nurse practitioners, social workers, health educators, dentist, aides
Guidance counselor*	Community police officer
Psychologist*	University faculty and students
	Other volunteers

---

*May be supported by school system or by outside agency.

rection of the Consortium, brokers new components of service with community agencies. Everyone has to communicate frequently to make sure that the school is perceived by the students and their parents as an integrated, full-service educational institution that is fully responsive to their needs.

The academic component of the school is paid for by the city Board of Education at the same rate as other schools—in this city, about $5,000 per child, or about $5 million per year. The support services are funded from many sources. The school budget covers the guidance counselor and the psychologist. United Way underwrites the coordinator's office and some support staff. A state grant funds the health clinic, and a foundation grant the family resource center. Other community agencies donate personnel. The twenty guides are primarily outstationed staff from local agencies, university interns, or AmeriCorps members. Many services are performed by volunteers. If all the services were contracted for, the additional bill would be close to $1 million, or another $1,000 per child per year.

WILL THIS SCHOOL ENSURE SAFE PASSAGE?

The chances are excellent that if a young person were to attend such a school, he or she would be more likely to succeed than someone who went to a traditional school. This vision incorporates almost every aspect of successful programs, all integrated into a student-family-centered institution. Although it would be preferable for schools to be small, in most cities that is an unrealistic goal. But if the design incorporates the principles of building small integrated units—houses or academies of no more than 200 students—I think it is possible to create an environment that can compensate for a large size. Granted, this example starts and ends with middle school. The assumption here is that all schools within a community would encompass the same principles of creativity, flexibility, and high expectations, along with one-stop access to necessary services. Even without total system changes, exposure for three years to a Safe Passage School could make a huge difference in the lives of young people (as we have seen from the examples in the earlier chapters).

CAN THE VISION BECOME A REALITY?

I used to work with a man who after reading my work would say, "Have you been smoking hashish?" That may be your reaction to the idea that one could take the Safe Passage School described here and replicate it across the nation. Of course, many of our 85,000 public schools, especially those in suburbia, already provide Safe Passage, in the sense that most of the students feel challenged by their experiences and they graduate and go on for higher education. I believe that school systems in suburbia are already moving in this direction, opening their doors to community agencies and responding to the needs of contemporary families. My thinking is shaped by the schools that are not so successful. Many of them are in deprived urban areas and in bleak rural communities. What will it take to create programs that are modeled after this vision in all the places that need them?

Safe Passage Schools cannot grow out of thin air. People in the community have to figure out how to put these institutions together. At least one research and development center is ready to help those who want to create a similar model. CRESPAR, the Center for Research on the Education of Students Placed at Risk, at Johns Hopkins University in Baltimore, co-directed by Robert Slavin and Wade Boykin, is in the process of organizing pilot projects called Talent Development schools that are built on the same concepts that I have used in my work.[2] I have mentioned other technical assistance groups in previous chapters and in chapters 13 and 14, we will review the federal and state sources for supporting youth development and school restructuring efforts.

INCREMENTAL CHANGES

Every school does not need to become a full-service community school. Many school systems are not interested in "going all the way" with the concept of integrated services—not all systems need to. But this review of successful approaches to improving educational outcomes has produced other concepts as well that are equally important to incorporate into schools to ensure Safe Passage for all children.

Excellent Teachers

The quality of teaching (as my 8-year-old friend Rachel points out at the beginning of this chapter) is very important. The bottom line for schools is whether the children learn. No consensus exists about how to measure achievement, and it is not my intention to get embroiled in the subject of standards and testing. Whatever measures are used, schools can easily identify failing children, and states can easily identify failing schools. Failing schools can be turned around, but that means improving the ways that children are being taught. It is not a mystery. How does a school upgrade the quality of teaching?

Authorities such as Robert Slavin, Henry Levin, Ted Sizer, Robert Felner, and James Comer—and all the other folks working with the New American Schools—may not operate on the same sets of assumptions about learning, but I believe they would all agree that it is possible to train teachers to be more responsive. This is a lengthy process, and it requires certain conditions: a principal who is willing to take chances and who will facilitate arrangements for in-service training; teachers who are open to new ways of teaching and want to acquire new skills; facilitators or coaches who are on hand to lead the teachers through training experiences in specific methodologies. Teachers unions have to be flexible about these arrangements; almost all school-change efforts require more time than union contracts generally cover. Serious curricular reform may require summer meetings and weekend retreats.

Prevention Curricula: Liberate the Teachers

Schools are currently overloaded with prevention curricula that have very little behavioral impact. One reason for that massive and expensive failure is the reliance on classroom teachers to implement these curricula. Teachers should be released from the responsibility of providing sex education, substance-abuse prevention, conflict resolution, and whatever else comes along. They should not be put in charge of "behavioral modification" or "self-esteem building" exercises. Teachers need to concentrate on their jobs—developing strong cognitive skills among their students.

One approach to incorporating prevention promotion in the school day is to divide up the territory between cognitive and didactic learning and psychosocial-skills training. All K–12 core curriculum (particularly science) should be revised to include appropriate information about health promotion, the consequences of using chemical substances, processes of reproduction, the impacts of violence, good nutrition, and other health subjects. Work is already underway to develop a comprehensive life sciences curriculum for the middle school level.[3] At the same time, all the training in psychosocial skills should be put together into one unit offered annually that includes instruction on decision making, deals with aggression, teaches coping skills, and uses other behaviorally oriented components. This training should be offered by health educators and other practitioners who are equipped to counsel young people and can refer them for specialized help if they need it.

Student Assistance is a model for bringing trained social workers into the school either to deal with substance-abuse issues or dropout prevention. This model could be expanded so that the Student Assistance worker uses a more holistic approach and takes over all the psychosocial counseling and group work, leaving the teachers to teach.

Real Parental Involvement

I have already advised parents to be more proactive in regard to their children's schooling. At the same time, school systems need to be more proactive in involving the parents. Much has been written on this subject, and any school that wants to institute an effort can find out what to do. Joyce Epstein, codirector of the Johns Hopkins Center for Research on the Education of Students Placed at Risk, has developed a useful framework of six types of approaches that encourage parental involvement in schools.[4]

1. *Parenting* Help families set up home environments that are conducive to studying through parent education courses, family support programs, home visits, neighborhood meetings.

2. *Communicating* Encourage better school-to-home and home-to-school communication through conferences, language translations, sending home student work, parent pickup of report cards, and provision of clear information about what's going on.

3. *Volunteering* Survey parents to determine interests and skills, stimulate parent presence in the classroom to help out teachers, set up a parent room for meetings, and use parents as safety patrols and hall monitors. Make sure schedules are flexible to accommodate working parents.

4. *Learning at home* Provide information on homework requirements and monitoring; set up family math, science and reading activities at school and over the summer.

5. *Decision making* Urge parents to participate in the PTA; organize advisory groups on curriculum, safety, or personnel; encourage formation of advocacy groups and active roles in elections; offer leadership training.

6. *Collaboration with the community* Help parents gain access to information and services relating to health, cultural events, recreation, social services, and summer programs for youth; promote integrated services; promote community service projects.

Many examples of successful parent involvement programs have been reviewed.[5] Perhaps the most important experiment is being conducted in Chicago, where Local School Councils made up of six parents, two community members, two teachers, and the principal are mandatory.[6] The councils are charged with reviewing contracts with principals, approving the annual budget, working on curricula and school improvements, and issuing an annual report. Experience to date has been mixed. The turmoil at the top levels of the school system was so great that Mayor Daley took over the reins, bringing in all new administrators at the district level. Some 109 of the 600 schools were put on academic probation and forced to accept an outside team. The turnover among principals has approached 80 percent, indicating massive dissatisfaction among both the councils and the principals. Yet in hundreds of schools, parents are heavily involved in decision making for the first time.

One South Miami Beach middle school has instituted a program called Rainmakers (RAIN—Referral and Information Network), a parent empowerment model. Disadvantaged Hispanic families are organized into a group to be partners in the design and delivery of educational and support services. Rainmakers are in evidence everywhere in the school, where they have a parent resource room, work on issues such as housing and immigration, and act as teachers' assistants. Members receive small stipends. As Katherine Hooper-Briar, a leading authority on parent-school collaboration, has noted, "Instead of being marginalized by the systems so vital to the family, . . . parents are now the motivators and mobilizers of others who feel disenfranchised."[7]

Security Dads is a unique parent-involvement program implemented in a high school in Indianapolis.[8] Adult male volunteers monitor the halls, playground, lunchroom, and special events. They are trained to intervene by talking to students and to discourage fighting. In their positions as male role models, these men are expected to help students learn to respect authority.

Parent resource rooms are being organized throughout the country.[9] A middle school in a disadvantaged Milwaukee neighborhood has also established a parent center—a room where parents can meet, make phone calls, and get information. In addition to a paid coordinator, three parents staff the room and receive small salaries for their work. The center is the headquarters for an extensive volunteer program that assigns ten to fifteen parents every week to act as file clerks, tutors, and class helpers. Adult education and computer classes are made available to the parents.

Parents respond very well when schools offer the kinds of services that the parents really need, starting with basic items such as clothing and food. The health services in the schools we visited were heavily used, as were job-related courses such as English, computer training, and other business skills. Schools with programs for adults are beginning to feel the impact of changes in welfare laws, which are putting pressure on welfare recipients to gain work skills.

Individual Attention

Any school can recognize the importance of connecting every child to a responsible adult. I have never visited any program or spoken to any youth worker who has not commented about "parents these days." Teachers frequently complain, "Parents do not come to school when invited; they do not check their children's homework and rarely know where their children are after school or at night." Most youth workers understand that parents are having a hard time fulfilling the demands on their lives to support their families and keep a roof over their heads. In turn, the families generally welcome help from the school as long as it does not take too much time.

We have strong evidence to support that when children are attached to well-trained and supervised mentors, case managers, or older peer tutors, their achievement and attendance levels improve. School systems that want to find adults who will mentor their students can form relationships with the organizations mentioned in earlier chapters: Cities-in-Schools, Big Brothers/Big Sisters, Boys and Girls Clubs, Girls Inc., 4H, religious organizations, senior citizen groups, and universities.

Community agencies are coming into schools to perform many different functions. Schools also reach out into communities to become part of networks and comprehensive programs.

Susie Fitzhugh, Photographer

12

SAFE PASSAGE COMMUNITIES

Step by step, recreating community must lie at the heart of any vision for overcoming the economic, social and spiritual challenges that threaten us today. Building strong community institutions . . . from families and volunteer associations to businesses and schools . . . will be essential to the long-term viability of our country and its people.

—Peter McLauglin, "State of the County 1995"

The youth development field is rich in the rhetoric of community development, with calls for multiagency youth initiatives that are "community based" and that bring together all the necessary elements to create a safe, healthy environment. But the field is quite limited when it comes to examples with actual results. A compendium of comprehensive, community-based initiatives put together by the Finance Project mentions fifty programs, but many are broad economic development models or statewide initiatives, and the few that are focused on youth should, by my definition, be included among community schools.[1] In preparing this book, I asked a number of experts on youth development to suggest communities that have successfully gone through the recommended planning process and could document changes in outcomes for youth. The answer typically was, "I'll get back to you." But few ever did.

Perhaps the question is premature. A number of new initiatives are just now getting underway that support community-wide efforts. In this chapter, I present examples of two specific communities (Minneapolis and Kansas City), several other multicommunity initiatives, and discuss what seem to be the most promising approaches to organizing neighborhoods.

WHAT IS A COMMUNITY?

One problem in discussions of community is definition. In my village, Hastings-on-Hudson, the political entity and the community are perceived to be the same. By design, all of the population feeds into one school at each level. This came about because in the 1930s, the elite "hill" and the ethnic "village" appeared to be at odds, so a progressive school superintendent pushed through school building plans that guaranteed that as the population grew all children would always go to the same physical plant for schooling. (Now we have one elementary school and one middle school–high school.)

Hastings has all necessary components of a Safe Passage community: It is small, has a centralized and excellent school system, community police, supportive families, and a good number of support services for children. A youth advocacy program and a community center are supported by village and state funds. The school houses many supportive programs and caring people, including alternative classrooms for less motivated students.

Yonkers, contiguous to Hastings, contains myriad communities, some just like Hastings, others very different. Waves of ethnic groups have settled there, giving neighborhoods distinct flavors (Italian, Jordanian, Portuguese). Endless desegration battles have been fought with efforts to balance the African American and Hispanic student enrollments with diminishing numbers of White students. Magnet schools have been one answer, but they can take children far out of their physical neighborhoods and limit the prospects for community schools. Certain neighborhoods lack most of what is requisite for Safe Passage. One observes decayed housing, burned-out or empty stores, and a lot of men hanging out on the streets during the working day. The school system, along with community agencies and community police, have fought hard to help children overcome barriers to education and success, but still the problems persist. Turbulent politics rule the scene, making it difficult to carry out long-term changes to improve community life.

My concept of community is an area defined by tradition as a neighborhood, with enough students to fill one high school (and its feeder schools) but small enough so people feel a sense of identity with the area. Think of concentric circles, starting with the individual, then the family, the schools, and then the community (and the city, county, state, and nation). Each circle is important in the lives of young people, and each level is interdependent on the others. Thus, even if families function well and schools are productive, Safe Passage cannot be ensured without healthy communities.

ENVISIONING A SAFE PASSAGE COMMUNITY

Many advocates for youth believe that communities must go through a process of change that will lead to better outcomes for children. I have tried to visualize this process in an imaginary setting, an inner-city neighborhood like those in Yonkers, populated by diverse low-income families. A Safe Passage initiative is stimulated by the local person who sits on the City Council as a representative of the area. He invites community leaders, school personnel, social and health agencies, parents, youth, local businesses, and the media to come together in a forum to develop a more comprehensive approach for the youth of this community. At the first meeting, the group agrees that, while a number of services are available to youth in the community, they are fragmented and not being used. The youth representatives complain that their voices are not heard and that there is little to do that is compelling enough to get them off the streets. Everyone acknowledges that the schools need improvement and that the job situation is critical. The point is made early on that some kind of financial support will be needed to turn all the talk into action.

In order to get started, the director of the Urban League agrees to coordinate this effort, which the group names the Youth Community Improvement Program (YCIP). A statement of goals is issued, calling for an intense, community-wide effort to ensure that all children make it through high school and are prepared to enter the labor force or to go on to higher education. Every agency represented has to sign on to that goal statement.

The first stage involves extensive data gathering and planning. Committee members volunteer to collect information about the needs of children and families and the services available. This work is carried out in conjunction with local university (or college or community college) researchers, who train the interviewers, computerize the findings, and draft reports. (The university people restrain their proclivities to take over the project and are strongly committed to the community-based YCIP goals.)

The plan that emerges after six months of data gathering, analysis, and debate involves centering activities on the local schools, with particular emphasis on upgrading the quality of the high school located in the area. The group wants to create clear paths for youth from preschool through high school, assuring that each level functions well and is related to the other levels. During the planning process, the issue of safety has arisen, and the plans call for attention to community policing. YCIP is officially constituted as a freestanding, nonprofit agency with an elected board. The Urban League goes after a small foundation grant to staff YCIP with an executive director.

A year after the YCIP process is initiated, a number of activities are underway that focus on high school restructuring, community policing, after-school recreation, and the creation of a job clearinghouse. Most of the efforts are built on existing resources, using funding in more creative ways that result in better service integration. Youth are actively involved in opening a community center in a housing project. A neighborhood "homecoming" weekend is held, with a street fair, a community dinner, musical presentations, and fireworks all part of the festivities. The mayor attends and gives the YCIP leadership an award for outstanding civic distinction.

Expectations from the Process

A representative group from a community could create a great plan but encounter numerous difficulties implementing the plan. In my example, it may be that the high school building is completely obsolete and that community research will reveal that a new building is necessary. Finding the resources to accomplish such a goal moves the process to another level, the city Board of Education, and the city may have to appeal to the state for resources. But the fact that the solution to a problem may not present itself within the boundaries of the community should not deter the community from pursuing its goal. Rather, the process should activate the community to articulate its demands. The availability of documentation is an important weapon for this advocacy.

I do not believe that many communities can initiate such a process without outside assistance. Just as the school restructuring models appear to flourish only when on-site facilitators are part of the package, the process of community change has to be "pushed" by trained community organizers and planners. The Chapin Hall Center for Children at the University of Chicago supports an independent research and development effort in the area of community building. The staff has been instrumental in working with both communities and researchers to test community-development theories and practices, with a particular emphasis on involving the local residents in effective governance.[2]

YOUTH-DEVELOPMENT COMMUNITY INITIATIVES

Interest in creating youth-development initiatives at the local level is on the rise, and many diverse public and nonprofit entities are sponsoring initiatives. While auspices differ, the process proposed is similar, involving the organization of a representative group, detailed planning, and complicated implementation practices.

Minneapolis Youth Coordinating Board

The Minneapolis Youth Coordinating Board (YCB) was established in 1985 by the then-Mayor Donald Fraser through an agreement among the city, school district, park and recreation board, library board, and the county commissioners. By 1987, the people of Minneapolis were brought together to create a twenty-year vision called City's Children 2007, which serves as a guide for comprehensive youth development. YCB is currently operated by twelve elected officials, including Mayor Sharon Belton, and a small centrally located staff. YCB's specific goals are to improve the ability of public agencies to promote youth development, facilitate coordination, identify barriers, and communicate information. Recent activities have been informed by a study of Minneapolis youth by the Search Institute, which documented the absence of strong supports and resources for many young people.[3]

YCB directly sponsors several projects. Way to Grow is a citywide, school-readiness initiative that helps families and young children to gain access to prevention and early intervention services. Family resource workers operate and make home visits out of seven neighborhood-based offices where screening, referral, and parent education activities are located. The Neighborhood Early Learning Center is another strategy to strengthen families and communities as part of the city's neighborhood revitalization program. Community services such as health clinics, Head Start, child care, and parent education classes are encouraged to locate their services together in four sites (centers will eventually be in place in all eleven planning districts). Places to Grow is the latest initiative, this one aimed at 7 to 14 year olds to promote youth-development activities.

Other partnerships and collaborative activities that YCB has stimulated include the Minneapolis Redesign, to bring more collaborative services into schools; Phat Summer, to open park and school facilities during summer evenings for 12 to 18 years olds; Community Change for Youth Development, to improve youth opportunities in one community (see below); YWCA Eastside, to facilitate partnerships with public schools to build a new community facility; Moral Response Network, to involve church and community leaders in crisis intervention; What's Up Youth Info Line, to inform youth about activities in the community; and the New Workforce Policy Council, to bring together efforts to create jobs. YCB is clearly a major player in youth-development activities in Minneapolis. Its total budget of more than $2.9 million is made up of federal, state, and local grants, foundation and United Way support, and business contributions.

Colleen Burns, former executive director of the YCB, while celebrating the significant successes of the many collaborative efforts, recognized the difficulty in creating true citizen participation at the decision-making level. She questioned the original assumptions that people would have the time to volunteer, to create, implement, and govern the programs. As she pointed out:

We assumed that when someone complained about the approach a school was taking with their child, the inconvenience of a social service location, or the conditions in their neighborhood, they would have the time and energy to spend many long hours, without pay, helping to resolve those concerns. We assumed people could surmount the barriers created by lack of transportation and the struggle of trying to make ends meet on too few dollars to come to our meetings month after month after month.[4]

Burns proposed to lift the burden of participation from the too few people who do it by reimbursing volunteers for their time and expenses. She also called for greater honesty in dealing with communities about the boundaries of decision making. Too often, participants are led to expect immediate results, but the reality of program implementation is limited by restrictions resulting from regulations, policies, and funding. Finally, Burns questioned the outside dimensions of the process of "coordinating," pointing out that it is not necessary, and is probably too cumbersome, to put all youth-development activities under one umbrella. It would be wiser, in her view, to place the coordinating board in the role of promoting partnerships and sharing the vision.

Independent Commission: Kansas City

The Local Investment Commission (LINC) is a unique, citizen-driven, community collaborative effort fostered by the Missouri State Department of Social Services (DSS) in Jackson County–Kansas City, Missouri.[5] The goal is to provide leadership to engage the Kansas City community in creating the best system possible to support children, youth, and families, with an emphasis on comprehensiveness, prevention and consumer involvement.[6] The DSS is responsible for appointing the twenty-three individuals who make up the commission, which represents business and civic affairs, neighborhood leaders, and program participants. More than 300 volunteers are involved in committees and activities, as are foundations, school districts, nonprofits, and other partners. Committees include community planning/coordination, human services, economic development, housing and safety, job development, and wage supplementation. Program services professionals sit on an advisory cabinet but are not commission members. State officials and politicians are also excluded from commission membership to protect against turf battles.

After four years of planning, negotiating, listening, and talking, the commission established sixteen school sites in four school districts where school-linked services are provided; acquired Medicaid provider certification for the school system; set up employment opportunities for 700 families on welfare; trained and monitored 100 home-based child care providers; trained human service providers in leadership, family systems, and cultural diversity; relocated 200 state social workers into neighborhood-based systems; enrolled families into Medicaid–managed-care programs; and improved conditions in foster care.

The commission is operated by an executive director and a small staff. Following the direction of the commission, the executive director's office administered over $273 million in state and federal funds in 1995. At the state level, five major agencies have turned over their spending authority for Kansas City to LINC (education, health, labor, mental health, and social services). The commission also receives support from the Ewing Marion Kauffman Foundation to create a technical assistance team and train local and state officials.

Gayle Hobbs, the current executive director, attributes the success of this unique collaborative model to the exceptional partnership that formed among Gary Stangler, Director of Missouri DSS; Bert Berkley, CEO of a local corporation; and Robert Rogers, head of the Kauffman Foundation.[7] In the early 1990s, Berkley proposed to Stangler that the state-level DSS turn all local decisions on the distribution of funding in Kansas City over to a commission of local volunteers. The work started with a planning process and committee formation. According to Frank Farrow, of the Center for the Study of Social Policy, "The community leadership that Bert Berkley has mobilized around LINC is unmatched anywhere . . . people are still charged up about it even after 27 months."[8] In addition to strong local supports, Martin Blank, an expert on collaborative programs from the Institute of Educational Leadership, spent many hours advising the community and documenting the development of the commission.[9]

In order to ensure the steady flow of state funds, a Family Investment Trust made up from foundation grants (Danforth, Annie Casey, Kansas City Community Foundation, and Kauffman) provides $1 million a year to build the capacity of the five state agencies to work together to integrate services.

LINC also administers Caring Communities in Jackson County, a program that uses funds pooled from state agencies to integrate services in schools (see chapter 5). LINC's role in this effort is to serve as a policy-making board, provide technical assistance and training, integrate this with other LINC programs such as welfare reform, and provide accountability. Through Caring Communities, agency workers are being repositioned in schools.

According to one analytic LINC report about "bumps in the road," it was not an easy task to define which problems the commission needed to solve:

> Managing diversified funding is a particular issue for LINC because it juggles federal, state, private, and foundation funding. . . . Developing a common language among the diverse groups . . . has been a challenge. The developers of the LINC initiative underestimated the time commitment needed. LINC focused on immediate needs in order to show that the strategy could work, then turned to more comprehensive reforms, which require enormous amounts of time. LINC is still looking for a sound bite. With so many audiences and such a complex undertaking, [they] have not found a way to articulate the effort as clearly as they think is necessary.[10]

Community Change for Youth Development

In 1996, Public/Private Ventures (P/PV), a research and program development agency (see chapters 7 and 9), launched a two-year, foundation-supported, feasibility study of an initiative to stimulate a process of change at the community level.[11] Five concepts govern the agency's approach: the expansion of supportive relationships between adults and youth; the use of work as a developmental tool; the use of nonschool hours for constructive activities; youth empowerment; and continuity of support.

The Community Change for Youth Development (CCYD) process starts with a local planning group made up of adults, youth, and organizations in the target neighborhood and key players from the broader community. Bernadine Watson, director of CCYD, discussed some of the governance issues she expects these groups to address:

> Who are the real resident leaders; how to motivate residents to get involved in yet another community change process; what's the right balance between residents and institutions; how to get youth involved; how to keep elected officials involved; how not to get bogged down in the process.[12]

Watson also recounted the importance of giving residents dominant control over resources in the initial stages of the projects so that they gain experience in real decision making and do not perceive of their participation as mere "window dressing."[13] P/PV will provide extensive technical assistance to sites to help them leverage local resources, implement programs, and foster evaluation. Research will be conducted on the process, implementation, short-term, and long-term outcomes.

P/PV has selected sites with different governance structures. Three are already in the implementation phase:

> *Austin, Texas.* A partnership has been established between Austin City Community Services Division and Austin Interfaith, an advocacy organization. A Youth Charter Neighborhood Steering Committee governs this project for a 100-block poverty area in south-central-east Austin. Half of the steering committee are youths. The major activity of this group has been the creation of a "one-stop" youth-development center, bringing together a variety of community agencies.

> *St. Petersburg, Florida.* The Juvenile Welfare Board of Pinellas County oversees this project. The Childs Park Youth Initiative Council runs the program in the neighborhood. Building on previous city efforts to upgrade the community, the council is strengthening links with the city recreation department to launch art projects, involve youth in media work, and start a Youth Sports Academy. The academy will require every participant to have a tutor, health promotion and nutrition services will be available, and an academy band and cheerleaders will be organized.

> *Savannah, Georgia.* The Chatham-Savannah Youth Futures Authority (see chapter 9) governed by local representatives, has been in existence since 1988. It was selected as part of CCYD to extend its outreach in one specific target neighborhood. So far, a Youth Council has been set up and is working on

planning youth activities and recruiting volunteers. A new Neighborhood Council runs the Mini-Action Grant Program, to provide twenty $500 grants to local block associations and youth organizations for tutorial, sports, special events, and community service projects.

Three other sites are in the early stages of planning:

Kansas City, Missouri. Youth development activities in the Blue Hills Neighborhood will serve as a model for other neighborhoods in the city.

Minneapolis, Minnesota. A partnership between the Minneapolis Foundation, Office of the Mayor, and Whittier Alliance will concentrate on youth development work in the Whittier neighborhood.

New York City. A partnership of three settlement houses under the auspices of United Neighborhood Houses will form in the neighborhood surrounding the Grand Street Settlement (lower east side).

Healthy Communities, Healthy Youth

The Search Institute, a research organization led by Peter Benson and sponsored by the Lutheran Brotherhood, has initiated Healthy Communities Healthy Youth.[14] This program attempts to motivate individuals and groups to work together to create community environments that nurture children. The Search Institute has identified forty assets of youth that have proved to protect young people from risk-taking behavior and to promote healthy development—for example, family support and communication, community service, creative activities, achievement, caring, social competence, and having a sense of purpose.

St. Louis Park, Minnesota, is considered the pioneer in the implementation of the Search approach.[15] A thirty-person vision team was organized—representing schools, youth-serving agencies, churches, and businesses—to participate in community education and raise awareness about the importance of youth development. This group calls itself Children First. Several results have already been seen: The city and school have produced a joint calendar of events distributed to every household so everyone knows what is going on in the community; schools, libraries, and churches have joined in a "Catch 22" campaign that seeks to motivate parents to spend at least 22 minutes per day with their children; neighbors have invited youth to bake cookies together, play basketball, and participate in other activities; youth have become involved with younger children in community service; and other programs have been designed to build on positive assets of youth and their families. While these may not seem like earth-shaking activities, the aggregate impact of many people moving together to improve the quality of life for youngsters could be quite significant.

Benson advises communities to start with a positive vision rather than a crisis orientation. He also believes that communities should resist the temptation to create new programs and instead devote their energies to strengthening existing institutions and tapping the capacities of people and organizations to contribute their time and ideas. Yet among the more than fifty communities that have embraced this asset-building approach, many appear to be creating new facilities: In Hopkins, Minnesota, the youth are working to create a new teen center, and in Mesa, Arizona, neighborhood community centers are being constructed as an integral part of a new community. The Search Institute sees its role in the Healthy Communities, Healthy Youth Initiative as conducting further research on assets, building a national awareness of the importance of youth development, and providing training, technical assistance, and networking for communities ready to get involved.

United Way

The United Way of America is the national service center supporting 1,356 United Way organizations throughout the country that raise funds to support more than 45,000 local agency service providers. United Way is involved with several initiatives that are of interest to youth advocates. Building on experience gained from their Mobilization for America's Children, United Way agencies are already active in more than 170 communities, bringing together key stakeholders (schools, community agencies, community leaders) to work together to promote Success by 6, a model early-childhood development program. Now, with support from the DeWitt Wallace–Reader's Digest Fund and in a joint effort with the Institute for Educational Leadership, United Way seeks to stimulate community-wide efforts to implement the principles of extended-service schools in five communities.

The model for the new initiative is Bridges to Success, an extended-service school strategy created in 1991 through the leadership of the United Way of Central Indiana.[16] This effort created a partnership of ten major public and nonprofit agencies with a view toward integrating education with human and community-service delivery systems and establishing schools as life-long learning centers and community hubs. Under the auspices of a twenty-eight-member council, the program is being implemented by neighborhood-based site teams beginning in communities that express interest. Currently operating in six schools in Indianapolis, the council hopes to eventually reform the entire school district and its relationship to community agencies. At the demonstration schools, outside agencies provide health care, dental care, case management, recreational and cultural after-school activities, mental health services, community service learning, tutoring, and job readiness training.

One of the unique aspects of Bridges to Success is its two-tiered governance structure, with the council operating at the community and policy level and school site teams working at the neighborhood and practice level. The site teams are cofacilitated by the school principal and an executive of a local community agency. The Indianapolis public school district provides funding for the coordinators and the space, while United Way has committed more than half a million dollars for employing a director, providing evaluation and technical assistance, and covering the costs of collaboration including money for meetings, communication, and transportation. Partner agencies contribute the cost of service delivery.

The United Way of Greater Rochester has launched a similar initiative, CHANGE, that is committed to ensuring that children and families are healthy, self-sufficient, and fully prepared for work and postsecondary education.[17] The long-term objective is to create family service centers in thirty neighborhoods, building on collaborations between schools and community agencies. CHANGE involves the business community, the city of Rochester, Monroe County, the school system, and the United Way in pooling funds and making decisions about who gets support. Each of these important agencies has signed a resolution that identifies community outcomes and pledges to support customer-driven restructuring of health, human, and educational services.

A coordinating team is made up of administrators from each of those agencies, including the director of the local youth bureau and three full-time United Way workers—a coordinator and two community organizers. The local site process starts with a Planning Team composed of parents and local school and agency staff, supported by a United Way staff member. The strategy is being tested at two Rochester school sites, selected because of their large number of problems. The Jefferson Middle School houses a Family Wellness Center that offers services from nine different agencies: crisis intervention, counseling, case management, prevention programs, special services for the developmentally disabled, welfare information and referrals, youth development, probation visits, and dental care. Health services are in the offing.[18] The Clara Barton Elementary School offers comprehensive health promotion programs offered on-site by different community resources.

CHANGE actually grew out of Rochester's somewhat negative experience with New Futures (the Annie Casey initiative discussed in chapter 9). After the city missed getting into the final round of funding, CHANGE planners realized that a separate agency was not the answer to the issues challenging the community. They were convinced that their approach had to be from the bottom up, school and neighborhood based, rather than trying to make top-down changes in the city and county governments. A unique aspect of this initiative is the employment of community organizers who can work with school principals in putting together the packages that are needed in their particular neighborhoods. It is too early in the CHANGE process to measure outcomes or call this a success, but apparently, this bottom-up approach has generated a lot of interest and enthusiasm and, at two schools, tangible evidence that working together to create centers is a viable activity. For instance, the superintendent of schools, on the basis of the Jefferson School Model, has called for the formation of Family Wellness Centers in every middle school.

Safe Futures

The U.S. Office of Juvenile Justice and Delinquency Prevention (OJJDP) has also launched a community-based effort to encourage planning and collaboration among agencies. Six communities have each been awarded $1.4 million a year for five years to improve service-delivery systems and to prevent youth violence. These resources are expected to be used in such program areas as after-school activities, mentoring, treatment, mental health services, and gang interventions. In Boston, the award went to the Blue Hill Avenue Coalition (made up of seventy public and private agencies) in conjunction with the Office of Community Partnerships. This partnership plans to set up a total support network in three neighborhoods involving residents and youth, community-based service providers, schools, churches, housing authorities, probation officers, and police. Neighborhood governance boards will assume administrative control and authority. The Safe Futures Initiative in Contra Costa County, California, will be managed by the County Board of Supervisors, while in St. Louis the Mayor's Office of Youth Development will take charge.

The Office of Justice has other community-based initiatives, but they are not as centered on youth. The Weed and Seed program is in place in more than seventy-six communities as a neighborhood approach to law enforcement and community revitalization that involves an array of local agencies. Project PACT (Pulling America's Communities Together), an outgrowth of Weed and Seed, addresses youth violence through comprehensive programming at four major sites—Atlanta, Denver, Washington, DC, and the state of Nebraska.

Centers for Disease Control (CDC)
Teen Pregnancy Prevention Program

In 1997, CDC awarded planning grants to thirteen community-wide coalitions in large cities to support their work with youth to delay pregnancy and childbearing. The idea is for lead agencies ("hubs") to establish partnerships with other agencies to plan for and then mobilize community resources to support a broad range of youth development activities and to create supportive environments. In many of the selected cities, the local public health department has assumed the role of hub, bringing together a mix of youth-serving agencies, schools, and existing consortia. Other hubs include a well-established Children's Network, a university-based institute, a nonprofit child advocacy institute, and two nonprofit family planning councils.

The first step is conducting needs assessments and designing strategies. Grantees are expected to document the lessons learned during the first phase of planning, showing how the hub and the partners were able to mobilize the community to assess itself; and to define a valid intervention program, to field test components, to figure out how to fund the components, and to build support for a Community Action Plan. After detailed plans are submitted to the CDC, further support will be given to the five communities that appear to have the most potential for success. CDC intends to evaluate this program carefully.

Community-wide teen pregnancy-prevention efforts are also underway in two major foundation efforts: Plain Talk, sponsored by the Casey Foundation in five communities (see chapter 7); and Community Action Programs, sponsored by the California Wellness Foundation in five other communities.

Other Examples

It is difficult to catalogue all that is occurring at the community level. Many community and economic development programs are not specifically aimed at adolescents, but if successful, they will greatly improve the quality of life for all youth and their families. The Atlanta Project (TAP) is one of the more publicized efforts. TAP, a creation of the Carter (Jimmy) Center in Atlanta, targets high-risk neighborhoods through the installation of twenty community offices that coordinate improvements in health, housing, economic development, education, community development, and public safety in conjunction with the corporate sector.

Youth Development Inc. (YDI) in Albuquerque, New Mexico, is a nonprofit umbrella organization that offers thirty different community- and school-based services to more than 14,000 youth in education, employment, drug-abuse counseling, gang intervention, runaway and homeless youth shelters, and low-income housing. Recently, YDI's publicly supported budget increased to over $10 million with the addition of the local Head Start program. Chris Baca, the CEO, was one of the founders of this unique community-based organization back in 1971.

ORGANIZATIONAL STRUCTURES

As we have seen, the movement toward creating a Safe Passage Community can be spearheaded in government or in the voluntary sector. A mayor can assume the leadership for the city and put together a citywide council made up of representatives of public and nonprofit agencies and the community at large (Minneapolis). Or an organization such as the United Way or the Urban League can launch the formation of a planning body made up of similar groups (Indianapolis or Rochester). Or a new, youth-serving, nonprofit agency, such as Youth Development Inc., can be organized to meet specific needs. Or, in the most unusual example, a state agency can create a local commission that becomes a freestanding entity with authority over its own funding (LINC).

I have cited dozens of communities where some sort of consortium is being formed with a view toward integrating services and creating better environments in neighborhoods for children and families. The organizational structures in several of the examples were dictated by the funding agency, in one case the federal government, and in several others, foundations required certain arrangements. According to Cheryl Hayes, director of the Finance Project, community-based initiatives are more likely to have organizational structures that are responsive to their specific communities needs if government policies facilitate connections across agencies and providers.[19]

State governments can play an important role in getting things going. The California legislature, for example, has created five county demonstrations with coordinating councils that were charged with administering blended categorical funding. In West Virginia, a Governor's Cabinet on Children and Families oversees the creation and operation of Family Resource Networks at the local level.

In Iowa, more than thirty separate state funding streams were consolidated at the county level to make funding more flexible. In Tennessee, the legislature and state agencies created a funding pool to support community-based initiatives directed toward keeping vulnerable children with their families as an alternative to foster care.

Importance of Planning

Every one of these initiatives starts with the collection of data.[20] This is the sine qua non of community development. It is essential to determine specific needs and available resources in order to map out Safe Passage strategies. I became convinced of the importance of this step long ago when I developed plans for family planning programs under the auspices of the U.S. Office of Economic Opportunity and, later, of the U.S. Department of Health and Human Services. In 1970, after a bill was finally passed appropriating public funds for the establishment of family planning clinics throughout the United States, we wanted to make sure that those resources were used appropriately. In a dozen large cities and several rural areas, using census data and surveys, we mapped out in great detail where the "women in need" lived, the location of current delivery sites, and the location of potential sites. The availability of this kind of information, complete with detailed maps, defused much of the controversy surrounding the issue and made it clear that if disadvantaged women were to have equal access to birth control services, then additional sites had to be opened. Of course, the actual availability of funds to provide the services made the proposition very attractive to community agencies. Grants were awarded by DHHS according to the defined needs—a practice that continues today in the distribution of public family planning funds to more than 4,000 clinic sites.

If we return to the hypothetical community envisioned in the beginning of this chapter, we can spell out what specific information a Safe Passage community should have at hand to begin planning.

- *Status of youth.* Census data on age and poverty status; special survey of teenagers (like the Youth Risk Behavior Survey from CDC or Search needs assessment) on sex, drugs, violence, and depression; school records on test scores, attendance, suspension, and retention; and police records on juvenile arrests and truancy.

- *Available services for youth.* Survey of youth agencies to determine activities, hours open, potential for expansion; survey of health, mental health, and social service agencies to determine utilization by children and families, and the potential for expansion.

- *Models for Safe Passage communities.* Given specific needs and current resources, how to move to structure community interventions that address those needs.

A community interested in pursuing a planning process that results in a plan of action or a set of strategies would greatly benefit from having access to hands-on help from a facilitator or coordinator. Almost all of the examples discussed here emanate from a government, foundation, or think-tank initiative that brings with it technical assistance, manuals, meetings, and frequent communication with authorities. I don't believe that many community groups could carry out detailed planning activities without some outside help. The National Center for Community Education in Flint, Michigan, offers community–school training that includes planning, funding, organization of services, assessment, and public re-lations.[21]

COMMUNITY RESOURCES

Not every community is going to enter into a complicated planning process and develop networks that integrate services. Just as some schools will not restructure but rather change incrementally, some communities can be improved by paying attention to and making better use of the resources that exist that influence the quality of life in the neighborhood. Obviously, the effectiveness of the schools is a major consideration. But other community agencies contribute substantially to the welfare of children and their families. I would particularly like to comment on the role of youth organizations, police departments, and housing authorities.

Youth Organizations

One important component of Safe Passage is the shelter provided by youth organizations around the country. As the Carnegie Corporation report *A Matter of Time* underscored, "Community programs represent an untapped potential for meeting needs so clearly articulated by young adolescents themselves. Effective programs already exist, but they reach all-too-few adolescents."[22] More than 17,000 national and local youth organizations operate in this country, their various facilities the safe havens for millions of young people who have no other place to go after school and on weekends. But they are much more than physical plants; they provide a wide choice of youth-development activities that encourage intellectual growth, social skills, and physical prowess. In these places, young people can relate to their peers and have fun with games and recreational activities. Most important, they can find there trained and committed staff who act as friends, mentors, and role models.

4H is one of the nation's largest youth organizations, involving almost 6 million youth in just about every county in the country. A nonprofit agency, the National 4H Council works in collaboration with state Cooperative Extension Services in thousands of clubs, special-interest groups, and school enrichment programs, and involves close to 700,000 volunteers along with the professional staff. YMCAs, YWCAs, and scouts account for millions more youth, staff, and volunteers. The Boys and Girls Clubs serve more than 2.4 million youth at more than 1,800 club sites. Based on their positive experience with SMART Moves, they have opened up clubs in more than 200 housing projects, as well as in malls, homeless shelters, and on Indian reservations. Girls Inc. serves more than 350,000 young women at more than 1,000 sites.

The Carnegie study recognized the importance of both established national organizations and thousands more independent, community-based agencies in addressing the needs of young people in the after-school hours. The study urged that these groups pay more attention to high-risk youth, involve youth much more in program planning and implementation, become more culturally sensitive, and strengthen the quality of the staff through more training. Youth organizations of all kinds were urged to become more involved in community networks, such as the emerging programs described in this book.

One of the strengths of the national organizations with local affiliates is their ability to disseminate tested models and to use research to inform action. I closely observed this process as an advisor to the Girls Inc. Preventing Adolescent Pregnancy Program. The staff started with the production of a program model after a careful review of the research on pregnancy prevention. They created a four-component effort that was age appropriate and responsive to developmental needs. Then, a pilot project was set up in several affiliates that involved considerable training and supervision over a four-year period. Research was conducted and published that confirmed the validity of the interventions. Subsequently, the intervention was packaged and, for those affiliates that wish to use it, training is available.

Community Police

In chapter 4, we visited the Caimito Koban, the successful community police project located in a youth center. The model is being replicated across this country, with excellent results reported from Baltimore, Maryland, Columbia, South Carolina, Philadelphia, Boston, Washington, DC, and other communities. In Washington, DC, the Koban is located in Paradise, a housing project with 650 units. Three officers are assigned to work in a "clubhouse," and fifteen others have responded to the invitation to move in with their families. In Baltimore, neighborhood ministations have been established.

One thing is certain, every community has police officers. In my own small community, with a force of twenty-one, one person is designated as youth officer, and another has been trained to offer the DARE curriculum in the school. Both spend a lot of time with the local youth and know them all by name. As one of them said, "Fifteen percent of police time in Hastings is spent on crime, and 85 percent on public service."

Yonkers has a Youth Unit of twenty-one officers, some of whom are assigned to DARE and the Police Athletic League, a police-sponsored, after-school sports program. A conversation with Officer Harrigan, chief of the youth division, showed him to be extremely sympathetic to the plight of deprived children living in the disadvantaged areas of the city. He lamented the inability of today's parents to take care of their children, citing examples of 6 year olds found walking the streets in the middle of the night and drug-abusing parents who are children themselves. Despite the importance of police activities in youth work, repeated budget cuts and administrative changes make it hard to offer any program continuity.

Housing Projects

Many of the children found in the youth programs cited in this book live in housing projects. Although I am a strong advocate of moving services into schools, the creation of community schools does not obviate the need to improve the quality of life around public housing projects, where the same principles of colocation of supportive services apply. The Boys and Girls Clubs have demonstrated that delinquency rates were lowered after establishing an intensive club program in housing projects. Not only does the availability of after-school programming help youngsters, but also the development of a recreation center in the projects can serve the needs of parents and create opportunities for children and parents to meet together for community dinners and other events.

COMMUNITY NETWORKS—A RATIONAL GOAL

A great deal of positive energy is directed toward putting together the pieces of effective programming at the community level. Diverse ways of governing reflect the strengths and attributes of local governing bodies and community agencies. Experience varies as to the degree of true consumer participation, ranging from neighborhood-based, designed, and implemented programs to central-office administered partnerships. One common characteristic is the designation of a central place in each community—a school or a community site—where services are colocated. As Hayes points out, the emerging models

> demonstrate that changing established systems is a slow and cumbersome process, and it requires participation and support from all parts of the community. It is often difficult for institutions with established missions to imagine their roles and relationships changing. It is equally difficult for service providers with established disciplinary orientations to change their behavior and for governance structures to loosen their control over funding and administrative procedures.[23]

Despite these organizational barriers, at the community and neighborhood levels, the commitment is present. Just as successful programs in schools and community agencies need powerful support from state and federal sources to "go to scale," community-wide projects will founder without some kind of subsidy to build the infrastructure. In the next chapter, we explore how these efforts can be supported through public and private ventures.

Bill Schropp, Photographer,
courtesy of the Children's Aid Society

13

TRACKING RESOURCES THROUGH THE STATE AND FEDERAL MAZE

Only public expenditures will allow us to achieve results on a scale that will make a difference. America has a long tradition of using public funds for purposes beyond the means of private resources—from building highways and railroads to saving the Chrysler Corporation—and there is no reason we can't extend that tradition to helping our teenagers grow up successfully.

—Gary Walker, "Commentary: Under the Influence of Adults"

Turning a vision into a reality takes a lot of time. It cannot be accomplished without infusion of resources. The volume of scattered efforts to create more effective schools and responsive communities throughout this country is impressive. Now we must find a way to put together the fragmented pieces into intensive, cohesive, and sustained long-term programs. This chapter deals with the political verities of doing just that. In my view, many of the strategies that must be implemented in order to assure Safe Passage are the responsibilities of legislative and administrative bodies. Although committed, caring people in families and in the community are the most important components, programs cannot function without financial and policy supports.

Here, I present a summary of the resources that emanate from state and federal governmental bodies so that you can get an idea of what's going on, but you must be aware that everything at every level is subject to change. This is a report as of spring 1997—after the 1996 presidential elections. I have tried to limit the bureaucratic jargon, the alphabet soup of government. It is absolutely obligatory, however, that those interested in the welfare of children—whether parents, advocates, or voters—appreciate the complexity of the U.S. system (or nonsystem) for supporting youth programs.

One very important detail is that most of the federal funds flow to states through block grants, which are usually distributed to states through a population-based formula such as the number of children or number of families in poverty. States then have some flexiblity in determining how to use and distribute the funds within their boundaries. Fewer and fewer dollars are disbursed by the federal government via grants directly to local community agencies or schools. As a result, states have increasing powers over the administration of these resources. And we must recognize that every one of the fifty states is a nation of its own, with its own bureaucracy and its own governance.

In reviewing this material, you will find similar programs in different administrative departments—for example, the repetition of collaborative community concepts in diverse departmental initiatives, and the inclusion of educational items in all kinds of health, labor, justice, and housing initiatives. By the time you finish this chapter, you may be totally disenchanted with government (if you weren't already). But do not give up. In the final chapter I present ideas about actions at the national and state levels that will support the development of Safe Passage Schools and Safe Passage Communities.

THE ROLE OF STATES IN YOUTH DEVELOPMENT

The goal of Safe Passage can never be met without serious sustained commitments from all the fifty states. Several years ago, I had the opportunity to review what states were doing to create more comprehensive approaches to youth development issues, particularly in regard to connecting up health and education efforts at the local level.[1] I found a growing consensus that states must do a better job of integrating service programs and assisting communities to develop more comprehensive systems of care—themes that I have mentioned before. In response, many activities are underway, including multiple efforts in single states, but no two state initiatives are alike, and each is shaped by the particular politics, personalities, history, and organizational structure of the state. The governor is often the key player in shaping responses to youth development needs. And all of the discussion at the moment is heavily influenced by the potential impact of budget cuts and changes in the welfare system.

States can contribute to integrated Safe Passage interventions through three major mechanisms: They can decide to use their block grants for comprehensive programming (for example, putting drug-prevention funds into school-based health center programs), they can design and fund their own integrated youth services initiatives, or they can use dedicated taxes to fund certain programs. I do not have the capacity (nor the patience) to tell you what is going on in each state, but I will try to summarize the national scene and offer a couple of examples of interesting approaches in selected states.

Support of Comprehensive Programs

Significant action is taking place in many states to meet the specific needs of high-risk adolescents. Driven by the impending crises in the lives of millions of youths, creative new programs are bubbling up all around the country that try to bring together the requisite health and social services into one place, usually the school.[2] As demand grows and dollars decrease, states are trying to foster coordination and collaboration among state agencies by cutting down on fragmentation and overlap, and are bringing support to disadvantaged communities and school districts in the form of grant programs that call for joint health, social services, and educational initiatives.

As usual, money turns out to be fundamental. Some of the governors appear to expect that outmoded service systems can be turned around completely with "reconfigured" dollars (taking existing funds and moving them from one program to another). But in light of program development experience, this seems like wishful thinking. It is being demonstrated, however, that communities can use relatively small grants to develop more efficient structures for putting program components together, as has been done in Kentucky. Schools are learning how to use Title I (education funds for disadvantaged students) and special-education dollars to develop more comprehensive schoolwide interventions.

States are increasingly turning to "sin taxes" to finance youth services—seventeen states earmark tobacco taxes, and sixteen states set aside alcohol levies to pay for education or health services. Of the thirty-seven states with lotteries, fifteen have designated the proceeds for education, for a total of $5 billion since 1994. Illinois, New York, and South Carolina earmark gaming revenue for education, mental health, and other social services.[3] In Florida, special taxes on gyms and spas help finance school construction.

Most of the impetus for program development at the state level has come either from the governor or from administrators. Unfortunately, state legislators are frequently uninformed about issues, policies, and programs that influence the lives of children and families, even in their own districts.[4] Instead, they are targeted by an onslaught of advocates for special programs like prevention of substance abuse or teen pregnancy, and have little awareness of the growing number of advocates for integrated and effective service systems.

How Much Does "It" Cost?

Among comprehensive programs supported by states the range of efforts is very broad, and so is the cost per program. One comparative cost analysis for the model program Success for All estimated that the additional staff and resources needed to implement it could cost between $250,000 and $650,000 per year per school.[5] The same source figured that the personnel and training for the Comer Social Development model would cost between $100,000 and $275,000 for a school of approximately 500 students.[6] The annual cost for the full-service school models described in chapter 5 ranges from $75,000 each for Kentucky's Youth and Family Service Centers to $800,000 for the most comprehensive community school. School-based clinics average about $150,000 per year, which does not include large amounts of in-kind and donated goods and services. The cost for a clinic user is about $100 per year, while the incremental cost for a student in a community school might be about $1,000. You should know that the average cost per student in public schools in the United States is about $5,500 per year. I might also mention that the cost per student in Hastings-on-Hudson, New York, where I live, is more than $12,000 annually!

Statewide initiatives may focus on only a few sites or on many. In New Jersey's School-Based Youth Services Program, only one school project is funded in each of twenty-nine counties, for a total appropriation of around $7 million per year. In Kentucky's Family and Youth Center's initiative, almost all schools are eligible for youth or family center grants, so that by 1996 about $40 million was being spread around 500 sites.

Block Grants

Many members of Congress believe that the best way to "shrink" the budget is to put grant funds in blocks and give them to states to administer. That means lumping several federal programs together and changing the regulations so that the states assume responsibility for making grants. The result of this approach is that states may receive a smaller sum of money for certain services even though the needs may be growing. The advantage to the states is that they are allowed to make many more decisions about how to spend the money.

Promoting Collaboration at the Local Level

Can states compel education and human services to work together? The balance between state interference and local control is always delicate. State initiatives that give grants to communities to develop their own collaborative program models make sense, especially when a strong administrative structure can be devised. Within a year, new programs can be set up. The important concept is, of course, that the money go directly to those communities that can show that their plans include both school and community resources and are focused on specific behavioral problems.

One problem with the simple RFP (Request for Proposals) approach is that the most needy communities may fail to win grants because of this competitive process. They may not have the grantsmanship skills required, or there may be a shortage of potential collaborators. Yet in the long run, the solution to the problems in the highest-risk communities may be tied inextricably to their gaining greater resources. It is also possible that "tinkering around the edges" will have little significant impact on the academic success of disadvantaged children when compared to the potential effect of redistribution of school funds. As one state official suggested:

> The most important criterion for state efforts [is] the extent to which a state provides disproportionate education, health and social service funding to poor communities. State agencies can coordinate, target and reprogram until everyone is blue in the face, but if basic school aid formulae leave poor school districts with 70 percent less per capita funding than wealthy districts, high risk kids will never be adequately served.[7]

Thus, the issue of equality in educational spending must be considered here as an alternative approach to addressing the youth-at-risk issues at the state level, an approach that is being pursued in certain states (Texas, New Jersey, and nineteen others) and is being met with enormous resistance and controversy.

Massive reallocation of educational funds may be a distant goal but state funding of comprehensive community school efforts is possible right now. However, local program development could be enhanced by access to technical assistance and training from state agencies. But state agency personnel often lack the necessary skills for working in high-risk communities and may need training in how to deal with local agencies in a collaborative setting. It has been observed that state bureaucrats are not encouraged to communicate across agency lines; if they do, they encounter inflexible regulations that make it difficult to change the way they do business. State agencies have to be sensitive to these problems and phase in the granting process with plenty of technical assistance to the most disadvantaged communities—both before and after the grant is awarded. Balance has to be achieved between a state laying a particular program on people and the people having a sense of community control.

The absence of evaluation in most of the ongoing state youth-at-risk efforts is a problem. A consensus exists that these systems should be driven by outcome evaluation. Some state officials feel that any money they can pry loose from the legislature should go directly into services in high-risk communities, that the local people know what to do, and that these new services will surely have a positive effect and improve the situation. Judging from the questions raised about local implementation and integrated service models, there is definitely a need for more program and policy research, monitoring, and evaluation.

Sustaining Programs

How can you get a high-quality, comprehensive youth initiative going that will be able to continue past the term of the governor? How can these initiatives be protected during budget crunches? The New Jersey School-Based Youth Services Program appears to have weathered both a change in administration and budget woes. Not only is it still up and running, but additional funds have been added to create more programs. Of all the state structures observed, the New Jersey program is the least complex bureaucratically, tucked into the Department of Human Resources and covered by a line item in that budget. It is enormously popular around the state and gaining a great deal of recognition around the country. One important factor in its success is local control—the school districts were allowed a lot of flexibility in designing programs, so no two programs are the same. The model is relatively simple, low cost, and makes a lot of sense. Several years ago, New Jersey Right-to-Life tried unsuccessfully to eliminate the program because it provided prenatal and postpartum counseling to teen mothers in schools. The state legislature was not pursuaded, and funding continued without further investigation. By law, contraceptives cannot be distributed nor is there any referral for abortion; thus a major controversy has been pretty much defused. The programs are finally being evaluated, but the results are not yet available.

It's possible that restructuring at the state level—for example, creating mega-agencies—is too complex and time consuming. Perhaps it is most practical to place the responsibility for creating collaborative, school-centered initiatives in one single state agency that can rapidly get the dollars out to communities to create new programs. In one state, a single agency head (Jocelyn Elders, when she was commissioner of health in Arkansas) is credited with bringing about significant changes in the availability of health services for adolescents through the development of school-based centers at the local level. As one observer pointed out, "She went around to all these little communities and talked to the power structure—the school people, the politicians, and the ministers—and then she just wouldn't take no for an answer."[8]

Bill Shepardson, a staff member of the Council for Chief State School Officers and a seasoned researcher on state collaborations, believes that the strategies employed by states to develop integrated programs may be more important than the structures.[9] Children's cabinets, youth commissions, governor's partnerships or whatever the latest initiative is called may not last long enough to bring about real changes in budgeting processes. In his view, more attention should be paid to changing the mind-sets of entrenched state bureaucrats, who are not accustomed to working outside of their own areas.

Shepardson has tracked the progress of ten states in developing structures that enhance collaboration.[10] He finds that most states are trying to follow the same objectives: identifying a central locus in government for child and family programs; promoting accountability by tracking results; making funding streams more flexible; fostering local coordinating bodies; and creating a technical assistance capacity. We can see how these themes are put into effect in the Maryland.

Maryland's Subcabinet and Office for Children, Youth, and Families

Some governors have demonstrated their commitment to children's issues by establishing a special division within their executive offices. Maryland has a very sophisticated version of this structure, building on an Office for Children and Youth that has been on the organizational chart since 1974.[11] In 1989, Governor Shaeffer created a Subcabinet for Children, Youth, and Families composed of the secretaries or directors of all the major state departments and offices, and had it chaired by a Special Secretary.

The organization of the Office of Children, Youth, and Families (OCYF) through the subcabinet makes the governor's office the central focus in state government for planning, monitoring, and coordinating services to Maryland's at-risk children and their families; emphasizes prevention services by redirecting resources from residential treatment placements to community-based preventive services; and reduces the duplication of services in state agencies. The OCYF is charged with developing an interagency plan; an interagency budget; reviewing and monitoring state expenditures for children, youth, and families; developing innovative interagency funding approaches; resolving interagency conflicts; and providing technical assistance to local jurisdictions.

The OCFY is directly responsible for four major statewide initiatives: Governor's Council on Adolescent Pregnancy; Maryland's Making the Grade, a school-based, primary care initiative; State Coordinating Council, which oversees appropriate residential placements for children; and Office of Ombudsman, to protect children at risk from problems resulting from out-of-home placement.

Local Management Boards (LMB) representing a cross-section of the community are being established to plan, coordinate, and implement "seamless" interagency programs at the local level, with members appointed by the local government. Each LMB is required to collect data on local demographics and services provided, and to demonstrate the effects that these services have on participants. According to an analysis of the Council of State Chief School Officers, "There is a deliberate and focused effort in Maryland to move, wherever possible, responsibility for decision making from the state level to the city and county levels."[12] This applies to the state educational authority as well, which has granted waivers to local districts that increase flexibility.

Other States with Cabinets

In Delaware, the governor established a state Family Services Cabinet Council to oversee Family Service Partnerships at the local level. Through this mechanism, state agencies are required to collaborate with one another, working together to coordinate twelve local service centers throughout the state that provide "one-stop shopping" for 140 different services.[13]

West Virginia has a Cabinet for Children and Families, chaired by its governor, that includes agency heads, the state superintendent of schools, and two legislators. It is staffed by the Early Childhood Implementation Commission, which provides technical assistance at the local level. Every county now has a Family Resource Network in place, which is responsible for planning and monitoring coordinated service delivery.

I am happy to report that in my own state, New York, the idea of a more centralized youth-development agency is finally beginning to take root. Governor Pataki has proposed the formation of a State Department of Children and Family Services, beginning with the Division for Youth, which runs detention services, and selected child welfare services from the Department of Social Services, including pregnancy prevention, child care, child-abuse prevention, and other youth-development programs. Advocates are interested in expanding his proposal to include children's mental health and drug and alcohol services.[14]

California's Healthy Start

The California Healthy Start program is an interesting example of how a state can use both approaches—starting a new initiative and using existing funds—to build programs at the local level. As mentioned in chapter 5, the Healthy Start Support Services Act was passed in 1991 to foster local interagency collaborations.[15] A California Partnership for School-Linked Services has provided policy direction for the program and worked on restructuring state policies in support of local initiatives. With the Department of Education as the lead agency, the partnership has involved the Governor's Office, the Office of Child Development and Education, the Health and Welfare Agency, and the Foundation Consortium for School-linked Services, representing more than twenty California foundations.

In four years, beginning in 1992, the partnership awarded 280 planning grants and 140 operational grants involving more than 1,200 school sites. In addition to the Healthy Start money, grantees had to provide a 25 percent "match"—using their own funds for in-kind contributions of such items as space, personnel, and materials—and draw on other sources of funding. More than half of the programs were positioning to become eligible for Medi-Cal (California's Medicaid program). Many other sources of funds were tapped: Title I or special education, county or other public agencies, general funds from the school district, child health and disability prevention, community-based or private service organizations, or grants from foundations.

The California experience gives evidence of the potential for moving public funds from community-based programs into school centers. As of 1996, the Healthy Start program had gained so much visibility in California that its budget was doubled, from $20 million to $40 million. One of the major factors in its success has been the availability of evaluation data showing positive effects on families and children in the programs.

Various approaches are being used at the local level to bring together all the possible participants to create Safe Passage Communities. In some counties, an Interagency Children and Youth Services Council acts as a structure through which local child and family service programs can communicate and begin to work together. As one Healthy Start coordinator reported in California,

> Both Healthy Start and the new Title 1 force us to look at the whole school. Eventually what we are moving toward is to have a single plan for school restructuring which every initiative supports. The thing is not to see these efforts as separate, to make sure everything is working together in the same direction.[16]

Other States with Initiatives

Oregon Benchmarks is a unique, statewide effort to measure improvements in health and education for children and families and provide goals for state agencies that influence planning and budgeting. One outgrowth of this work has been the creation of a Commission on Children and Families that sets policies and coordinates services. Local commissions have been organized in all counties to develop local plans that will achieve the goals set by benchmarks.

Georgia has an Initiative for Children and Families to build community-based comprehensive systems in community or school hubs and to integrate state programs. This effort grew out of the work of a Policy Council for Children and Families, which puts together major decision makers to plan strategies and utilize federal block grants. In Indiana, a Step Ahead initiative is geared toward stimulating local planning through organized councils. Most states have some form of statewide council or commission that pulls together the relevant state agencies to better assist communities.

Florida, in addition to its Full Service Schools, has developed the Florida Healthy Kids Corporation, a school enrollment-based health insurance plan for uninsured children. Each school district in the plan offers schoolchildren insurance premiums on a sliding scale, with the total cost shared among the family, local funds, and state funds. In 1997, the state contributed $39 million to be used primarily for starting up programs. The Robert Wood Johnson Foundation recently allocated $3 million to seven other states to replicate this significant model.

States and School Reform

The state picture would be quite incomplete without an overview of the status of school reform initiatives. Fortunately, *Education Week,* in collaboration with the Pew Charitable Trusts, produces an annual report card that documents the condition of education in each state.[17] According to that source, standards-based reform has emerged as the principle strategy at the state level for improving schools. States are moving ahead fastest in the area of setting their own standards and designing assessments that show how well students perform to meet those standards. However, the resistance to national standards is far-reaching, with almost all states preferring to establish their own.

The state record on improving the quality of teaching is only fair. Half the states have increased the numbers of teachers who graduate from recognized schools of education, yet in at least fourteen states, four out of ten high school teachers do not have a degree in the subject they teach. The report documents that school systems are most frustrated in their struggle to reorganize schools and to improve the school climate. State policies that promote site-based management are not universal. Class sizes are still too large, and schools are still too big in more than half the states.

In regard to funding, a number of states have attempted to equalize the distribution of funds, but even so, huge differences remain. The annual average cost per student (adjusted for region) ranges from $3,537 in Utah to $8,118 in New Jersey. While more funds are going into systems than previously, the new money does not seem to reach the classroom: only half of the total staff is made up of teachers, which means that a lot of money is going toward administrative and overhead costs.

Each state is clearly embarking on its own school reform effort, in most cases independent of the health and social service reforms of the comprehensive initiatives described above. In Utah, a Strategic Planning Act for Educational Excellence was adopted by the state legislature in 1992, calling for a five-year plan that emphasizes student outcomes, school choice, site-based management, and greater parental and business involvement. Utah has adopted content standards and assessments in the core subjects. The governor has put forward a Centennial School initiative that awards funds to advance local reforms. Up until recently, Utah as a rural place could coast along on low school expenditures, but immigration patterns are radically changing the complexion of the state and the need for attention to the problems of high-risk students is mounting as in every other state.

Since 1988, New Jersey's Department of Education has had the power to assume direct control over failing districts. It now runs three inner-city school systems, with less-than-ideal results. In 1996, the state adopted standards in which an explicit link was made between what schools would be expected to teach and how much they should be expected to spend. The state is moving in the direction of supporting more teacher training and upgrading the certification procedures.

States Need Federal Support

States are moving ahead in innovative ways to bring together the necessary resources to create better systems of serving children and families. At the same time, states depend on federal leadership and support, and very little direction has come from Washington about how states can address the need to integrate services at the community level beyond a few demonstration projects. Several federal initiatives mandate state multiagency planning for coordinating services.

ROLE OF FEDERAL GOVERNMENT IN YOUTH DEVELOPMENT

Summarizing how the federal government impacts on youth development is an overwhelming task. Almost everything the government does and fails to do influences the outcomes of children, families, and communities. Here, I attempt only to highlight significant programs supported by the federal government that will have relevance in shaping Safe Passage strategies for the future.

We start with an overview of governmental departments that support various components of youth programming.[18] The appendix at the end of this chapter presents the most current appropriations for selected federal programs that support youth services as they appeared in the budget for the fiscal year ending in the fall of 1997.[19] (The 1998 budget is currently being negotiated.) Totals for the departments are included so you can contrast the enormous amounts of money that are earmarked for items such as welfare, Medicaid, justice, labor, and housing with the amount of funding available for specific youth programs. No one can make much sense of this hodgepodge, nor do we know exactly how many dollars go directly to youth services right now. The National Commission on Children, a congressionally appointed forum "on behalf of the children of the Nation," estimated that in 1989 the federal government spent about $60 billion, or 5.2 percent of the total federal budget, on programs and services for children—and that those funds supported at least 340 programs in eleven different federal departments. (In 1989, the federal budget totaled about $1,100 billion.) A more recent analysis by Margaret Dunkle for the Institute for Educational Leadership identified eighty-two separate federal entities with responsibility for federal programs that serve children and families. These include nineteen congressional committees and twenty-six subcommittees, twelve departments, and twenty-five agencies within departments.[20]

You should know that the total U.S. budget by 1997 was about $1,614 billion—on its way to $2 trillion! Of that amount, the largest departmental appropriations were for the treasury ($381 billion), Social Security ($396 billion), and defense ($254 billion). The Department of Health and Human Services budget is also up there ($351 billion), but that includes Medicare and Medicaid ($270 billion). I point to these astronomical figures so you can see how minuscule the monies being spent on specific youth programs are. The most significant education program for disadvantaged youth, Title I, gets around $7 billion—just one-third of 1 percent of the whole budget. To put this sum in perspective, about $15 billion is being spent annually on the "war on drugs." As another point of comparison, Americans spend about $45 billion a year on gambling.

The departmental overviews that follow present only the barest outlines of how each agency addresses youth issues. (Dollar amounts are only mentioned for a few programs; see the chapter appendix for more detailed funding information.) The primary objective is to demonstrate that many diverse programs aimed at helping young people and their families are scattered throughout the federal bureaucracy, but in isolation from other departments, which means that resources for services are fragmented.

The Federal Role in Education

The role of the federal government in public education is quite misunderstood by the American public. Of the $254 billion spent on public elementary and secondary schools in this country in 1993, *only 7 percent came from the federal government*; 46 percent came from states, 44 percent from localities, and 3 percent from other sources, such as foundations and businesses.[21]

The U.S. Department of Education (DOE) has been a true political football, having been kicked around through several administrations. One platform in the "Republican revolution" after the 1994 election was to get rid of the DOE. Failing to do that, successive budget proposals massively cut education appropriations, and one budget was vetoed by President Clinton because of its potential negative effect on education. The public began to realize where all this could lead, and in the final negotiations on the 1997 budget, education came out reasonably well. But the movement toward budget reduction will certainly continue across line items. The Republican platform in 1996 once again called for the elimination of the DOE, in order to get the government "off the back of educators."

The largest federal expenditure for education (over $7 billion) is distributed through states to the schools under the auspices of Title I, the *Elementary and Secondary Education Act* (ESEA). This major federal program is designed to meet the needs of economically disadvantaged children for educational remediation. Following the recommendations of an independent commission, Title I was amended in 1994 so that some portion of it could be used to involve parents and community agencies in schoolwide programs instead of the traditional approach that took disadvantaged students out of their regular classes for remediation.[22] Title XI of the ESEA gave school districts the flexibility to use 5 percent of their Title I funding for coordinated services programs. According to information put out by the DOE, Title I is supposed to promote better integration of federal, state, and local programs as a strategy for producing better student results. States and school districts are both expected to have plans for Title I schoolwide programs and blueprints for implementing Goals 2000.

Schools in which 50 percent of the children come from low-income families are eligible to use Title I for schoolwide programs, estimated at 22,000 schools. According to Cynthia Brown, a member of the commission, very few communities have changed the way they use Title I money even though they can now using it for building an infrastructure to coordinate many services (as in Safe Passage Schools). About 8,500 are believed to be using these funds for comprehensive programs now, but we do not know what services are included. Altogether, 51,000 schools receive some Title I funds for remedial programs for targeting poor children.[23]

Title I money is distributed to states according to a formula that relies primarily on the number of children 5 to 17 in impoverished families, weighted by the per-pupil expenditure for education in the state. The states disburse the money to counties that then use their own data to distribute the money to school districts, which must come up with a plan for which schools get the money. The plan then goes to the state for approval. States get 1 percent of Title I funds for state administrative purposes.

In 1997, the budget for the first time included substantial funding for charter schools. Some $51 million was divided up among those states with laws permitting charters to stimulate front-end spending by charter groups—funds needed to plan and organize the infrastructure prior to their being able to collect public funds from local school districts. Even Start provides federal funds for local collaborative efforts to improve family literacy through early childhood education, parenting programs, and basic adult education. The funds go directly to local partnerships that bring together school districts and community agencies.

Other major federal funds go to schools for implementation of the Individuals with Disabilities Education Act (IDEA). About $4 billion was appropriated in 1997 for the special education of handicapped children. Under the law, states and local education agencies are required to have on file an Individual Education Plan for each student with a disability, and to pay for whatever services are needed—including speech and physical therapy, and psychological and nursing services. This has resulted in a separate and costly support services program only for children marked by the label "special education."

The Goals 2000: Educate America Act of 1994 authorized states to engage in a five-year school improvement effort that focuses on eight goals mentioned in chapter 6. States were allowed a great deal of leeway in this legislation (and very small grants), and are required to pass much of the funding through to local districts for implementation of standards and training. Some thirty-one states have adopted standards for core subjects; others have begun to develop curricula and assessment procedures or to develop professional training programs. Some states rejected the grants entirely because they did not want federal intrusion.

The DOE also administers an important substance-abuse and violence-prevention program known as Safe and Drug-Free Schools and Communities (Title IV). Besides providing block grants to states, it also supports grants for training school personnel, parents, and community members; for evaluation; for curriculum development; and for direct services. By law, 5 percent of the funds must go through states to support DARE programs (see chapter 9). Funds are distributed to local school districts by states based on the number of school-age children, and the districts may use the funds for after-school programs, counseling, and mentoring as well as classroom curricula. The Safe and Drug-Free

Schools program also administers the Gun-Free Schools Act, which requires states to mandate expulsion of youths caught bringing guns to school.

A School-to-Work Transition initiative joins the U.S. Department of Labor with the U.S. Department of Education to create statewide systems that offer education and training programs. The DOE also funds a number of educational research centers in universities around the country and has a large-scale departmental research operation in Washington.

The Federal Role in Health

Adolescents have access to a variety of federally funded health services administered by the U.S. Department of Health and Human Services (DHHS). Separate streams of funding are directed to adolescent health centers, family planning clinics, special clinics for sexually transmitted disease diagnosis and treatment, special clinics for AIDS, community health centers, and school-based clinics. The most disadvantaged teens are eligible for Medicaid reimbursement for services from private physicians, hospital emergency rooms, and managed-care groups, although many teens do not take advantage of that coverage. Since Medicaid is a state-administered program, however, drastic changes being proposed both at the federal and state levels could limit the amount of funding available and decrease an individual's eligibility.

The Bureau of Maternal and Child Health (MCH) in the U.S. Public Health Service has been a leader in the field of adolescent health for some years, encouraging states to include adolescent health coordinators on their staffs and to use block-grant funds for services for children and adolescents. The commitment to adolescent health has been reiterated frequently by the current DHHS Secretary Donna Shalala and reinforced by the appointment of a director for the Office of Adolescent Health, located in the MCH Bureau. The office, with minimal funding, is charged with studying the special needs of adolescents and forging partnerships within the department and with other agencies to promote coordination and program development. Now faced with budget cuts and reorganization, however, MCH departments in states have begun to eliminate the position of adolescent health coordinator.

Although many states have opted to use Maternal and Child Health (MCH) block-grant funds for school-based services, only $13 million out of the total appropriation ($678 million) is used by states for those purposes. (In addition, states spend about $28 million of their own revenues on school-based health centers.) Healthy Schools, Healthy Communities is a recent initiative of the Bureau of Primary Health Care and the MCH bureau, which for the first time awarded federal grants directly to school-based clinics. Only $3 million was made available for health services at twenty-seven school sites, $1 million for health education in school health centers, and $1.5 million for staff-training grants. This is just a demonstration program and could easily be discontinued next year when the funds run out. The Bureau of Primary Health Care has also stimulated the involvement of more than 200 of its community health centers in the provision of primary health care services in schools, using state, city, or foundation grants. MCH supports a number of other small programs for local partnerships, infant mortality reduction, and service improvement.

Family planning programs are administered directly by a separate Office of Population Affairs, which also runs a very small Adolescent Family Life program that is primarily concerned with funding abstinence programs.

The Division of Adolescent and School Health (DASH) of the Centers for Disease Control and Prevention (CDC) is a government unit with a significant interest in youth development, school health, and prevention programs. (DASH does not appear as a line item in the CDC budget.) DASH administers the Youth Risk Behavior Survey (YRBS), the source for the information in chapter 3. CDC has been the lead agency in AIDS prevention and supports DASH's funding all states and a few cities to organize and evaluate relevant health education and health promotion programs. As part of its efforts for comprehensive school health, it also funds the National Training Partnership to stimulate replication of proven health education models. In addition, CDC has a Division of Violence Prevention that operates a small research and demonstration program. In a separate Division of Reproductive Health Care, CDC has launched a pregnancy prevention initiative at the community level (described in chapter 12).

Many of the prevention programs of interest are housed in the Substance Abuse and Mental Health Services Administration (SAMHSA) of DHHS. The Center for Substance Abuse Prevention (CSAP) supports the High Risk Youth Demonstration Program, which has awarded grants to hundreds of communities for comprehensive efforts specifically targeted on behavioral risk factors. Unfortunately, many of the grants were discontinued following the recent budget cuts. Grantees were told to look to other sources such as Drug-Free Schools and the community development block grants for support. CSAP's Community Partnership Demonstration Program encourages the development of community-wide prevention activities. SAMSHA also supports a Center for Mental Health Services that funds sites to provide interagency systems of care for children with serious emotional disturbances.

DHHS administers the massive National Institutes of Health, which concentrates primarily on research and also supports program services and treatment facilities for adolescents. The National Institute of Mental Health (NIMH) has played an important role in developing prevention interventions that relate to mental health problems among children and youth. Under the auspices of the NIMH, the Child and Adolescent Service System Program (CASSP) has awarded grants to states to improve services to children with severe emotional disturbances. A number of research and development centers have been created in the health field that impact on adolescent health. Most recently, two national centers were designated specifically by the MCH Bureau to support school-based mental health programs.

Funding for AIDS prevention and treatment is included in a number of different DHHS initiatives, including the Ryan White Comprehensive AIDS Resources Emergency Act.

The Federal Role in Welfare

In 1996, national legislation was passed by Congress and signed by President Clinton, and many states adopted new rules for welfare that dramatically affect the lives of poor young people. These include rigid time limits of two years, restrictions on benefits to legal immigrants, work requirements without sufficient support for child care and transportation, requiring teen parents to live with their parents (no matter how abusive) and go to school (without adequate child care). Critics were assured that changes would be made in the legislation to lessen some of the most regressive conditions. Yet the outlook in mid-1997 is grim in many states, where the restrictions are already in place without providing any safety net for those families unable to become self-sufficient within the allotted time period.

Still, in the DHHS, several programs have been initiated that might be accessed through community programs. The Family Preservation and Support Program allots funds for states to plan coordinated community-based prevention activities that alleviate stress and promote parental competency. One of the goals of this legislation is to lower the rates of out-of-home placement of children by strengthening families' capacities to take care of them.

Probably the best-known children's program in the nation, Head Start, is administered by the DHHS's Administration of Children, Youth, and Families (ACYF). This program has survived the budget-cutting frenzy because of the documented impact of early childhood education and parenting programs on future outcomes.

The Crime Bill of 1994 authorized $567 million over six years for a Community Schools Program that was to be divided between the Department of Education and DHHS. That program never happened, but a small program did survive on the welfare side of DHHS. Currently, the Bureau of Family and Youth Services in the ACYF administers a modest Community Schools Youth Services program in which $10 million in grants was awarded to forty-eight community-based agencies in 1995 and $12.8 million in 1997 to integrate youth development principles into the extended-service school model.[24] In 1996, the effort was not included in the budget.

The Bureau of Family and Youth Services is also responsible for the Runaway and Homeless Youth Program that provides housing and support in local crisis-intervention centers. ACYF's National Center on Child Abuse and Neglect runs the Community-Based Family Resource Program, which helps states develop systems of services in communities. Under this authority, states also develop trust funds that provide flexible funding to localities. Finally, DHHS supports a small youth-gang prevention program, awarding grants to twenty-one communities to plan comprehensive, community-specific strategies.

The Federal Role in Justice

The Office of Juvenile Justice and Delinquency Prevention (OJJDP) has launched a major effort in recent years to develop effective prevention programs. Most of its funding is in the form of block grants to states, but about $40 million has been used for discretionary grants to communities. The Title V Delinquency Prevention Program, for instance, gives states funds to award grants to eligible local governments to develop community-wide prevention strategies. Training and technical assistance is also made available to community leaders and practitioners. Over $2 million is earmarked in the Department of Justice budget to promote the establishment and continuation of Boys and Girls Clubs in public housing and other at-risk communities. Cities-in-Schools and the Children at Risk Program also receive support from the OJJDP. A small Safe Futures initiative has been launched in five communities (see chapter 12).

In 1994, the president's Crime Prevention Council was created by Congress as part of the Violent Crime Control and Law Enforcement Act. The Council is chaired by the vice president, and is responsible for coordinating federal crime-prevention programs and assisting communities to step up their own efforts. In late 1995, the council issued a catalog of fifty federal programs that might be used for crime-prevention activities.[25] It is not my intention to list each of those programs here, but only to highlight the possibilities that existed in late 1995 for communities to secure support for some aspect of youth development. The council's review of reports on what works identified 300 specific strategies, ranging from academic achievement to self-defense training, and their catalog includes all of the programs discussed in this section on federal resources.

The President's Crime Prevention Council and HUD operate the Council's small Ounce of Prevention program ($1.2 million), which awarded nine grants to community-based efforts to improve the coordination and integration of youth crime and violence prevention programs. Funds are targeted at the federally designated Empowerment Zones and Enterprise areas around the country.

Community Policing is an important program within the Department of Justice. According to the Department, "community policing consists of two core components—community partnership and problem solving—and brings together the community, police, and government to address crime-related issues."[26] An Office of Community Oriented Policing Services (COPS) has been devised to funnel grants to local communities. Ultimately, 100,000 new officers are supposed to be on the street, with the addition of about 30,000 each year for the three years beginning in 1997.

The Federal Role of Labor

The Job Corps is the government's major effort to provide voluntary education, training, and employment for disadvantaged youth ages 16 to 24 who are in residential settings.[27] Authorized under the Job Training Partnership Act (JPTA), major corporations and nonprofit organizations contract with the DOL to operate 111 Job Corps Centers. Some thirty additional centers are operated by the Departments of Agriculture and the Interior as conservation programs on public lands. JPTA also authorizes a Youth Training Program and other small specialized efforts for disadvantaged youth.

The School-to-Work Opportunities Initiative integrates career employment and education with a special curriculum to prepare youth for the technological demands of the workplace. The replication of the Quantum Opportunities Program (chapter 4) is taking place under the aegis of the Department of Labor.

The Summer Youth Employment and Training Program provides summer jobs, academic enrichment, and other related services to disadvantaged youth ages 16 to 21. Most youth employment programs operate at the local level through a mayor's Office of Employment and Training or the Private Industry Council. Summer jobs have always been an unpredictable resource, since communities rarely know until the beginning of summer whether funds will be forthcoming.

In 1995 and again in 1996, the Department of Labor included a program called Youth Fair Chance in its proposed budget. This was to be a new initiative that would support comprehensive education, employment, and social services programs in high-poverty areas. Funds were never appropriated.

Corporation for National Service

This independent federal corporation was set up to recruit and train individuals to work in community projects. AmeriCorps members receive a stipend and are available as staff to youth programs. VISTA volunteers also serve in disadvantaged areas. Learn and Serve America involves K–12 students in community service. And the National Senior Service Corps encourages older people to use their skills to address community needs.

Housing and Urban Development

HUD has been the major source for YouthBuild, a national effort to create programs for young people interested in rebuilding their communities. Participants receive training in construction and then rehabilitate abandoned buildings or construct housing. Following passage of the YouthBuild Act in 1992. HUD allotted it $50 million in 1995, then cut the appropriation in half in the proposed 1996 budget, but strong support in the Senate resulted in a final appropriation of the original amount. Some 100 organizations receive YouthBuild grants, and another 100 are in the planning stages.

HUD administers major funding for community development, with a block grant to states that supports housing and economic development. It also creates Empowerment and Enterprise Zones in selected communities, which have received huge grants to create plans that include youth-development and safe haven programs.

HUD funds several other important youth initiatives. As part of its Family Investment Center grants to public housing authorities, it supports five Youth

Development Initiative sites and four after-school programs. The National Youth Sports Program gives direct grants to community agencies for sports, recreational, and educational programs in public housing communities. HUD is also contributing to the Eisenhower Foundation's evaluation of community police Kobans in cities around the country.

The Department of Agriculture

The Department of Agriculture has a long history of involvement in youth development through its support of 4H clubs. The Cooperative Extension Service (CES) provides funding to states through a formula grant program and through state land-grant universities that provide educational and technical assistance.[28] In 1991, a special initiative was launched to develop programs at 4H clubs for youth at risk, focusing on school-age child care and education, reading and science literacy, and coalition building.

The Department of Agriculture also sponsors major food programs for children. WIC (food for low-income children and mothers), National School Lunch, School Breakfast, and the Summer Food Service Programs are designed to ensure that disadvantaged children obtain a nutritious meal at least once a day.

The Department of Defense

Even the Department of Defense has some responsibility for youth activities. An Office of Family Policy, Support, and Services operates youth programs for almost 1 million children of the military in 481 youth centers around the world.

The Department of the Interior

Support for the Native American population has traditionally been the responsibility of the Department of the Interior. Indian reservations have their own school and health jursidictions. Additional funds are made available from other federal departments for specific line items.

1998 Budget

This review is being conducted just as the 1998 budget is undergoing the annual congressional orgy of partisan debate. I do not know what the final outcome will be—but it doesn't seem like much will change in regard to youth issues. The proposed Clinton budget holds the line at $1.69 trillion with a promise of deficit termination in five years. The most dramatic cuts would be in Medicare and Medicaid spending, with small reductions proposed for the Departments of Defense, Energy, Interior, and NASA. Increases are proposed for Education, other Health and Human Services programs, and Justice. For education, President Clinton has put forward a new $260 million program called America Reads as a first step in his $2.7 billion volunteer mentoring effort. He has also called for significant increases in monies for Title I, Head Start, charter schools, parental involvement in achieving the Goals 2000 educational reform, bilingual education, and tuition assistance for postsecondary schools. School construction was slated to receive $5 billion but was eliminated in the first round.

Many of the changes in DHHS are on the welfare side, with alterations in the budgeting process that shifts the onus of welfare funding more to the states. The Community Schools program appears in the Administration for Children, Youth, and Families section—this time under Violent Crime Reduction Programs—at the same low level as 1997 ($13 million). More funds are also set aside for the prevention of family violence and sexual abuse. A new Medicaid benefit for children and legal immigrants would be funded out of Medicaid savings, and, additional health insurance for children would be assured. Another new item, $50 million for Abstinence Education, allocated through the Bureau of Maternal and Child Health, may be used only for mentoring, counseling, and adult supervision to promote abstinence from sexual activity, with a focus on those groups most likely to bear out-of-wedlock children.

The Healthy Schools, Healthy Communities program that funded school-based centers has been subsumed under the Community Health Centers cluster, with language that suggests that an increment of $8 million added to the budget should be used for serving uninsured and underserved children through school-based centers. Advocates for school-based health centers are pushing for a line item for school health at a much higher dollar level.

In Justice, the 1998 budget calls for a huge hike for juvenile justice and delinquency-prevention programs, with a heavy emphasis on training and equipping prosecuters to reduce juvenile offenses. Some $75 million of new money would go to schools and communities for crime reduction. A new $50 million violent-youth court program would be established, and $8 million would be for setting up residential programs for at-risk youth. Of particular interest to community-school advocates, the Justice budget includes $60 million in new funds for after-school programs, probably modeled after the Beacons. I have been told that $50 million of this appropriation would be shifted to the Department of Education to fund "21st Century Schools."

All of these new programs are predicated on a falling deficit, which the president believes will result from declining Medicaid and Medicare expenditures by low-income adults and us older folks. As Jeff Simering, legislative director of the Council of the Great City Schools, told *Education Week*, "We could use any help we can get, but if [small amounts are] spread across creation, who knows what it will produce?"[29]

BURNING ISSUES AT THE FEDERAL LEVEL

I think it is safe to say that no consensus exists in the United States on the role of government in financing programs. My own position is quite clear: Safe Passage cannot be assured without federal support. But the current organization of resources is so fragmented and arcane, it has been difficult even to determine what efforts take place where. I have spent many frustrating hours trying to clarify the current status of youth programs, and all I can say for sure is that a number of federal resources are being used to assist youth and their families through appropriations across all departments.

Except for a recent minor initiative for clinics in the Bureau of Primary Health Care, and a small grant program in the Family and Youth Services Bureau for community schools, no federal grants went directly to communities and schools earmarked by Congress for integrated services in 1997. However, the full-service community school concept has been recognized in many recent legislative endeavors, including the crime bill, Title I, versions of health reform, and the new Empowerment Zone grants. The proposed 1998 budget adds dollars for after-school programs to prevent delinquency, and abstinence programs to prevent teen pregnancy. Federal regulations could be changed to facilitate the increased pooling of categorical dollars—for example from special education, HIV prevention, substance abuse, and mental health—to be used for more comprehensive programs. Medicaid is already being used in many schools and clinics, although providers experience difficulties both with determining eligibility and with reimbursement procedures. The advent of managed care adds to the complexity, with providers struggling to establish either fee-for-service or capitation contracts with managed-care providers. Health care reform legislation could guarantee that school-based centers become "essential community providers" and that enrollees in managed-care plans could obtain mental health, health education, and other preventive services within these plans. Congress has just approved new legislation that provides health insurance coverage for low-income children.

Describing the current role of the federal government in assuring Safe Passage is further complicated by the rapid changes taking place in Washington. It is a good bet that new resources will be hard to claim, and that many of the programs mentioned above or listed in the Appendix will either be eliminated or packaged in different ways, probably through looser block grants.

Integration of Services

It's clear that many federal programs have the potential to encourage youth development and ensure Safe Passage, but they are very fragmented and uncoordinated. The federal government has long recognized the need for stronger collaboration among agencies. An Interagency Committee on School Health, organized in 1992, is cochaired by the assistant secretaries of Education and Health and Human Services. The committee consists of more than forty high-level representatives from nine federal departments and agencies and focuses on three areas: integrated services, curriculum, and health services. One function of the committee is to act as a clearinghouse—for example, by compiling a chart listing all the federal programs that provide funds for school health programs. In addition, a National Coordinating Committee on School Health has been put together by representatives from the education and health administrations that brings together thirty national organizations covering health, mental health, and schools.

A Coordinating Council on Juvenile Justice and Delinquency Prevention, chaired by the Attorney General, includes the secretaries of Health and Human Services, Education, Labor, and HUD, along with juvenile justice professionals from state and local governments. This group developed *Combatting Violence and Delinquency: The National Juvenile Justice Action Plan*, which outlined strategies that provide opportunities for youth and strengthened communities, as well as for treatment and punishment.[30] (I have no idea how this council relates to the Crime Prevention Council.)

But committee meetings, communication, and reports are not sufficient to bring together the necessary resources. It would be more effective to create formal links among the various departments and to pool money at the national level to support comprehensive projects such as full-service community schools or multicomponent, community-based efforts. Several pieces of legislation have been introduced in recent years to address these issues, but they have either never been fully implemented or failed to win support of the Congress.

Unsuccessful Legislative Attempts

The Claude Pepper Young Americans Act was signed by President George Bush in 1990, enabling the Administration on Children, Youth, and Families to appoint a commissioner who would advocate for children and youth and coordinate programs within DHHS and other agencies. The act called for grants to states and community programs for children, the establishment of a national clearinghouse, and the holding of a White House conference on children, youth, and families. No funds were ever authorized to carry out these functions. No White House conference was held.

In 1991, Senator Bill Bradley introduced the Link-up for Learning Act, a grant program to be administered by the Department of Education to provide coordinated services for youth.[31] Grantee schools or community agencies would be expected to expand and improve educational programs and develop partnerships with other agencies that provided a broad array of support services. Phrases such as "co-location," "one-stop," and "case management" appear frequently in the proposed act. A Federal Interagency Task Force consisting of the secretaries of Education, HUD, and HHS would work toward creating jointly funded programs and make recommendations to Congress to facilitate collaboration. An appropriation of $50 million was sought. This bill did not pass.

The Comprehensive Services for Youth Act was put forth by Senator Edward Kennedy in 1992, calling for an authorization of $250 million to be used at the local level for youth-development-oriented, school-based health and social service centers; at the state level for coordination; and at the federal level to fund the creation of demonstration models with the ability to serve targeted high-risk populations (e.g., runaways, the homeless, immigrants, youth with HIV, adolescent parents, etc.). A Federal Council for Children, Youth, and Families was to be charged with making recommendations on how to remove barriers to coordination and comprehensive service delivery within one year of enactment. This act did not pass.

The Healthy Students–Healthy Schools Act was sponsored by Senator Jeff Bingaman in 1994. The legislation would establish an office in the CDC and create a national advisory council to review, coordinate, and streamline federal health education efforts. The measure would also ensure that the DOE's drug-free schools money could be used in conjunction with comprehensive school health programs. This act did not pass.

Finally, in late 1994, two initiatives were passed under the Violent Crime Control and Law Enforcement Act (the "Crime Bill"): the Family and Community Endeavor Schools Program, assigned to the Department of Education, and the Community Schools Youth Services and Supervision Program, assigned to DHHS. Both gave grants to community-based organizations or schools to provide after-hours services in schools, modeled after the Beacon program in New York City. Proposed authorizations started with $37 million in the first year, growing to $200 million six years later. As I pointed out above, only a small amount of funding was expended. In 1995, $10 million in grants was awarded by DHHS to a few agencies. In 1996, no grants were awarded, and in 1997, the authorization grew to only $12.8 million.

The latest attempt to develop a more rational federal system for supporting children and youth services was the Youth Development Community Block Grant of 1995. Senator Nancy Kassebaum took the lead to reallocate existing federal funding for preventive youth programs into a more coherent approach. The legislation supported the idea of local control through direct funding of youth services and focused on prevention rather than crisis intervention. Each community would be expected to form a local board, appointed jointly by the county chief in conjunction with the local community leaders. All funds would pass through states and be distributed to counties based on a federal formula (youth population, poverty, and crime rates). The total pot to be distributed, $2 billion, would be pulled from twenty-three existing programs in DHHS, Labor, Education, and Justice, minus a reduction of 10 percent to further budget-cutting efforts. During the legislative process, several changes were made in the funding and administration, but Congress did not approve the measure. Youth advocates were not in agreement on this bill—some favored it because it gave communities more control over the funds, others feared that the county chiefs would gain too much power over the programs and many important interventions might be cut out in the block-grant process.

Lessons Learned

Somewhere in my voluminous files, I came across an anonymous document from the Domestic Policy Council that presents an analysis of past experience with intergovernmental partnerships and provides important insights that can guide those who seek to eliminate some of these administrative tangles.[32] If you want federal agencies to work closely together, the initiative must be directed from the White House and located there. Interagency initiatives cannot function without budget, staff, and resources for administrative purposes above and beyond the regular agency funding. Everyone believes that flexibility is important, but this is not possible without the authority to waive regulations. Comprehensive initiatives should be careful not to promise more than they can deliver. Tracking and accountability mechanisms need to be in place from the outset and supported by all parties. The federal government is advised to get its own house in order—to have a clear set of goals and a well-defined infrastructure—before advising states and communities that they must do the same.

In the final chapter, I propose an approach that I think would be effective in targeting resources for critical needs. After so many abortive efforts, it is time for Congress to come to grips with both the problems of providing services to youth and the necessity of creating more integrated systems. But what happens in Washington is only one piece of the action. We have to pay equal attention to the fifty states to stimulate initiatives, work for school reform, and support integrated services.

APPENDIX	Selected Federal Funds for Youth-Related Programs, FY 1997 (millions)	
Total		**1,631,000**
Department of Education		***28,340***
Title I, Elementary and Secondary Education (ESEA) and other grants for disadvantaged		7,690
Impact aid		617
Special Education, Individuals with Disabilities (IDEA)		4,036
Vocational education		1,139
Adult education		354
Bilingual/Immigrant education		262
Goals 2000: Educate America Act		
State and local improvements		476
Parental assistance		15
School-to-Work Opportunities Act		200
Research and statistics, and other educational improvement items		398
School-improvement programs (16 programs)		1,425
Safe and Drug-Free Schools and Communities		556
Charter schools		51
Student financial assistance		7,560
Libraries		136
Department of Health and Human Services (DHHS)		***351,086***
<u>Health Resources and Services Administration</u>		<u>3,481</u>
Maternal and child health block grant		681
No specific sum for adolescent health		
Healthy Start		96
Community (Consolidated) Health Centers		757
Office of Population Affairs		
Family planning		198
Adolescent Family Life		14
Ryan White AIDS Program		896
Healthy Schools, Healthy Communities (included with MCH and Community Health Centers)		
<u>Medicaid</u>		<u>102,000</u>
<u>Centers for Disease Control</u>		<u>2,230</u>
Preventive services block grant		145
Chronic and environmental disease prevention		230
Sexually transmitted diseases and TB		186
Violent crime reduction		32
Prevention centers		7
<u>Substance Abuse and Mental Health Services</u>		<u>2,098</u>
Mental health block grant		275
Children's mental health		60
Substance abuse block grant		1,271
Center for Substance Abuse Provention		176

**APPENDIX Selected Federal Funds for Youth-Related Programs, FY 1997
(millions)**

<u>Administration for Children, Youth, and Families</u>	<u>36,238</u>
Family support (welfare programs)	16,876
Head Start	3,981
Foster care and adoption aid	4,445
Social services block grant	2,500
Family Preservation and Support Program	240
Child care and development block grant	956
Runaway and homeless centers	69
Community-based resource centers	51
Teen-pregnancy-prevention initiative	30
Community schools	14
Department of Justice	***14,520***
Office of Juvenile Justice and Delinquency Programs	
Block grants to states	100
Delinquency-prevention program in communities	20
Youth-gang prevention	10
Youth mentoring	4
Safe Futures Partnership	8
Department of Labor	***32,874***
Job Corps	1,154
Summer Youth Employment	871
School-to-Work Opportunities Act	200
JPTA Youth Training	126
Department of Housing and Urban Development	***29,928***
Community development block grant	4,600
Youthbuild	30
Department of Agriculture	***56,954***
Children, Youth, and Families at Risk Initiative	10
4H Youth Development	64
Food stamps	23,500
School lunch	4,905
School breakfast	1,225
WIC—food for low-income women and children	2,600
Department of Interior	***7,404***
Bureau of Indian Affairs, including school	450

APPENDIX   Selected Federal Funds for Youth-Related Programs, FY 1997 (millions)

Department of Treasury	*380,559*
Gang resistance education and training	11
Department of Defense	*254,824*
Corporation for National Service	*258*
AmeriCorps	215
Learn and Serve America	43

Source: *Department of Labor, Health and Human Services, and Education and Related Agencies Appropriation Bill*, 1997, Senate Report 104–368, Calendar No. 589, September 12, 1996; "Data Bank: Final Fiscal 1997 Appropriations and President Clinton's Fiscal 1998 Proposals," *Education Week*, February 19, 1997, pp. 16–17; Office of Management and Budget, *A Citizen's Guide to the Federal Budget* (Washington, DC: U.S. Government Printing Office, 1997).

Note: Numbers do not add to totals within departments because only programs that cover children and youth were selected.

14

ENSURING
SAFE PASSAGE

*To do good things is noble. To advise others to do good things is even nobler—
and a lot easier.*

—Mark Twain

The social needs of children and their families are approaching crisis proportions. In 1996, President Clinton was reelected, and we voted in a new Congress. If the president wants to leave a substantial legacy, he will have to act quickly to demonstrate his commitment to ensuring Safe Passage for the children of this country. Volunteerism is not a sufficient response. In any case, this crisis cannot be met overnight. The year 2000 is rapidly approaching, bringing with it another president and, possibly, a different Congress. If we as a nation believe that these issues are real and critically important, we have to join together and demand a meaningful response over the long haul.

I have tried to offer convincing evidence that investing in programs that work is both a constructive public policy and a strong ethical position. I hope you are willing to join this movement—to celebrate the contributions of youth work; to build stronger and more effective institutions; to involve families, schools, communities, and youth themselves; and to use scarce resources rationally and productively so that every child gets an even chance to succeed in life. I personally expect to be involved in the creation of a large-scale initiative to introduce new kinds of extended, full-service community schools as hubs for strengthening the children, their families, and their neighborhoods. It is essential that we bring together the school restructuring movement and the advocates for comprehensive health, mental health, and social services.

Now my job is to pull this whole argument together into a cogent charge for the future. We are almost into the twenty-first century, when projected changes in families, immigration, the economy, technology, and information systems will affect the quality of life. Although social, demographic, and economic trends are somewhat predictable as extrapolations of the past, changes are taking place so rapidly that the crystal ball is unclear. All we can say with certainty is that future generations will not succeed without careful planning by, and constant attention from, responsible adults.

I maintain that the elements we need for social planning are not a mystery. The components that have to be put together to produce effective programs are summarized in this chapter. A call is issued for the passage of a Safe Passage Act and the creation of a Safe Passage Commission to validate the nation's commitment to the future of young people. Although the legislation would emanate from the White House and the Congress, the Safe Passage Movement must unite all caring people from the public and private sectors at the local, state, and national levels.

WHAT ADOLESCENTS NEED

All adolescents have certain universal requirements. As I have stressed throughout this work, every child must be connected to a responsible adult—if not a parent, then someone else. All young people must have access to cognitive learning, literacy and numeracy, and the development of critical thinking and reasoning skills. Adolescents also have to be taught the skills of social competency, how to relate to peers and adults in a demanding and often perplexing world. At the same time, in order to develop value systems, young people need room to experiment and make decisions based on rational choices. They must see visible opportunities for success, perceive that the society has high expectations for them, and understand what's required in the world of work. They must feel that their voices are being heard and that their feelings respected. And finally, young people have to be surrounded by a sense of safety in their homes, their schools, and their communities.

Millions of young people can be assured that these needs will be met. Most families nurture their children, and many schools can provide the stimulating atmosphere they require. Yet the futures of millions of other young people are in jeopardy. We know in great detail about what they are doing and experiencing that makes them vulnerable to poor outcomes. The score card on the new morbidities—sex, drugs, violence, and depression—is readily available to all who want documentation of adolescent troubles. I have estimated that fully one-third of youth in mid-adolescence (14 year olds) are not going to make it because of their personal, social, educational, and environmental circumstances. We know quite a lot about the characteristics of these young people.

The teenagers who demonstrate the most high-risk behaviors are those who start acting out at early ages. One kind of troublesome behavior seems to lead to others, and eventually these young people are differentiated from achieving youngsters in many ways. High-risk adolescents tend to come from high-risk families, where they lack parental nurturing and support and are deprived of cultural enrichments. School is a danger zone, as these youngsters fall further and further behind with little hope of graduating with their peers. They are susceptible to negative peer influences. Many of these youth live in very deprived circumstances, in dangerous communities with poor schools and few supports. This lamentable life script is so often repeated that people have grown immune to its implications.

But not all children growing up in difficult situations get into trouble. We know that some young people are protected by their own resiliency and invulnerability and make it despite all odds. In most cases, some adult has extended a helping hand.

PROGRAM COMPONENTS OF THE SAFE PASSAGE MOVEMENT

In order to design more effective interventions, we have to start with an understanding of the characteristics and needs of youth. I believe that programs must focus on those more general characteristics rather than on specific behaviors like smoking or truancy or unprotected sex. Programs have to build on young people's strengths and resiliency and offer them opportunities for positive youth development. We have identified a host of programs that have been evaluated and appear to work. From these programs, I have extracted a number of components that should be incorporated into all programs as we try to move the demonstration models to scale. Table 14.1 displays the effective components according to the point of entry: individual, family, school, and community. The

---

TABLE 14.1   Effective Components of Safe Passage Programs

Individual
Early intervention: preschool and home visits
One-on-one attention: attachment to a parent or another adult
Youth empowerment: listening to their voices

Family
Training in parenting
Parental involvement and support, responding to family needs
Intergenerational involvement

School
Educational achievement: acquisition of cognitive skills
Effective principals as innovators and gatekeepers
Teachers with high expectations for all students
Teachers trained to manage classrooms
School-based but not necessarily school-operated
Social skills/competency training
Group counseling on psychosocial issues
Community service experience

Community
Community location as alternative to school
Community outreach: indigenous workers
Cultural responsiveness
Community police
Safe havens
Incentives and entrepreneurial approaches
Work force experience

Comprehensive interventions
Multicomponent; multiagency
One-stop health and social services
Intense and sustained media backup
Changing/enforcing policies

---

provision of one-on-one individual attention, a focus on acquisition of basic cognitive skills, training in social skills and competency, and the development of multicomponent school and community interventions is especially important in the design of successful programs.

I have shared with you my own visions of a Safe Passage School and a Safe Passage Community that encompasses all of these components. I strongly believe that we have the knowledge necessary to create schools and communities in which all children flourish, but not without resolving many issues. Research on, and observations of, programs have provided insights into why many programs fail and what difficulties some programs experience in trying to replicate successful models. Aside from lack of funds, programs don't work because they are based on faulty theory, have poor personnel practices, are not organized efficiently, and do not faithfully replicate successful models. A recognition of these kinds of shortcomings and pitfalls must be built into the design of effective programs. The theory may be great, but if the practice is weak or faulty, the impact will be nil. The major implementation issues identified in this book are summarized in Table 14.2.

REPLICATING SUCCESSFUL PROGRAMS

Questions about theory, practice, organization, and administration all must be dealt with by practitioners if the Safe Passage Movement is to be effective. Many

---

TABLE 14.2   Implementation Issues

Theory
Targeting behaviors or targeting environments?
Targeting only high-risk youth or everybody?
Expectations of success: realistic?
Systems change or relocation of personnel?

Practice
Leadership: charismatic? One of a kind?
Need for continuous technical assistance
On-site coordinator/facilitator
Staff turnover
Union regulations
Time-consuming processes
Turf ownership

Organization and Administration
Centrality of planning
Mode of governance
Dealing with controversy
One-stop or referral system?

Replication
Cookie cutters or anarchy?
Fidelity to model (curriculum)
Model overadvertised: promises too much
Requires continuous monitoring

TABLE 14.3   Factors Influencing Replication of Programs

Support
Funds
Legislation that provides funds for new starts
Foundation favor
Marketing, particularly of curricula

Research
Evidence of success: evaluation that shows outcomes
Documentation of models

Practice
Charisma of the leader: well-known personality, big following
Presentations at national conferences, papers, media
Responsive to special groups: e.g., rites of passage for African American males

Politics
Political savvy: knowing who controls program supports
Powerful board membership
Lobbying

Organization
Attention to training and providing on-site technical assistance
National youth organizations: have capacity to assist affiliates
National research organizations: have capacity to design, research, and implement
Universities: have capacity to design, research, and implement, usually under
    auspices of special university-based centers

---

factors influence replication—evaluation, leadership, organizational affiliation, marketing practices, and availability of support. Table 14.3 reviews those factors.

But keep in mind that every well-documented, theory-based program does not get replicated, and that some programs with negative or inconclusive evaluations do. Researchers may be disappointed to learn that research findings alone definitely do not drive replication. Who you know does matter, and it matters if you are in touch with the establishment among foundation folks, university gurus, national youth-serving agencies, or public officials. For the little guy in the inner city or in a remote rural area, it is difficult to get a handle on support mechanisms such as technical assistance. I get calls all the time from individuals who have interesting ideas about programs they would like to implement, but no clue as to how to obtain funding. (They think I am a foundation.) It is difficult for nonaffiliated people to learn about the sources of financial support. This reality adds more importance to the development of strong coalitions at the local level that become the stimulus for community-wide activities. A group of practitioners, a mix of school and community people, will have much more strength in asking for support than an individual—no matter how great the idea.

A keyword in all this is "flexibility." Practitioners, policy makers, and community people of every description have to bend. They have to find new ways of doing business with each other and new ways of working with the public. The concept of community policing is an excellent example of the new flexibility. The cop is back on the beat, trained with a view toward mentoring and ameliorating social conditions. The probation officer can move his office into the school and act as a counselor. With more flexible school-community partnerships, the teacher is encouraged to spend time with and instruct the parent how to help the child with homework. The nurse practitioner stationed in a school can help an asthmatic child breathe and give medication that prevents absences. Schools can be located in lofts, and police bureaus can move into community centers.

Change is required. And change is taking place at the local level in selected pockets of activity around the country. I have offered you many examples of effective programs that are really helping children, youth, and families overcome the odds. Will all this wonderful energy and imagination be dissipated as we try to institutionalize effective change? That is a tough question. We have to create the mechanisms that translate this knowledge of youth-development programs and practices into broad-scale changes. Actions will be required at the national and state levels to stimulate movement from the top down and at the local level to capture the energy and organize the movement from the bottom up.

CREATING A SAFE PASSAGE MOVEMENT

The question is, Where do we go from here, and how do we get there? A number of strategies could be considered for moving toward building strong comprehensive service systems that involve schools and community agencies. Many federal agencies (as in chapter 13) already support programs that could be strengthened and could offer real leadership in youth development. It is also possible to design and support new legislation that would place youth development programs in a position that transcends existing federal departmental structures. Or we could assume that the impetus is already in place in the nonprofit sector to stimulate state and local groups to move forward without looking for federal leadership.

Building on Existing Federal Structures

One could advance compelling arguments for or against placing the administration of an integrated youth initiative in the departments of Education or Health and Human Services or Justice or Housing and Urban Development. All have programs that address the delivery of comprehensive services in one-stop locations. The major benefit of any one choice would be that the bureaucracy is already in place. Advocates could focus on the Community Schools program in DHHS and work to expand the funding, or, perhaps, the new program in the Department of Justice that will support after-school services that could be extended, or through the Department of Education, Title I regulations could be further amended to create more responsive whole school programs. Settling on one government agency, however, would not solve the problem of merging interdepartmental funding streams. The record for crossing departmental lines and integrating education and health and human services is very poor.

An argument could be made in favor of locating a new major initiative in the White House, or the creation of a separate commission, such as the Corporation for National Service or NASA, may be worth consideration. One would have to determine whether these are really effective mechanisms for establishing connections to communities, fostering collaboration among existing agencies, and carrying out the goals of a new initiative.

Designing New Legislation

What kind of legislation would we need to establish the authority for funding partnerships between schools and community agencies to create comprehensive programs? The thrust would be to create a new initiative at the highest government level that would give visibility to the movements for full-service community schools and other integrated programs, override departmental interests, make the best use of existing program funds, and make it possible to mix those resources at the state and community level.

I propose a Safe Passage Act, based on the premise that school reform cannot succeed without attention to child and family support services, and the provision of prevention and support services will have little impact without attention to reformation of schools. The Safe Passage Act provides support to local communities for the development of responsive twenty-first century institutions that bring together the best in school enrichment and support programs.

Components of the Safe Passage Act

The legislation would require a president to take active, visible leadership in the following actions:

(1) Promote an initiative that would result in the rapid implementation of effective comprehensive school/community programs across the nation.

(2) Bring together the branches of the federal government to integrate service systems and fiscal resources.

(3) Assist states to leverage their resources to support comprehensive programs.

(4) Assure maximum accountability and priority for the cause of youth development.

(5) Stimulate and support communities to develop local coalitions to create community schools.

Safe Passage Cabinet

The President would also need to organize a Safe Passage Cabinet, including the Secretaries of Health, Education, Labor, Justice, Housing and Urban Development, Agriculture, and other relevant government agencies. The Cabinet would be held responsible for pooling categorical funds and revising policies to ensure communities greater access to comprehensive services.

Safe Passage Commission

The legislation would create a "blue-ribbon" Safe Passage Commission committed to assisting states and communities to bring together and integrate the resources they need to help children, families, schools, and communities. The commission, appointed jointly by the president and Congress, would be made up of prominent citizens from various sectors who would serve for five-year terms and act as the governing body for the initiative. The Safe Passage Commission would be constituted as an independent agency with emergency powers.

Appropriations

The act would call for an immediate one-year appropriation of $10 million that would support a small staff of the Safe Passage Commission in the White House, for planning the Safe Passage program and organizing the Commission. The second-year appropriation would be $700 million, divided among state grants, direct grants to communities, and continued work of the Safe Passage Commission.

Initial Work of the Commission

The Commission staff would bring in experts to document in detail: (1) the communities with the highest priority for immediate attention; (2) the programs that work; (3) the technical assistance resources that must be available to foster implementation; (4) the policies and regulations in government agencies that must be changed to de-categorize funding sources and build more comprehensive, intensive approaches; (5) the monitoring, accountability, data collection, and evaluation requirements. Much of this material has already been completed by various university centers and youth-development agencies. The first work of the Commission would be to devise procedures for awarding grants.

State Grants

The state money ($100 million) would be distributed according to the number of children in poverty in each state. States would be expected to use these funds to set up a Safe Passage Initiative in the Governor's Office or to support existing integrated children's agencies (as in Maryland). The state would be required to develop a plan for integrated school/community services, to identify technical assistance resources, and to help communities apply for grants. Title I planning could be adapted for these purposes. An important role for states would be to foster activity in the most underdeveloped, needy communities.

School/Community Grants

At least $500 million would be distributed directly to community coalitions, school districts, and/or community agencies with the capacity to develop appropriate Safe Passage programs using models that have documented results. Initially, about 2,000 grants of $250,000 each would be made available to create local infrastructures such as community schools, community networks, or local commissions. (A city could be eligible for multiple grants; existing community schools would also be eligible.) Proposals from local groups would have to demonstrate an understanding of "what works" and incorporate those principles into their plans of action. The proposals would have to demonstrate how the organizing group would tap into existing resources, for example Title I and Drug-Free Schools, and the new literacy effort, if funded.

Or, Alternatively . . .

States would administer all grants. Communities would have to apply to states and demonstrate their capacity to design effective community schools. States would be required to meet performance standards in regard to funding procedures, technical assistance, accountability, and monitoring.

Continuing Work of the Commission

In the second year, the Safe Passage Commission (with a budget of about $100 million) would turn to issues such as training, program research and evaluation, and dissemination of materials. Grants would be given to universities and youth program development agencies to create training opportunities for Safe Passage workers. A grant program in program research would be organized by the commission, either independently or through one of the national institutes.

As a major presidential initiative, the Safe Passage Act would give enormous visibility to youth development programs and would allow local communities to turn their own visions into realities. This legislation would have to comprehend the concept that one size does not fit all, and fund a range of models. The appropriations would be expected to grow each year to about $1 billion in year five.

The total amount required to create Safe Passage neighborhoods can be estimated based on local school populations. Using the Title I criterion, 22,000 of the nation's 80,000 public schools house very disadvantaged children. If each of these school was used as the hub for a community center, and required $250,000 per year to support nonacademic expenses, the total amount necessary would be more than $5 billion—more than the Head Start appropriation or about two-thirds of Title I. However, if the Safe Passage Commission were to use its strength to identify and pool other sources of funding, much lower amounts would be necessary.

Administration of the Safe Passage Act

The Safe Passage Commission, as an independent corporation, would have the responsibility for administering the funds, building a staff from personnel outstationed from the involved federal agencies. This would mirror the same practice advised in the creation of Safe Passage schools—the relocation of people who work in community agencies into school buildings in order to offer comprehensive programs. Transferring existing federal personnel to the new corporation would save funds and give experienced federal employees a new challenge.

FUNCTIONS OF A SAFE PASSAGE INITIATIVE

Our review of what works and what doesn't in youth programming can serve as guide to the kinds of activities that must be undertaken to produce an appropriate response to the critical and multiple needs of children and families. These functions are necessary no matter what long-term strategy is pursued, whether a new federal initiative, or building on existing administrative structures, or relying on the nonprofit sector at the state and local level.

Leadership

A primary goal of this Safe Passage initiative is to gain national recognition of the importance of emerging school-community models. This requires strong political support, visibility, and funding.

Intelligence

Gathering accurate and current information about federal programs is hard work. To develop a rational and orderly approach to assuring Safe Passage, someone has to determine, *across departments*, exactly what youth-serving programs are already in existence, whom they serve, what the eligibility is, and what the regulations are. A compilation of programs must be prepared for the commission in order to make decisions about overlapping efforts and reduction of fragmentation. The Finance Project and the Institute for Educational Leadership, both in Washington, could provide useful assistance with this task.

Technical Assistance

This new federal initiative has to be ready to advise communities about governance issues. While many parties agree that collaborative efforts between schools and community agencies are essential, less consensus exists on how to put these efforts together. Experience has shown that outside agents, called facilitators or coordinators, are very important elements in successful school restructuring and community development enterprises. A cadre of trained experts has to be prepared to stay with a local project over time. The model used in the Department of Agriculture's Extension Service might be useful here, that of the county agent who traditionally works to organize 4H programs for youth and other activities for the people in the community. Many of these extension services operate out of land-grant universities.

Staffing

If comprehensive programs are to be implemented in thousands of communities, a new breed of professional youth worker is required. These people need a knowledge of planning techniques, exposure to effective programs, superior negotiation skills, cultural sensitivity, and a willingness to work hard. An appreciation of the different climates of schools and community agencies would be essential. Many youth workers already have those qualifications. The task for the commission would be to legitimate Safe Passage workers as a broad professional group.

Training

A considerable amount of training is already being sponsored under federal auspices in each of the specialized fields. Millions of dollars are being spent on workshops, teleconferencing, Internet, newsletters, and the production of videos. But, little of that training leads to the production of people who would become Safe Passage workers.

In the future, all relevant training and professional education should be infused with the Safe Passage philosophy, the concepts that go with intensive comprehensive program development. Many universities are already involved in rethinking how teachers are trained, recognizing that schools of education require at least as much restructuring as the local schools that receive their products. Clearly, teacher education must encompass not only the new methodologies that work but also help modern teachers understand and be able to deal with the contemporary scene in which they will be working. Rethinking the training and certification of principals is a critical issue, since they appear to be the primary bridge between educational and service initiatives. All other professional training also must be revamped so that psychologists, social workers, health practitioners, youth counselors, and recreation specialists all understand the core elements of Safe Passage, particularly the importance of educational achievement.

A function of the commission would be to recognize the importance of youth work and lay out the dimensions for the design of a new profession, including accreditation requirements. The commission would encourage universities to modernize their curricula across disciplines, prepare Safe Passage facilitators and coordinators, and conduct relevant research.

Accountability

It is evident that certain basic pieces of data are indispensable in launching a major initiative of these dimensions. For planning, it would be necessary to compare communities in terms of quality of life for youth (school achievement, risk behaviors) and availability of resources. For monitoring grants, it would be necessary to know not only how funds are being spent but also to what effect.

A Safe Passage record system could be devised that would track individual students through their school experiences. The adoption of such a system could be a grant requirement, giving grantees the opportunity to monitor their own programs as well as to provide state and federal agencies with routine reports. This new system could be built on the experience of the Centers for Disease Control with the extension of the National Youth Risk Behavior survey through states.

Evaluation and Research

It is quite obvious that much more effort is required to define the essential components for assuring Safe Passage. Although I have maintained that we know in general what works, much still remains unknown. We know that one size does not fit all. A research effort must be launched to carefully examine the components of Safe Passage programs—to continue to evaluate the relative effectiveness of one-on-one approaches, social skills and competency training, career preparation, and many other issues that are not resolved.

ROLES FOR NONGOVERNMENTAL ORGANIZATIONS

Organizing a Safe Passage Movement

Charles Bruner, director of the Child and Family Policy Center, Des Moines, Iowa, has been a major contributor to the nation's thinking about reform of service systems for children and families. He, too, calls for a new vision at the national level that transcends categorical boundaries, yet he acknowledges the lack of what he calls "grassroots mobilization." He uses as an example the Christian Coalition and the numbers and passion it can mobilize because it has "established a vision more compelling than others currently available, one that resonates with a broad swath of working Americans anxious about their, and their children's future."[1] According to Bruner (and I agree), "we" have not brought together a coalition that articulates themes such as family values and individual responsibility, although that is what we are addressing in our work.

Achieving a Safe Passage climate requires the creation of an inclusive movement across all sectors. "We" have to lay claim to the "high ground" and mobilize Americans to support this call for immediate, intensive action at the local, state, and federal levels. As Evelyn Frankford, director of a statewide youth initiative for the State Communities Aid Association in New York points out, "We reformers too often express our ideas too abstractly, and our language is unclear. If our intended audience is a larger public beyond the 'converted,' there is a disconnect between the way we present our agenda and what the public is concerned about."[2]

A Coalition for Safe Passage has to be drawn together that builds on the many lessons from the past, draws in a much larger constituency from all sectors, gives youth and parents opportunities to articulate their needs and hopes, and, as Bruner would say, "resonates" with the American people.

Foundations

Creating a Safe Passage Movement is not just a federal initiative. Private and nonprofit sectors would have to join in this cause if it is to be successful.

Foundations, as we have seen, are important factors in initiating demonstration programs and research, but, as with the federal government, the results are fragmented. Much of the foundation-sponsored, youth-related research never gets applied to program practice. Just as the government should institute a Safe Passage Cabinet that crosses functional domains, foundations should get together and think about a more comprehensive, long-term role. And foundation youth-program experts should definitely sit on the Safe Passage Commission.

Universities

If we are to develop the kinds of cross-disciplinary approaches demonstrated in exemplary programs, universities will have to alter professional training in many ways.[3] As we have seen in chapter 8, universities are already moving ahead to create interprofessional training opportunities, along with experiential learning through collaborations with schools and community agencies. Some of the most innovative models of new kinds of institutional arrangements are found in university-assisted schools (see the Turner School in chapter 4).

Youth Development Agencies

National organizations that serve youth can have a powerful role in the Safe Passage Movement. At the national level, their representatives can be articulate spokespersons for young people because they speak with authority about their constituencies. The fact that these agencies have hundreds and even thousands of local affiliates makes them important partners in the development of comprehensive programs. National youth agencies have considerable experience in training youth workers and are eager to work collaboratively to strengthen their methods.

The private, nonprofit, "think-tank" operations—Public/Private Ventures, RAND Corporation, Academy for Educational Development, SRI, Urban Institute, Search Institute, among others—are important players in the youth-development field. Along with universities, they are the primary researchers and program evaluators. Many of their staff members can contribute substantial knowledge to the growing "state of the art."

Churches

Religious groups have a strong interest in the ethical and moral development of young people. The potential strengths of churches in the Safe Passage Movement must be incorporated in community endeavors. Churches can supply volunteers who wish to act as mentors, tutors, and youth advocates. Church buildings are excellent places for after-school and evening programs. And often they are the only safe havens left in the neighborhood for children and their families. Church leaders definitely have "bully pulpits" from which they are in a position to influence the thinking of their parishioners and congregants. They can help people understand the importance of assisting all children to overcome social, economic, racial, and gender barriers to success.

Business

American industry knows that it has much to gain from a Safe Passage Movement. Unless the vast majority of American youth are readied for their places in the labor force, the economy will suffer and the quality of life decline. Many corporations, small businesses, and unions have already joined partnerships with school and community groups in school-to-work and other school-linked programs. Articulate business leaders can be the strongest advocates for Safe Passage programs because they have credibility with sectors of the American public that may not be so sympathetic to youth work.

Senior Citizens

Millions of retired people want to contribute to their society by working with young people. Senior citizen groups make ideal partners in community-wide programs. Seniors are available during the daytime hours to go into schools and help out in classrooms, clinics, recreational, and cultural programs. We must not forget that, in many communities, senior citizens control the purse strings and must be convinced that social programs are a sound investment.

Media

Every aspect of media can be turned toward shaping a better future for young people. Television, the most potent influence, can definitely be used to convey positive messages by featuring successful teenagers and effective programs. Videos can be created that trigger useful discussions between teenagers and adults, modeled after *In The Mix* and other existing programs. Newspapers can feature stories or op-ed pieces that promote Safe Passage. Media stars can contribute their time and energy to helping advocates design strategies to interest the public in the youth cause.

THE ROLE OF THE STATES

The same Safe Passage principles apply to states as to the nation as a whole. Decisive action must come from the top in order to bring together the forces that will allow local school and community agencies to shape new institutional arrangements. The passage and funding of the Safe Passage Act would stimulate states to strengthen existing structures or to create new structures for enabling communities to develop comprehensive programs.

State initiatives can be shaped as statewide youth commissions or Cabinets to oversee the requisite functions: planning integrated programs, decategorizing funding, promoting strong program models, offering technical assistance, and setting up mechanisms for accountability. Many states are already moving in the direction of creating structures that assure greater coordination among state agencies. Several governors have advanced strong and well-funded youth initiatives that bring together agencies at the local level.

In each state, certain measures should be sought that would indicate that the state was moving in the direction of supporting Safe Passage concepts. First, state decision makers would have to be made aware of the need for more comprehensive approaches at the state level. Someone in the state legislature or state government will have to understand the interrelationships between school failure and other problems. Advocates have an important role in consciousness-raising about youth issues and must get involved in the documentation of needs and the promotion of responsive action. In some states, governors have delegated responsibility for planning and research to an entity like an interagency task force, an advisory council to the governor, or a temporary commission. In other states, nonprofit advocacy organizations have taken on the task.

An essential first step is the production of a state plan that addresses the need for comprehensive services for high-risk youth. It must spell out in detail the options for mechanisms that will assure coordination among state departments, particularly education, health and human services, justice, and labor. It helps at the outset to designate a lead agency, one governmental body, that can get the operation up and running.

Some of the most successful state initiatives have been based on new legislation that specifically provides state grants for demonstration projects. In most cases, this has meant appropriations being designated through a single line item in the state budget for education, health, or human services. The most effective law would require the pooling of state funds from different categorical sources to create a new Safe Passage Initiative capable of passing the pooled funds on to communities.

THE ROLE OF YOUTH WORKERS

Without sounding overly sentimental, I have tried to convey that the strength of the youth development field rests with the people who take care of your children. A number of names have cropped up here—theoreticians, administrators, professors, researchers, and program developers, along with principals, teachers, health workers, and youth workers. These are the true heroes of today, the thousands of people who spend their lives trying to help young people succeed, to make it. While parents are the first line of protection, as we have seen, not all children can rely on their parents, and even those with responsible parents have to turn to other people for support at some time.

The outcome of living in a society with a deepening gap between the haves and the have-nots is the creation of a kind of underground work force that tries to take care of the have-nots. These are the people—broadly defined as youth workers—who are committed to seeing children through their crises and introducing them to a higher quality of life. I meet these folks everywhere. I often think if we could just connect up the "good" people from one end of the country to the other, they would outnumber the uncaring population and become the prime decision makers. But youth workers do not enjoy major decision-making power in this society.

People Who Make a Difference

Let me introduce you to someone I met in my travels who personifies American Youth Work. Cornelius Crockett is the coordinator of the Quantum Opportunities Program in Houston, Texas. This program, which is supposed to be a replication of the QOP model in Philadelphia, is being run by a small Houston grassroots organization called Youth Advocates, supported by the Department of Labor, rather than by the Ford Foundation, which supports the Philadelphia program.

This tall, good-looking, 32-year-old African American man grew up in Gary, Indiana, in a segregated community. His father left home when Cornelius was 4, and he was brought up mostly by his mother and grandmother. He went to a mix of public and parochial schools in Gary, Chicago, and, finally, in New Orleans when his mother moved there. During his final two years in a totally unchallenging high school, he played basketball and had a great time exploring the streets. Although he expected to get a basketball scholarship to a Big 10 university such as Michigan, he ended up at Prairie View A&M, an all-black campus of Texas A&M. After his first semester, he realized that he did not want a career in sports and became seriously interested in the academic side of college life. One professor influenced him significantly, and that same man is now a prominent lawyer in Houston and still acts as his mentor.

Cornelius finished college with a strong interest in public policy and law. He worked his way into a job with the Texas Department of Parole, going around to small Texas towns to set up and supervise probation offices. At the same time, he started attending law school part time. But law school became too much when his exam in contract law was scheduled for the same time as the birth of his second child.

When the QOP grant was awarded to Youth Advocates, Cornelius applied for the job of counselor because he wanted hands-on experience in prevention. Within a short period of time, he became coordinator of the whole program, supervising the five full-time case managers who work with him. He feels somewhat frustrated because he has to spend so much time on administration and so little time actually working with the participants. But observing him with his fellow workers, patiently collecting data and filling out forms, listening carefully to their experiences, dealing with school officials, you can understand why he is where he is.

Cornelius works long hours, running back and forth between two schools and a youth center. The program still faces a number of obstacles, including no funds for transportation, so he spends a lot of time driving the students around in his car for various activities. Although computers are supposed to be in place, none has yet arrived. Because the program is supported by a government agency (the Department of Labor), participants who are undocumented aliens are not permitted to receive certain benefits such as stipends. The staff often contribute funds out of their own pockets for bus tickets, special events, and food items.

Youth work is full of frustrations. On any given day, the young people can be surly, manic, out of control, or severely depressed. Because Cornelius wears a beeper, he can expect to hear from one of his "kids" at any time of night or day about anything from trivia like lost homework to life-and-death matters like drive-by shootings. The facilities are grungy and old, with never enough desk space and little room for privacy. And the pay is really low.

Cornelius is torn between continuing with QOP or finding a way to get back to law school full time. He is pretty sure that a law degree is a necessary legitimation of what he most wants to do in life—have a strong influence on public policy. He is particularly knowledgeable about the justice (or injustice) system in the state of Texas, and the impact of race discrimination on the quality of life for minority children.

Meeting people like Cornelius Crockett is what convinces me that there is hope for the future of America. Despite all the frustrations, hard work, and lack of compensation, these youth workers are not going to give up. I call it the persistence of the caring community. It is difficult to single out individuals because so many deserve recognition. I will just mention one other person who speaks for many.

Dorothy Stoneman, founder of YouthBuild, received a "genius grant" ($325,000) in 1996 from the MacArthur Foundation. Stoneman spent twenty-five years in Harlem developing a community service program that put very deprived young people to work on construction projects in their own neighborhoods. Today, YouthBuild is a major national organization with 100 programs in thirty-four states. As Stoneman told the *New York Times*,

> It's sort of my job to produce hope. It's my function to be determined, to never give up, to make sure we don't let anyone turn us back. This mass of young people have been treated as if they were worthless, have been thrown away, and assumed without value because they dropped out of school, have a deep, very powerful desire to play a constructive role in the world. It's the adults' responsibility to make . . . a mini community in which young people can get the support, the love, the opportunity, the structure, the friends to build their own path to the future.[4]

Youth workers come in varied colors, genders, statuses, professional categories, and personalities. Although very different from one another, what these people have in common is a deep commitment to making life better for children in the United States and for overcoming social, racial, and ethnic divides. They are all "doers"; they don't let minor problems get in their way. And many of them never go off duty—they are always at their trade, promoting their ideas or programs and looking for support. Every encounter is an opportunity to sell the concept.

THE ROLE OF YOUTH

All the research and program development in the world will not assure Safe Passage unless young people buy into the proposed plans and solutions. Focus groups of youth are very popular in contemporary research, as are all kinds of surveys and polls of teenagers. We have many avenues to hearing their voices. What youth are saying is: "We are talking, but are you listening?"

I have seen many young people in my travels to programs around the country. No matter where you go, they are not very different from each other. Native American youth in Flagstaff, Arizona; African Americans in Chicago and Houston; Whites in Hastings-on-Hudson and Marshalltown, Iowa; Hispanics from the Dominican Republic in Washington Heights, New York; Hispanics from Mexico in Modesta, California; Puerto Ricans in San Juan; Asians from Vietnam in St. Paul; Asians from China in San Francisco—all of them go to schools that have the same basic structures; all of them hang out in malls that have the same stores; all are exposed to the same television and videos, the same music, and the same clothes. They even express the same concerns; "What will there be for me to do in the future?" "How can I grow up safely?"

The American public's view of teenagers is shaped by seeing them as a threatening mass of loud, strangely attired, disorderly young people. Very few adults understand what these youths are experiencing. Many of these teenagers are hungry and depressed, and have little in the way of comfort awaiting them at home. They go to schools that seem like prisons; gray walls lined with lockers, bells ringing, marching in line to change classes, waiting in line for a thirty-minute lunch period, waiting in line to go to the bathroom. No talking in the lunch room. No textbooks that can be taken home. What do their voices say? "Get me outta here." Many leave long before graduation, starting life with a mountain of severe limitations to overcome. The job situation is tough, especially for those without diplomas.

Yet in my travels I have encountered many, many teenagers who are climbing that mountain, who know what they have to do to succeed, and how to find adults who can help them achieve their goals. Young people, when given the opportunity, are extremely articulate. I have heard teenage representatives on conference panels who can spell out in great detail what the society needs to do to assure young people a better future. I have heard young people cogently present the cost-benefit argument for social investment, comparing the $80,000-a-year cost for juvenile detention to the $8,000 cost per year for a decent education.

Whatever we do in the future, obviously young people will have to have a strong voice in it. On one visit to a wonderful middle school, I asked a student what she liked about the place. First she said, "The school lunches are delicious, better than my old school," and then she said, "They really respect us here." The desire to be respected by adults is frequently reiterated by young people. No greater show of respect would be to include them in this dialogue about their futures and rely on them for their ideas about what Safe Passage entails.

THE CHARGE TO THE NATION

The Safe Passage challenge is enormous. The odds are already stacked against successfully achieving the goals of assisting every youth to pass over the threshold into becoming responsible adults. Demography is at work producing a large wave of adolescents tumbling into a population increasingly weighted by long-lived senior citizens like me. The active work force will have a much greater responsibility than ever before to support the young and the old. The uncertain job picture compounds the complexity of our nation's economic outlook, as does our relationship with a volatile world economy. The potential for racial and ethnic strife lies near to the surface, and it is hard to predict whether we will come together more as one "indivisible nation" or be torn apart. No wonder the young people are uneasy about their futures. Complacency is not the answer.

This country has the capacity for responding to crises when the call is issued. As one who has lived through the Depression, World War II, the Cold War, the response to Sputnik, the War on Poverty, the Vietnam War, and the Republican Revolution, I know that we can mount massive campaigns in almost any direction, given the temper of the time. The temper of this time must be to create healthy citizens for the twenty-first century. I do not know how to pull the rabbit out of the hat, to raise the consciousness of the American people about the importance of this cause. I leave that to the advocates, the practitioners, and the youth themselves. The art of pursuasion has been refined by the public relations experts and pollsters, who could surely be called upon to assist with this mission. My contribution is this book, which I hope will convince you that we know how to create strong and effective institutions for our children and families. My charge to you is to join the movement that will assure Safe Passage for all.

NOTES

CHAPTER 1

1. S. Zeldin, *Opportunities and Supports for Youth Development: Lessons from Research and Implications for Community Leaders and Scholars* (Washington, DC: Center for Youth Development and Policy Research, Academy for Educational Development, 1995), p 4.

2. E. Zigler and Matia Finn-Stevenson (eds.), *Children in a Changing World: Development and Social Issues* (Pacific Grove, CA: Brooks Cole, 1993); Carnegie Task Force on Meeting the Needs of Young Children, *Starting Points* (New York: Carnegie Corporation of New York, 1994).

3. See J. Dryfoos, *Adolescents at Risk: Prevalence and Prevention* (New York: Oxford University Press, 1990).

4. H. Leitenberg, "Primary Prevention of Delinquency," in J. Burchard and S. Burchard (eds.), *Prevention of Delinquent Behavior* (Newbury Park, CA: Sage, 1987), pp. 312–331.

5. Carnegie Council on Adolescent Development, *A Matter of Time: Risk and Opportunity in the Nonschool Hours* (Washington DC: Carnegie Council on Adolescent Development, Task Force on Youth Development and Community Programs, 1992).

CHAPTER 2

1. U.S. Bureau of the Census, *Statistical Abstract of the United States 1996*, Washington DC, 1996 Tables 173 and 736.

2. J. Dryfoos, "The United States National Family Planning Program, 1968–74," *Studies in Family Planning*, vol. 7, no. 3, March 1976.

3. Alan Guttmacher Institute, *11 Million Teenagers: What Can Be Done About the Epidemic of Adolescent Pregnancies in the United States* (New York: Alan Guttmacher Institute, 1976).

4. J. Dryfoos, *Adolescents at Risk: Prevalence and Prevention* (New York: Oxford University Press, 1990).

5. Census data in this chapter are largely abstracted from the *Statistical Abstract of the United States, 1996*. Other sources will be specifically referenced.

6. National Center for Educational Statistics, *National Education Longitudinal Study of 1988: A Profile of the American Eighth Grader* (Washington, DC: U.S. Department of Education, NCES 90-458, 1990).

7. N. Zill and C. Nord, *Running in Place: How American Families Are Faring in a Changing Economy and an Individualistic Society* (Washington, DC: Child Trends, 1994).

8. P. Scales, *Portrait of Young Adolescents in the 1990s* (Carrboro, NC: Center for Early Adolescence, 1991).

9. Dropout rates vary according to source. A special study of 16 and 17 year olds showed higher dropout rates than in the source in note 5: 11 percent for Hispanics, 10 percent for African Americans, and 7 percent for Whites. U.S. General Accounting Office, *Hispanics' Schooling: Risk Factors for Dropping Out and Barriers to Resuming Education* (Washington, DC: GAO/PEMD -94-14, 1994).

10.   Annie E. Casey Foundation, *Kids Count Data Book* (Baltimore, MD: Annie Casey Foundation 1994).

11.   National Education Goals Panel, *The National Education Goals Report* (Washington, DC: U.S. GPO, 1995).

12.   U.S. Department of Education, *The Condition of Education, 1995* (Washington, DC: National Center for Education Statistics, 1995).

13.   D. Grissmer, S. Kirby, M. Berends, and S. Williamson, *Student Achievement and the Changing American Family* (Santa Monica, CA: RAND Corporation, 1994).

14.   The National Education Longitudinal Study of 1988 is the best source for detailed information about school life. Eighth graders were surveyed in 1988 and are being followed upon every two years. See Office of Educational Research and Improvement, *A Profile of the American Eighth Grader: NELS: 88 Student Descriptive Summary* (Washington, DC: U.S. Department of Education, NCES 90-458, 1990).

15.   D. Blyth and E. Roehlkepartain, *Healthy Communities: Healthy Youth* (Minneapolis MN: Search Institute), undated. This was a composite look at almost 90,000 youth in grades 6–12 in 112 relatively small communities conducted by Search Institute for RespecTeen, an effort of the Lutheran Brotherhood.

16.   Personal communication, Aaron Shirley, director of Jackson-Hinds Comprehensive Health Center, Jackson, MS, June 15, 1993.

17.   L. Olsen, "Keeping Tabs on Quality," *Education Week,* Supplement, January 22, 1997, p. 7.

CHAPTER 3

1.   U.S. Department of Health and Human Services, "Youth Risk Behavior Surveillance—United States, 1995," *Morbidity and Mortality Weekly Report,* September 17, 1996, 45: SS-4.

2.   S. Stolberg, "Cigar Fad Reported to be Recruiting Legions of Teen-Agers," *New York Times,* May 23, 1997, p. A24.

3.   Alan Guttmacher Institute, *Sex and America's Teenagers* (New York: AGI, 1994).

4.   U.S. Department of Justice, *Juvenile Justice Bulletin* (Washington, DC: Department of Justice, 1996).

5.   J. Fox, *Trends in Juvenile Violence* (Washington DC: U.S. Bureau of Justice Statistics, 1996).

6.   Ibid., p. 2

7.   E. Ozer, C. Brindis, C. Irwin, and S. Millstein, *The Health of Adolescents in the U.S.: 1994* (San Francisco, CA: National Health Information Center, Institute for Health Policy Studies, University of California, n.d.).

8.   National Center for Educational Statistics, *National Education Longitudinal Study of 1988: A Profile of the American Eighth Grader* (Washington, DC: U.S. Department of Education, NCES 90-458, 1990).

9.   Ibid., p. 8.

10.   C. Sipe, J. Grossman, and J. Miliner, *Summer Training and Education Program (STEP): Report on the 1987 Experience* (Philadelphia, PA: Public/Private Ventures, 1988).

11.   For a detailed discussion of the research on overlapping behaviors, see J. Dryfoos, "The Prevalence Of Problem Behaviors: Implications for Programming," in R. Weissberg, T. Gullotta, R. Hampton, B. Ryan, and G. Adams (eds.), *Healthy Children 2010: Enhancing Children's Wellness* (Thousand Oaks, CA: Sage, 1997). pp.17-46.

12.   P. Benson, *The Troubled Journey: A Portrait of 6th–12th Grade Youth* (Minneapolis, MN: Lutheran Brotherhood, 1990).

13.   J. Keith and D. Perkins, *13,000 Adolescents Speak: A Profile of Michigan Youth* (East Lansing, MI: Community Coalitions in Action, Michigan State University, 1995).

14.   J. Dryfoos, "The Prevalence of Problem Behaviors."

15.   E. Werner and R. Smith, *Vulnerable But Invincible: A Longitudinal Study of Resilient Children and Youth* (New York: McGraw-Hill, 1982).

16.   N. Garmazy, "Stress-resistant Children: The Search for Protective Factors," in J.

Stevenson (ed.), *Recent Research in Developmental Psychopathology* (Oxford, UK: Pergamon, 1985), pp. 213–233.

17. R. Blum, "Risk and Resilience: A Model for Adolescent Health Interventions," unpublished paper, National Center for Youth with Disabilities, University of Minnesota, 1996.

18. M. Resnick, L. Harris, and R. Blum, "The Impact of Caring and Connectedness on Adolescent Health and Well-being," *J. Paediatr. Child Health* 29, Suppl. 1. S3–S9 (1993).

19. J. Hawkins and J. Weis, "The Social Development Model: An Integrated Approach to Delinquency Prevention," *Journal of Primary Prevention* 6:73–97 (1985).

20. M. Rutter, "Young People Today: Some International Comparisons on Patterns of Problems, Education, and Life Circumstances," *Preparing Youth for the 21st Century* (Washington, DC: Aspen Institute, 1996), p. 25.

CHAPTER 4

1. The description is based on site visits I made in February 1996 and January 1997. Additional material has been supplied by Sister Teresa Geigel, executive director of the Centro; Lynn Curtis, president of the Milton Eisenhower Foundation; and Keith Baker, associate director of evaluation, Milton Eisenhower Foundation.

2. The material about Quantum was gathered at a site visit on April 22, 1996, unless otherwise cited.

3. Quoted in B. Howard, "A 'Cadillac' Job-Training Program Delivers for Disadvantaged Youth," *Youth Today,* January/Febuary 1995, p. 28.

4. A. Hahn, *Lessons from a Pilot Project,* paper given at conference on America's Disconnected Youth: Toward a Preventive Strategy, American Enterprise Institute, May 16, 1996.

5. Center for Human Resources, *Quantum Opportunities Program* (Waltham, MA: Brandeis University, 1995), p. 5.

6. Cited in A. Hahn, *Lessons, What Does It Take? Forging Long-Term Allegiance Among Youth From Public Assistance Households* (Waltham, MA: Brandeis University, Center for Human Resources, March 1993).

7. B. Howard, "A 'Cadillac,' " *Youth Today*, January/February 1995, p. 28.

8. L. Sullivan, quoted in *Quantum Opportunity Program* (Philadelphia, PA: OIC of America, no date, p. 1.

9. Much of the material presented here was gathered at a site visit held on March 14, 1996.

10. At El Puente, the designation of *Latino* is used rather than *Hispanic*.

11. D. Gonzalez, "A Bridge from Hope to Social Action," *New York Times*, May 23, 1995, p. B1.

12. M. Fleischer, "The New Visionaries," *Village Voice*, April 3, 1995. pp. 3–6.

13. Ibid.

14. Ibid.

15. D. Gonzalez, "A Bridge."

16. S. Ramirez and T. Dewar, *El Puente Academy for Peace and Justice: A Case Study of Building Social Capital,* report prepared for the Kettering Foundation, October 23, 1995.

17. "El Puente: A Holistic Center for Growth and Empowerment," *Perspective Latina*, June 1993.

18. J. Berger, "Metro Matters," *New York Times,* August 31, 1993.

19. Fleischer, "New Visionaries," p. 5.

20. Fleischer, "New Visionaries," p. 6.

21. K. Greider, "Against All Odds," *City Limits*, August/September 1993, pp. 34–38.

22. Marshalltown School District, *The Marshalltown Plan: Marshalltown Community Schools*, 1994

23. Grant Application, School-Based Youth Services Program, submitted by Marshalltown Community School District to Iowa Department of Education, July 25, 1994.

24. Unpublished data from 1993–94 school year supplied by Todd Redalen, director, Caring Connections.

25.   Office of Educational Services for Children, Families, and Communities, Guidelines for Serving At-Risk Students (Des Moines, IA: Iowa Department of Education, 1996), p. 1.

26.   I. Venafra, "Real Estate Mathematics, *WEPIC in Action* (WEPIC/Turner Newsletter), June 1995, p 6.

27.   M. Sommerfield, "Beyond the Ivory Tower," *Education Week*, April 24, 1996, p. 35.

28.   L. Benson, I. Harkavy, and J. Puckett, "Communal Participatory Action Research as a Strategy for Improving Universities and the Social Sciences: Penn's Work with the West Philadelphia Improvement Corps as a Case Study," *Educational Policy* 10.2: 202–222 (1996), p. 208

29.   Sommerfield, "Beyond the Ivory Tower," p. 35

30.   Brown, "After-School Community Activity," *Class Act*, Nov. 15, 1994, p. 6.

31.   Ibid., p. 34.

CHAPTER 5

1.   J. Dryfoos, *Full Service Schools: A Revolution in Health and Social Services for Children, Youth, and Families* (San Francisco, CA: Jossey-Bass, 1994).

2.   Florida Department of Health and Rehabilitative Services and Department of Education, *Request for Program Designs for Supplemental School Health Programs,* Instructions, Tallahassee, 1991.

3.   M. Tyack, "Health and Social Services in Public Schools: Historical Perspectives," *Future of the Children*: 2(1): 19–31 (1992).

4.   Office of Technology Assessment, U.S. Congress, *Adolescent Health-Volume I: Summary and Policy Options* (OTA-H-468) (Washington, DC: U.S. Government Printing Office, 1991).

5.   *Access: To Comprehensive School-Based Health Services for Children and Youth*, (Washington, DC: Making the Grade, Fall 1996).

6.   J. Dryfoos, "New Approaches to the Organization of Health and Social Services in Schools," *Schools and Health: Our Nation's Investment,* Appendix D (Washington, DC: National Academy Press, 1997).

7.   E. Zigler, S. Kagan, and N. Hall, *Children, Families, and Government: Preparing for the 21st Century.* (New York: Cambridge University Press, 1996).

8.   P. Edwards and K. Biocchi, *Community Schools Across America* (Flint, MI: National Center for Community Education, n.d.).

9.   M. Cahill, *Schools and Community Partnerships: Reforming Schools, Revitalizing Communities* (Chicago: Cross City Campaign for Urban School Reform, 1966).

10.   P. Coltoff, "Full Service Schools Broaden Definition of Education Reform," *Christian Science Monitor*, Feb. 24, 1997.

11.   H. Lawson and K. Briar-Lawson *Connecting the Dots: Progress Toward the Integration of School Reform, School-linked Services, Parent Involvement and Community Schools* (Oxford, OH: School of Education and Allied Professions, Miami Univ. 1997).

12.   I. Harkavy and J. Puckett, "Toward Effective University-Public School Partnerships: An Analysis of a Contemporary Model," *Teachers College Record* 92:4 (1991).

13.   Florida Department of Health and Rehabilitative Services and Department of Education, *Request for Program Designs for Supplemental School Health Programs,* Instructions, Tallahassee, 1991.

14.   M. Wagner, S. Golan, L. Shaver, M. Wechsler, and F. Kelley, *A Healthy Start for California's Children and Families: Early Findings from a Statewide Evaluation of School-Linked Services* (Menlo Park, CA: SRI International, 1994).

15.   Personal communication from Eric Friedlander, Kentucky Cabinet for Human Resources, January 10, 1995.

16.   *The Exchange,* (Silver Spring, MD: National Clearinghouse on Families and Youth, Summer/Fall 1996).

17.   Dryfoos, *Full Service Schools*, J. Dryfoos, "Full Service Schools" *Educational Leadership* April 1996: 18–23. J. Dryfoos, "School-Based Services: Exemplary Program Models" in R.

Illback (ed.) *Integrated Services for Children and Families: Opportunities for Psychological Practice* (Washington, DC: American Psychological Association, 1997).

18. G. Babiak, "They're Seen. And Heard. News from Recycle A Bicycle," *City Cyclist*, March/April 1995, p. 22.

19. P. DeMuro, "Site Visit Report: Sioux City-School Based Prevention," September 16; from materials provided by Pete Hathaway, principal, Woodrow Wilson Middle School, Sioux City, Iowa, 1996.

20. F.I.N.E. schools application, January 15, 1996; provided by Pete Hathaway, principal, Woodrow Wilson Middle School, October 1996.

21. DeMuro, "Site Visit Report," p. 6.

22. Mathtech, Inc. and Policy Studies Associates, Inc., *Selected Collaborations in Service Integration*, report for the U.S. Department of Education and U.S. Department of Health and Human Services, ED Contract LC89089001, Feb. 1, 1991.

23. D. Cohen, "A Lesson in Caring," *Education Week,* August 2, 1995, p. 43.

24. J. Dryfoos, C. Brindis, and D. Kaplan, "Research and Evaluation in School-Based Health Care," in L. Juszczak and M. Fisher (eds.), *Adolescent Medicine: State of the Art: Health Care in Schools* (Philadelphia, PA: Hanley and Belfus, 1996).

25. See N. Berger and M. Hetrick, "The Evaluation of Florida's Full Service Schools: The 1992–1993 Evaluative Report and the Future," paper presented at Conference on School Health and Full Service Schools, St. Petersburg, Florida, 1994; R. Illback *Kentucky Family Resource and Youth Service Centers: Summary of Evaluation Findings* (Louisville KY: REACH of Louisville, 1996); M. Wagner and S. Golan, *California's Healthy Start School-Linked Services Initiative: Summary of Evaluation Findings* (Menlo Park, CA: SRI International, 1996).

26. See J. Klein and E. Cox, "School-based Health Care in the Mid-1990s," *Current Opinion in Pediatrics* 7:353–359 (1995); B. Rienzo and J. Button, "The Politics of School-based Clinics: A Community-level Analysis," *Journal of School Health* 63(6): 266–272 (1993); S. Godin, L. Woodhouse, W. Livingwood, and H. Jacobs, "Key Factors in Successful School-based Clinics, *NMHA Prevention Update,* 4 (1): 3 (1993).

27. Bureau of Primary Health Care, *School-based Clinics That Work* (Washington, DC: DHHS Public Health Services, 1993); Government Accounting Office, *School-based Health Centers Can Expand Access for Children* (Washington, DC: U.S. Government Accounting Office, GAO/HEHS-95-35 (1994); *The Exchange,* Summer/Fall 1996, p. 11.

28. Farrell Area School District, *A Tradition of Care and Education for All: Prescription for America,* Flier, 1993; Children's Aid Society, *Building a Community School: A Revolutionary Design in Public Education* (New York: Children's Aid Society, 1993).

29. D. Barfield, C. Brindis, L. Guthrie, W. McDonald, S. Philliber, and B. Scott, *The Evaluation of New Beginnings* (San Francisco, CA: Far West Laboratory, 1994).

30. E. Brickman, *A Formative Evaluation of PS5: A Children's Aid Society/Board of Education Community School* (New York: Fordham University Graduate School of Social Services, 1996).

31. A. Melaville, M. Blank, and G. Asayesh, *Together We Can: A Guide for Crafting a Profamily System of Education and Human Services* (Washington, DC: U.S. Government Printing Office, 1993).

32. D. Cohen, "Live and Learn," *Education Week*, June 7, 1995, pp. 27–30.

33. Committee for Economic Development, *Putting Learning First: Governing and Managing the Schools for High Achievement* (New York: Research and Policy Committee, CED, 1994), p. 1.

34. R. Chaskin and H. Richman, "Concerns About School-linked Services: Institution-based versus Community-based Models," *The Future of Children: School-linked Services* (Los Altos, CA: Center for the Future of Children, 1992).

CHAPTER 6

1. A. Shanker, "Where We Stand," *New York Times*, April 12, 1996, C, p. 5.

2. See also M. Duckenfield, J. Hanby, and J. Smink, *Effective Strategies for Dropout Prevention* (Clemson, SC: National Dropout Prevention Center, 1990).

3. J. Dryfoos, *Adolescents-at-Risk Revisited: Continuity, Evaluation, and Replication of Prevention Programs*, report to the Carnegie Corporation, January 16, 1996.

4. J. Caredenas, M. Montecel, J. Supik, and R. Harris, "The Coca-Cola Valued Youth Program: Dropout Prevention Strategies for At-Risk Students," *Texas Researcher 3*: 111–130: (Winter 1992).

5. Cities in Schools, "3-Year Evaluation of CIS Documents Successes, Outlines Challenges," *Network News* (Winter 1995), p. 1; and "Preventing School Dropouts," *Urban Institute Policy and Research Report* 24: 34–36 (1994).

6. *Cities in Schools Turning Kids Around*, (1995).

7. R. Felner, S. Brand, A. Adan, P. Mulhall, N. Flowers, B. Sartain, and S. DuBois, "Restructuring the Ecology of the School as an Approach to Prevention During School Transitions: Longitudinal Follow-ups and Extensions of the School Transitional Environment Project (STEP)," in L. Jason, K. Danner, K. Kurasaki (eds.), *Prevention and School Transition: Prevention in Human Services* (Binghamton, NY: Haworth Press, 1993), pp. 102–136.

8. Ibid., p. 195.

9. A. Hahn, "Lessons from a Pilot Project," paper presented at American Enterprise Institute on America's Disconnected Youth: Toward a Preventive Strategy, May 16, 1996.

10. Telephone interview with Arlene Weigh, Liberty Partnerships Program, Department of Education, Albany, NY, on December 8, 1995.

11. V. Denes-Raj, D. Jackson, and M. Bazigos, "Utilization of Cooperative Learning Groups to Ameliorate Summer Setbacks for African-American Female Students in Mathematics: A Program Evaluation," unpublished paper, Pace University, New York, 1995.

12. M. Bazigos, "An Equity Level: SAT Coaching with a Minority At-Risk Population in an Urban Public High School," paper presented at the New England Educational Research Organization, Portsmouth, NH, May 1995.

13. J. Pfannenstiel, T. Lambson, and V. Yarnell, *Second Wave Study of Parents as Teachers Program* (St. Louis: Parents as Teachers National Center, 1991; and J. Rouse, "Parents as Teachers: Investing in Good Beginnings for Children," *Spectrum* (Fall 1994), pp. 25–30.

14. Letter from Sharon Rhodes, Parents as Teachers National Center, St. Louis, MO, April 26, 1995.

15. S. Stringfield, S. Ross, and L. Smith (eds.), *Bold Plans for School Restructuring: The New American Schools Designs* (Mahwah, NJ: Lawrence Erlbaum Associates, 1996).

16. Press release, The New American Schools Development Corporation, July 9, 1992.

17. L. Olsen, "11 Design Teams Are Tapped to Pursue Their Visions of "Break the Mold Schools," *Education Week,* August 5, 1992, pp. 1, 47–52.

18. L. Olsen, "On assignment: Everett, Wash," *Education Week,* February 8, 1995, pp. 31–34.

19. New American Schools Development Corporation, *A Thousand Actions . . .* , annual report, 1994/1995; New American Schools Development Corporation, *Getting Stronger and Stronger*, annual report, 1995/1996.

20. S. Bodilly with S. Purnell, K. Ramsey, and S. Keith, Lessons from New American Schools Development Corporation's Demonstration Phase (Santa Monica, CA: Institute on Education and Training, RAND, 1996).

21. S. Pogrow, "Reforming the Wannabe Reformers," *Phi Delta Kappan* (June 1996).

22. L. Olsen, "Designs for Learning," *Education Week,* February 12, 1997, pp. 40–45.

23. R. Slavin, N. Madden, L. Dolan, B. Wasik, S. Ross, and L. Smith, "Whenever and Wherever We Choose: The Replication of Success for All," *Phi Delta Kappan* (April 1994), pp. 639–647.

24. R. Herman and S. Stringfield, "Ten Promising Programs for Educating Disadvantaged Students: Evidence of Impact," paper presented at the meeting of the AERA, San Francisco, CA, April 19, 1995, p. 21.

25. Slavin et al., "Whenever and Wherever We Choose."

26. H. Levin, "Learning from Accelerated Schools," in J. Block, S. Everson, and T.

Guskey, *School Improvement Programs: A Handbook for Educational Leaders* (New York: Scholastic, 1996), pp. 267–288.

27. National Center for Accelerated Schools Project, "Accomplishments of Accelerated Schools," summary, October 1995.

28. Task Force on Education of Young Adolescents, *Turning Points: Preparing American Youth for the 21st Century* (Washington, DC: Carnegie Council on Adolescent Development, 1989).

29. Carnegie Corporation, p. 8

30. R. Felner, A. Jackson, D. Kasak, P. Mulhall, S. Brand, and N. Flowers, "The Impact of School Reform for the Middle Years," *Phi Delta Kappan* (March 1997), pp. 528–550.

31. J. Lipsitz, A. Jackson, and L. Austin, "What Works in Middle-Grades School Reform," *Phi Delta Kappan* (March 1997), pp. 517–519.

32. Statement by Dr. James Comer in "Improving American Education: Roles for Parents," hearing before the Select Committee on Children Youth and Families (Washington, DC: U.S. Government Printing Office, June 7, 1984), pp. 55–60.

33. Herman, "Ten promising programs."

34. N. Haynes (ed.), *School Development Program Research Monograph* (New Haven, CT: Yale Child Study Center School Development Program, 1994).

35. B. Neufield and M. LaBue, The *Implementation of the School Development Program in Hartford: Final Evaluation Report* (Cambridge, MA: Education Matters, 1994), p. 9.

36. School Development Model, *Mobilizing the Whole Village* (New Haven, CT: Yale Child Study Center, 1996).

37. Herman, "Ten promising programs."

38. Cited in Herman and Stringfield. M. Sikorski, T. Wallace, W. Stariha, and V. Rankin, "School Reform and the Curriculum," *New Directions for Program Evaluation* 59 (1993).

39. Cited in Herman and Stringfield. K. Cushman, "Taking Stock: How Are Essential Schools Doing?" *Horace* 8 (1): 1–12 (1991).

40. D. Bensman, report to the Andrew Mellon Foundation, 1993.

41. P. Tainsh, "Central Park East Elementary Schools: Social Benefit Analysis Study," report to the Bruner Foundation, 1994.

42. P. Nesselrodt and E. Schaffer, "What's Essential Here Anyway? Secondary Students Whole School Days," presented at the 1995 annual meeting of the AERA, San Francisco, CA, 1995.

43. Ibid., p. 21.

44. D. Muncey, and P. McQuillan, "Preliminary Findings from a Five-Year Study of the Coalition of Essential Schools," *Phi Delta Kappan* (February 1993), pp. 486–489.

45. D. Viadero, "Mixed Record for Coalition Schools Is Seen," *Education Week*, November 1, 1995, p. 1.

46. Herman, "Ten promising programs," p. 86.

47. National Education Commission on Time and Learning, *Prisoners of Time: Schools and Programs Making Time Work for Students and Teachers* (Washington, DC: U.S. Government Printing Office, 1994), p. 10.

48. J. Lipsitz, H. Mizell, A. Jackson, and L. Austin, "Speaking with One Voice," *Phi Delta Kappan* (March 1997), pp. 533–540.

49. Ibid., p. 535.

50. Ibid., p. 537.

51. Ibid., p. 538.

52. National Education Goals Panel, *The National Education Goals Report: Building a Nation of Learners* (Washington, DC: U.S. Government Printing Office, 1995).

53. M. Millot, P. Hill, and R. Lake, "Charter Schools: Escape or Reform?" *Education Week*, June 5, 1996, p. 56.

54. "Innovative Schools Initiative," *Kaleidoscope* 2:1 (Winter 1996), p. 4.

CHAPTER 7

1. J. Dryfoos, *Adolescents at Risk: Prevalence and Prevention* (New York: Oxford University Press, 1990).

2. J. Dryfoos, *Adolescents at Risk Revisited: Continuity, Evaluation, and Replication of Prevention Programs*, report to Carnegie Corporation, January 16, 1996.

3. W. Kopp and R. Kazis with A. Churchill, *Promising Practices: A Study of Ten School-to-Career Programs* (Boston, MA: Jobs for the Future, n.d.).

4. M. Freedman, *The Kindness of Strangers* (San Francisco, CA: Jossey-Bass, 1993).

5. M. Freedman, "Demography Is Destiny: How Senior Citizens Could Save the Civil Society," *The American Prospect* (forthcoming).

6. See *Youth Roles*, publication of National Helpers Network, Inc.

7. Carnegie Council on Adolescent Development, *A Matter of Time: Risk and Opportunity in the Nonschool Hours* (New York: Carnegie Corporation, Task Force on Youth Development and Community Programs, 1992).

8. S. Schinke, M. Orlandi, and K. Cole, "Boys and Girls Clubs in Public Housing Developments: Prevention Services for Youth at Risk," *Journal of Community Psychology*, OSAP special issue, 118–128 (1992).

9. S. Kim, C. Crutchfield, C. Williams, and N. Hepler, "Innovative and Unconventional Approaches to Program Evaluation in the Field of Substance Abuse Prevention," *Journal of Community Psychology*, special issue (1994)

10. T. St. Pierre, D. Kaltreider, M. Johnson, "The Smart Leaders Booster Program: A Pennsylvania State University and Boys Clubs Prevention Project," *Working with Youth in High-Risk Environments: Experiences in Prevention*, Office of Substance Abuse Prevention, Monograph 12, pp. 186–199, 1992.

11. Center on Addiction and Substance Abuse, *Summary Statement: Children at Risk* (New York: Columbia University, 1995).

12. A. Harrell, *Impact of the Children at Risk Program: Preliminary Findings of the First Year* (Washington, DC: Urban Institute, 1995).

13. Personal communication, Adele Harrell, Urban Institute, Washington, DC, May 29, 1997.

14. J. Dryfoos, site visit, Caimito, Puerto Rico, February 1, 1996 (see chapter 4).

15. Information provided by Keith Baker, associate director of evaluation, Milton Eisenhower Foundation, 1996.

16. Milton Eisenhower Foundation, *Youth Development and Police Mentoring* (Washington, DC: author, 1997).

17. N. Guerra, P. Tolan, and R. Hammond, "Prevention and Treatment of Adolescent Violence," in L. Eron, H. J. Gentry, and P. Schlegel (eds.), *Reason To Hope: A Psychosocial Perspective on Violence and Youth* (Washington, DC: American Psychological Association, 1994), pp. 383–403.

18. B. Yung and R. Hammond, *PACT Positive Adolescent Choices Training: A Model for Violence Prevention Groups with African American Youth (Program Guide)* (Champaign, IL: Research Press, 1995).

19. E. Cowen, A. Hightower, J. Pedro-Carroll, W. Work, P. Wyman and W. Haffey, *School-Based Prevention for Children at Risk: The Primary Mental Health Program* (Washington, DC: American Psychological Association, 1996).

20. Primary Mental Health Project, *Primary Mental Health Project: A Primer for Setting Up New Programs* (Rochester, NY: Primary Mental Health Program, 1995).

21. National Research Council and John F. Kennedy School of Government, *Violence in Urban America: Mobilizing a Response* (Washington, DC: National Academy Press, 1994).

22. R. Mendel, *Prevention or Pork? A Hard-Headed Look at Youth-Oriented Anti-Crime Programs* (Washington, DC: American Youth Policy Forum, 1995).

23. D. Elliott, *Youth Violence: An Overview* (Boulder, CO: Center for Study and Prevention of Violence, 1994).

24. Office of Juvenile Justice and Delinquency Prevention, *Guide for Implementing*

the *Comprehensive Strategy for Serious, Violent, and Chronic Juvenile Offenders* (Washington, DC: U.S. Department of Justice, 1995); Office of Juvenile Justice and Delinquency Prevention, *Delinquency Prevention Works* (Washington, DC: U.S. Department of Justice, 1995).

25. See *Youth Violence Prevention*, supplement to the *American Journal of Preventive Medicine* (September 1996).

26. J. Harris, "Clinton Announces Offensive Against Rising Juvenile Crime," *Washington Post*, February 20, 1997.

27. Milton Eisenhower Foundation, *Policy Framework* (Washington, DC: author, 1996), p. 3.

28. D. Satcher, K. Powell, J. Mercy, and M. Rosenberg, "Violence Prevention Is as American as Apple Pie," *Youth Violence Prevention,* supplement to the *American Journal of Preventive Medicine* 12–5 (September 1996), pp. v–vi.

29. G. Botvin, E. Baker, L. Dusenbury, E. Botvin, and T. Diaz, "Long-term Follow-up Results of a Randomized Drug Abuse Prevention Trial in a White Middle-class Population," *JAMA* 273 (14): 1106–1112 (1995).

30. G. Botvin, L. Dusenbury, E. Baker, S. James-Ortiz, E. Botvin, and J. Kerner, "Smoking Prevention Among Urban Minority Youth: Assessing Effects on Outcome and Mediating Variables," *Health Psychology* 11: 290–299 (1992).

31. C. Perry, "Project Northland: Outcomes of a Community Wide Alcohol Use Prevention Program During Early Adolescence," *American Journal of Public Health*, 86 (7): 956–965 (1996).

32. M. Pentz, "Benefits of Integrating Strategies in Different Settings," in A. Elster et al. (eds.), *American Medical Association State-of-the-Art Conference on Adolescent Health Promotion: Proceedings*, (NCEMCH Research Monograph, pp. 15–34, 1993).

33. Telephone interview with Mary Ann Pentz, Department of Preventive Medicine, University of Southern California, November 22, 1995.

34. "Big Brothers/Big Sisters Make a Difference," *Public/Private Ventures News* 11 (1): 1–7 (1995).

35. J. Hawkins, R. Catalano, D. Morrison et al., "The Seattle Social Development Project: Effects of the First Four Years on Protective Factors and Problem Behaviors," in J. McCord and R. Tremblay (eds.), *The Prevention of Antisocial Behavior in Children* (New York: Guilford, 1992).

36. J. O'Donnell, J. Hawkins, R. Catalano, R. Abbott, and L. Day, "Preventing School Failure, Drug Use, and Delinquency Among Low-income Children: Long-term Intervention in Elementary Schools," *American Journal of Orthopsychiatry* 65 (1): 87–100 (1995).

37. Letter from Carol Wells, Social Development Research Group, University of Washington, School of Social Work, March 8, 1995.

38. Substance Abuse and Mental Health Services Administration, *Signs of Effectiveness II: Preventing Alcohol, Tobacco and Other Drug Use: A Risk Factor/Resiliency-Based Approach* (Washington, DC: U.S. DHHS Public Health Service, 1992).

39. Southeast Regional Center for Drug-Free Schools and Communities, *Shining Stars: Prevention Programs That Work* (Louisville, KY: University of Louisville, 1993).

40. Drug Strategies, *Making the Grade: A Guide to School Drug Prevention Programs* (Washington, DC: Drug Strategies, 1996), p. 3.

41. U.S. General Accounting Office, *Adolescent Drug Use Prevention: Common Features of Promising Community Programs* (Washington, DC: U.S. GAO/PEMD 92-2, 1992).

42. Drug Strategies, *Keeping Score 1996* (Washington, DC: author, 1997).

43. S. Philliber and J. Allen, "Life Options and Community Service: Teen Outreach Program," in B. Miller et al. (eds.), *Preventing Adolescent Pregnancy: Model Programs and Evaluations* (Newbury Park, CA: Sage, 1992), pp. 139–155. J. Allen, S. Philliber, and N. Hoggson, "School-based Prevention of Teenage Pregnancy and School Dropout: Process Evaluation of the National Replication of the Teen Outreach Program," *American Journal of Community Psychology* 8: 505–524 (1990).

44. Association of Junior Leagues International, *Fact Sheet: Teen Outreach Program: The Evaluation of Teen Outreach 1984–1994* (New York: Association of Junior Leagues International, 1995).

45. Brochure from Cornerstone Consulting Group, Houston, Texas, 1995.

46. Philliber Research Associates, "Carrera/Dempsey Replication Programs: 1993–94 Summary of Client Characteristics and Outcomes," unpublished report, 1995.

47. Telephone interview, Michael Carrera, Children's Aid Society, May 1995.

48. J. Bender, "Interview with a Master," *NOAPPP Network* 17 (1): p. 12. (Fall/Early Winter 1997).

49. H. Nicholson, L. Postrado, and F. Weiss, *Truth, Trust and Technology: New Research on Preventing Adolescent Pregnancy* (New York: Girls Inc., 1991).

50. Letter from Faedra Weiss, research associate, Girls Inc. National Resource Center, September 26, 1995.

51. I. Green, M. Smith, and S. Petters, "I Have a Future's Comprehensive Adolescent Health Promotion: Cultural Considerations in Program Implementation and Design" *Journal of Health Care for the Poor and Underserved* 5 (2): 267–281 (1995).

52. K. Moore, B. Sugland, C. Blumenthal, D. Glei and N. Snyder, *Adolescent Pregnancy Prevention Programs: Interventions and Evaluations* (Washington, DC: Child Trends, 1995), pp. 6–44.

53. Letter from Murray Vincent, University of South Carolina, February 10, 1995.

54. H. Koo, G. Duntman, C. George, Y. Green, and M. Vincent, "Reducing Adolescent Pregnancy Through a School- and Community-based Intervention: Denmark, South Carolina, revisited," *Family Planning Perspectives* 26: 206–211 (1994).

55. A. Paine Andrews, M. Vincent, S. Fawcett et al., "Replicating a Community Initiative for Preventing Adolescent Pregnancy: From South Carolina to Kansas," unpublished paper, 1995.

56. Kansas Health Foundation, *Health Issues*, quarterly report 1 (1) (1996).

57. L. Tiezzi, J. Lipshutz, N. Wrobleski, R. Vaughan, J. McCarthy, "Pregnancy Prevention Among Young, Minority, Urban Adolescents: Results of the *In Your Face* Pregnancy Prevention Program," *Family Planning Perspectives*, (1997) 29:173-176.

58. R. Barth, N. Leland, D. Kirby, and J. Fetro, "Enhancing Social and Cognitive Skills," in B. Miller, J. Card, R. Paikoff, and J. Peterson (eds.), *Preventing Adolescent Pregnancy* (Newbury Park, CA: Sage Publications, 1992), pp. 53–82.

59. D. Kirby, G. Barth, N. Leland, and J. Fetro, "Reducing the Risk: A New Curriculum to Prevent Sexual Risk-Taking," *Family Planning Perspectives* 23 (6): pp. 253–63, 1991.

60. S. Brown and L. Eisenberg (eds.), *The Best Intentions: Unintended Pregnancy and the Well-Being of Children and Families* (Washington, DC: National Academy Press, 1995).

61. L. Kotloff, P. Roaf, and M. Gambone, *The Plain Talk Planning Year: Mobilizing Communities to Change* (Baltimore, MD: Annie E. Casey Foundation, 1995).

62. *NOAPPP Network* 17 (1), 3–6 (Fall/Early Winter 1997).

63. D. Kirby, *No Easy Answers: Research Findings on Programs to Reduce Teen Pregnancy*, (Washington, DC: The National Campaign to Prevent Teen Pregnancy, 1997), p. 46.

64. J. Dryfoos, C. Brindis, D. Kaplan, "Research and Evaluation in School-Based Health Care," in L. Juszczak and M. Fisher, *Adolescent Medicine: State of the Art Health Care in Schools* (Philadelphia, PA: Hanley and Belfus, 1996).

65. NCSL Women's Network, "Adolescents and the HIV/AIDS Epidemic—Stemming the Tide," p. 23 (1993).

66. M. Rotheram-Borus, C. Koopman, C. Haignere, and M. Davies, "Reducing HIV Sexual Risk Behaviors Among Runaway Adolescents, *JAMA* 266 (9): 1237–1242 (1991).

67. Moore, et al., *Adolescent Pregnancy Prevention Programs*, pp. 20–21.

68. Select Committee on Children, Youth and Families, *A Decade of Denial: Teens and AIDS in America* (Washington, DC: U.S. Government Printing Office, 1992).

69. H. Kunins, K. Hein, D. Futterman, E. Tapley, and A. Elliot, *Guide to Adolescent HIV/AIDS Program Development,* special issue of *Journal of Adolescent Health* 14 (5) supplement (1993).

70. D. Kirby, *Sex Education in the Schools* (Menlo Park, CA: Henry J. Kaiser Family Foundation, 1994).

CHAPTER 8
1. D. Farran, "Effects of Intervention with Disadvantaged and Disabled Children: A Decade Review," in S. Meisels and J. Shonkoff (eds.), *Handbook of Early Childhood Intervention* (Cambridge, UK: Cambridge University Press, 1990), p. 533.
2. M. Pines, "Programs That Work: Taking Service to Families," Institute for Policy Studies at Johns Hopkins University. n.d.
3. Ibid., p. 28.
4. M. Adams, *Gentlemen, Shall We Begin Again? The Fifth Ward Enrichment Program* (Austin, TX: Hogg Foundation for Mental Health, 1994). p. 17.
5. M. Freedman, "The Aging Opportunity," *American Prospect* (29) 38-43 (1996).
6. Office of Research, *Educational Reforms and Students at Risk: A Review of the Current State of the Art* (Washington, DC: U.S. Department of Education, 1994).
7. D. Davies, "The 10th School Where School-Family-Community Partnerships Flourish," *Education Week*, July 10, 1996, p. 44.
8. U.S. General Accounting Office, *Residential Care: Some High-Risk Youth Benefit, But More Study Needed* (Washington DC: Department of Health and Human Services, GAO/HEHS 94-56, 1994).
9. M. Cahill, Fund for City of N.Y., personal communication, May 12, 1997.
10. R. Illback, *Kentucky Family Resource and Youth Service Centers: Summary of Evaluation Findings* (Louisville, KY: Reach of Louisville, 1996), p. 3.
11. G. Walker and F. Vilella-Velez, *Anatomy of a Demonstration* (Philadelphia, PA: Public/Private Ventures, 1992), p. iv.
12. R. Brandon and M. Meuter, *Proceedings: National Conference on Interprofessional Education and Training* (Seattle, WA: Human Services Policy Center, University of Washington, March 22, 1995), p. 8.
13. P. Hogan, "Transforming Professional Education," unpublished paper, September 20, 1994, p. 5. Hogan is Chief, Professional Studies Department, Wheelock College, Boston, MA.
14. J. Ponessa, "Cautiously, AFT Embraces Charter Schools," *Education Week*, August 7, 1996.
16. J. Dryfoos, *Adolescents at Risk Revisited: Continuity, Evaluation, and Replication,* report to Carnegie Corporation, January 16, 1996.
17. Carnegie Council on Adolescent Development, *A Matter of Time: Risk and Opportunity in the Out-of-Schools Hours* (New York: Carnegie Corporation of New York, 1994).

CHAPTER 9
1. L. Dusenbury, "Recent Findings in Drug Abuse Prevention: A Review from 1989 to 1994," prepared for Drug Strategies, October 27, 1994.
2. P. Ellickson, R. Bell, and K. Mcguigan, "Preventing Adolescent Drug Use: Long-term results of a Junior High Program," *American Journal of Public Health* 83 (6): 856–861.
3. Best Foundation, *Project Alert: A Solution from the Best Foundation for Drug-free Tomorrow*, brochure (n.d.).
4. C. Ringwalt, J. Greene, S. Ennett, R. Iachan, R. Clayton, and C. Leukefeld, *Past and Future Directions of the D.A.R.E. Program: An Evaluation Review* (Research Triangle Park, NC: Research Triangle Institute, 1994).
5. Glass, S., "Don't You D.A.R.E.," *The New Republic*, March 3, 1997, p. 19.
6. J. Swisher, M. Doebler, M. Babbit, and H. Walton, "Here's Looking at You, 2000: A Review of Evaluations and a Conceptual Critique," unpublished document, Pennsylvania State University, 1991.
7. T. Connelly, "Wappingers Central School District Drug and Alcohol Survey," unpublished report from the Office of Special Counseling Programs, 1990. Note that HLAY was one of twenty-seven different substance-abuse prevention programs in the school district.

8. Ringwalt et al., *Past and Future Directions*.

9. D. Kirby, M. Korpi, R. Barth, and H. Cagampang, *Evaluation of Education Now and Babies Later: Final Report* (Berkeley, CA: University of California, School of Social Welfare, Family Welfare Research Group, 1995).

10. Ibid., p. 52.

11. M. Hughes, F. Furstenberg, J. Teitler, "The Impact of an Increase in Family Planning Services on the Teenage Population of Philadelphia," *Family Planning Perspectives* 27 (2): 60–65 (1995).

12. D. Webster, "The Unconvincing Case for School-Based Conflict Resolution Programs for Adolescents," *Health Affairs*: 126-144, (Winter, 1993).

13. Ibid., p. 127.

14. "Peer Review," *Health Affairs* 13 (4): 163–177, 1994.

15. W. DeJong, "School-Based Conflict Resolution: Give Educators More Credit," *Health Affairs* 13 (4): 163–164.

16. R. Wilson-Brewer, "Comprehensive Approaches to School-Based Violence Prevention," *Health Affairs* 13 (4): 169.

17. E. Colyer, T. Thompkins, M. Durkin, and B. Barlow, "Can Conflict Resolution Training Increase Aggressive Behavior in Young Adolescents?" *Letters to Editor, American Journal of Public Health* 86 (7): 1028 (1966).

18. D. Klaidman, "Is It Time to take a Bite Out of McGruff?" *Legal Times,* Nov. 29, 1993, p. 1.

19. Bureau of Justice Assistance, *The Social Impact of the National Citizens' Crime Prevention Campaign: Focus on What Works* (Washington; DC: U.S. Department of Justice, 1993).

20. A. Wilkie and T. Orr, "Effects of a Multi-Faceted High School Dropout Prevention Program: Findings from Four In-Depth Case Studies," paper presented at 1994 Annual Meeting of American Educational Research Association, New Orleans, LA, 1994.

21. R. O'Sullivan, "Evaluating a Model Middle School Dropout Prevention Program for At-Risk Students," paper presented at annual meeting of American Educational Research Association, Boston, MA, 1990.

22. J. Grossman and C. Sipe, *Summer Training and Education Program (STEP): Report on Long-Term Impacts* (Philadelphia: Public/Private Ventures, 1992).

23. G. Walker and F. Viella-Velex, *Anatomy of a Demonstration: The Summer Training and Education Program (STEP) from Pilot Through Replication and Post-program Impacts* (Philadelphia: Public/Private Ventures, 1992).

24. C. Brown, of the Council of Chief State School Officers, "Supporting Significantly Improved Student Achievement in High Poverty Schools," remarks at meeting of state coordinators of Title I, New Orleans, LA, January 22, 1996.

25. Iowa Department of Education, *Inventory of Policies and Practices Related to Student Failure and Dropping Out*, (Des Moines, IA, August 1996).

26. J. Weisman, "Though Still a Target of Attacks, Self-Esteem Movement Advances," *Education Week,* March 6, 1991.

27. Ibid., p. 17.

28. *Utne Reader*, July/August 1994.

29. R. Weissbourd, "The Feel-Good Trap," *New Republic,* August 16 and 26, 1996, p. 12.

30. James Bell Associates and Lewin-VHI, *Working Paper: Draft Site Visit Summaries*, submitted to assistant secretary of planning and evaluation, U.S. DHHS, July 1993.

31. Center for the Study of Social Policy, *Building New Futures for At-Risk Youth: Findings from a Five-Year, Multi-Site Evaluation* (Washington, DC: Center for the Study of Social Policy, 1995).

32. Annie E. Casey Foundation, *The Path of Most Resistance: Reflections on Lessons Learned from New Futures* (Baltimore, MD: Annie Casey Foundation, 1995), p. vii.

33. D. Davies, "The 10th School Where School-Family-Community Partnerships Flourish," *Education Week*, July 10, 1996, p. 44.

34.   M. Burt, G. Resnick, and N. Matheson, *Comprehensive Service Integration Programs for At-Risk Youth: Executive Summary* (Washington DC: Urban Institute, 1992), p. 3.

CHAPTER 10
1.   W. Grant, A Parent's Guide to Understanding the Teenage Years (New York: Penguin USA, 1996).
2.   L. Steinberg, *Beyond the Classroom* (New York: Simon & Schuster, 1996).
3.   Ibid., p. 118.
4.   Ibid.
5.   D. Scott-Jones, "Parent-child Interaction and School Achievement," in B. Ryan et al. (eds.), *The Family-School Connection* (Thousand Oaks, CA: Sage Publications, 1997).
6.   M. Csikszentmihalyi, K. Rathunde, and S. Whalen, *Talented Teenagers: The Roots of Success and Failure* (Cambridge, UK: Cambridge University Press, 1993), p. 175.
7.   D. Roberts, "Adolescents and the Mass Media: From 'Leave It to Beaver' to 'Beverly Hills 90210,' " in R. Takanishi (ed.), *Adolescence in the 1990s* (New York: Teachers College Press 1993), pp. 171–186.

CHAPTER 11
1.   IS218 and Hanshaw are described in J. Dryfoos, *Full Service School.* (San Francisco, CA: Jossey-Bass, 1990); IS218 also described in chapter 5; Turner school is described in chapter 4.
2.   Center for Research on the Education of Students Placed at Risk, *CRESPAR Research & Development Report*, no. 1, Johns Hopkins University, October 1996.
3.   D. Hamburg, *Today's Children* (New York: Times Books, 1992); see chapter 12 on "Science and Health in Adolescent Education," pp. 221–228.
4.   J. Epstein, "School/Family/Community Partnerships: Caring for the Children We Share," *Phi Delta Kappan* (May 1995), pp. 701–712.
5.   See, for example, "A Family Plan: Involving Parents in Education: 10 Ideas that Work," *Education Week,* October 5, 1994, pp. 29–33.
6.   Telephone interview with Roger Weissberg, professor of psychology, University of Illinois, Chicago, October 28, 1996.
7.   K. Hooper-Briar, "The Missing Link," *Education Week*, October 5, 1994, p. 32
8.   "Project Description: Bridges to Success, Appendix" (Alexandria, VA: United Way of America, 1996).
9.   L. Lynn, "Building Parent Involvement," *Brief to Principals*, no. 8. Center on Organization and Restructuring of Schools (Winter 1994).

CHAPTER 12
1.   C. Hayes, E. Lipoff, and A. Danegger, Compendium of Comprehensive Community-Based Initiatives (Washington, DC: The Finance Project, 1995).
2.   R. Stone (ed.), *Core Issues in Comprehensive Community-Building Initiatives* (Chicago: Chapin Hall Center for Children at the University of Chicago, 1996).
3.   P. Benson, *Developmental Assets Among Minneapolis Youth* (Minneapolis, MN: Search Institute, 1996).
4.   C. Burns, "Facing the Flawed Premises and Practices of Community-driven Initiatives," *Connections* 3(1): 1 (March 1995).
5.   For a detailed account of LINC, see M. Blank and J. Danzberger, *Creating and Nurturing Collaboration in Communities* (Washington, DC: Institute for Educational Leadership, 1996). Also describes collaborative programs in Flint, Michigan; Fort Worth, Texas; South Tucson, Arizona; and Washington, DC.
6.   A. Bailey, "A Quiet Revolution in Social Services," *Chronicle of Philanthropy*, March 23, 1995, pp. 7–12.

7. Ibid.

8. Ibid., p. 13.

9. M. Blank and J. Danzberger, *Stories from the Collaborative Leadership Project* (Washington, DC: Institute for Educational Leadership, 1996).

10. "The LINC in Kansas City," *Moving from Principles to Practice: A Resource Guide*, distributed in 1996, p 15.

11. Public/Private Ventures, "Community Change for Youth Development: The Process Begins," *Public/Private Venture News* 11(3): 1 (1996).

12. Ibid., p. 1.

13. Telephone interview with Bernadine Watson, Public/Private Ventures, October 25, 1996.

14. E. Roehlkepartain and P. Benson, *Healthy Communities, Healthy Youth* (Minneapolis, MN: Search Institute, 1996), pamphlet.

15. "Creating Healthy Communities," *Search Institute Source*, 12 (2): 1-2 (August 1996).

16. "Project Description, Bridges to Success. Appendix." Supplied by United Way of America, 1996.

17. Information supplied by Sheri DeBoe, director of Network Services, Mobilization for America's Children, United Way of America, July 22, 1996.

18. Observations from site visit to Jefferson Middle School, Rochester, New York, May 14, 1996.

19. Hayes et al., *Compendium*, pp. 3–4.

20. U.S. Department of Education, *Putting the Pieces Together: Comprehensive School-linked Strategies for Children and Families* (Washington, DC: U.S. Government Printing Office, 1996).

21. L. Decker and M. Boo, *Community Schools: Linking Home, School, and Community* (Fairfax, VA: National Community Education Association, 1996).

22. Task Force on Youth Development and Community Programs, *A Matter of Time: Risk and Opportunity in the Nonschool Hours* (New York: Carnegie Corporation, 1992).

23. Hayes et al., *Compendium*, pp. 9–10.

CHAPTER 13

1. J. Dryfoos, *States' Responses to Youth-at-Risk Issues*, preliminary report to Carnegie Corporation, 1991.

2. In other chapters, I mentioned several specific programs in California, Florida, Iowa, Kentucky, and New Jersey. In addition, the following states directly support school-based health centers: Arkansas, Colorado, Connecticut, Louisiana, Massachusetts, New York, Pennsylvania, and Texas.

3. "Community Resources," *Education Week*, December 11, 1996, p. 28.

4. State Legislative Leaders Foundation, *State Legislative Leaders; Keys to Effective Legislation for Children and Families* (Centerville, MA: State Legislative Leaders Foundation, 1995).

5. J. King, "Meeting the Educational Needs of At-risk Students: A Cost Analysis of Three Models," *Educational Evaluation and Policy Analysis* 16(1):1–19 (1994).

6. Ibid.

7. P. Dryfoos, deputy director, Massachusetts State Budget Office, memo, October 1990.

8. M. Fowler, assistant director of Child and Adolescent Health, personal conversation, November 12, 1991.

9. Telephone interview with Bill Shepardson, director, Ensuring Student Success Through Collaboration Project, Council of Chief State School Officers, October 5, 1996.

10. See *Issue Briefs* put out by Council of Chief State School Officers, Washington, DC., Summer 1995 and Winter 1996.

11. State of Maryland, *Portrait of Progress*, annual report (Annapolis, MD: Governor's Office for Children, Youth, and Families, 1995).

12. Council of Chief State School Officers, "Changing Decision Making to Improve Results for Children and Families: How Ten States Are Tackling Tough Governance Issues," *Issue Brief*, Winter 1996.

13. J. Knitzer and S. Page, *Map and Track: State Initiatives for Young Children and Families* (New York: National Center for Children in Poverty, 1996).

14. E. Frankford and K. Schimke, Memorandum from Mobilization for Our Children, State Communities Aid Association, Albany, NY; January 27, 1997.

15. *California's Healthy Start Newsletter*, July 1995.

16. *California's Healthy Start Newsletter*, September 1995, p. 13.

17. *Education Week*, supplement titled *Quality Counts*, January 22, 1997, vol. 16.

18. President's Crime Prevention Council, *Preventing Crime and Promoting Responsibility: 50 Programs That Help Communities Help Their Youth* (Washington DC: 1995).

19. *Departments of Labor, Health and Human Services, and Education and Related Agencies Appropriation Bill*, 1997, Senate Report 104-368, Calendar No. 589, September 12, 1996.

20. M. Dunkle, *Steer, Row or Abandon Ship* (Washington DC: The Institute for Educational Leadership, 1997).

21. U.S. Bureau of the Census, *Statistical Abstract of the U.S.: 1996* (Washington, DC: U.S. Department of Commerce 1996), Table 235, p. 156.

22. U.S. Department of Education, *National Assessment of the Chapter 1 Program: The Interim Report* (Washington, DC: U.S. Department of Education, 1992).

23. Commission on Chapter 1, *Making Schools Work for Children in Poverty* (Washington, DC: Commission on Chapter 1, 1993).

24. *The Exchange* Silver Spring, MD: National Clearinghouse on Families and Youth, (Summer/Fall 1996).

25. President's Crime Prevention Council, *Preventing Crime and Promoting Responsibility*.

26. Office of Juvenile Justice and Delinquency Programs, *Matrix of Community-Based Initiatives* (Washington, DC: U.S. Department of Justice, NCJ 154816, 1995), p. 5.

27. Ibid.

28. Carnegie Council on Adolescent Development, *Consultation on Afterschool Programs* (Washington, DC: Carnegie Corporation, 1994).

29. J. Portner, "Clinton Budget Proposes 94% Increase to Combat Youth Crime, Delinquency," *Education Week*, February 19, 1997, p. 17.

30. Coordinating Council on Juvenile Justice and Delinquency Prevention, *Combatting, Violence and Delinquency: The National Justice Action Plan* (Washington, DC: U.S. Department of Justice, 1996).

31. C. Shearer and S. Hochschneider, *Starting Young: School-Based Health Centers at the Elementary Level* (Washington, DC: National Health and Education Consortium, 1995).

32. "Promoting Intergovernmental Partnerships: Preliminary Recommendations for Federal Action," September 30, 1996. Unpublished and unsigned document from Domestic Policy Council meeting, September 24, 1996.

CHAPTER 14

1. C. Bruner, *Realizing a Vision for Children, Families, and Neighborhoods: An Alternative to Other Modest Proposals* (Des Moines, IA: Child and Family Policy Center, 1996), p. 43.

2. E. Frankford, "Realizing the Reform Vision for Children, Families and Neighborhoods; Strategies for Going Forward," draft of unpublished paper, State Communities Aid Association, Albany, NY, 1996.

3. K. Hooper-Briar and H. Lawson, *Serving Children, Youth, and Families Through Interprofessional Collaboration and Service Integration: A Framework for Action* (Oxford, OH: Danforth Foundation and the Institute for Educational Renewal at Miami University, 1994).

4. *New York Times*, June 19, 1996, p. B8.

Index